You Can't Spell Jesus in Hebrew

And Other Hidden Truths
About Christianity

By

James W. Dobbs, Jr.

With additional commentary by
Laura Dobbs Pemberton

Copyright © 2019 Laura Dobbs Pemberton
All rights reserved.

ISBN 10: 1732996466
ISBN 13: 978-1732996465

Dedication

*Hold on to what is good
even if it is a handful of earth.*

*Hold on to what you believe
even when it is a tree
that stands by itself.*

*Hold on to what you must do
even when it is a long way from here.*

*Hold on to life
even when it is easier letting go.*

*Hold on to my hand
even when I have gone away from you.*

- A Pueblo Indian Prayer -

I dedicate this book to all who seek the truth and with thanks to the people who helped make it happen: the wonderful staff at OLLI/Kennesaw State University, and all my children and grandchildren.

Forward

By Laura Dobbs Pemberton

A few weeks prior to the planned publication of my father's book, he went into the hospital unexpectedly and died two weeks later. His untimely death dealt a devastating blow to the entire family.

While in the hospital in those final days, he told me, "If I don't make it out of here, please make sure my book gets published." Such a simple request, and yet I now realize that aside from memories, this book is all I have left of my dad.

The project was something we talked about each time we got together, and he often gave me updates on the content. In the process, I saw my dad as something of a genius, and I found his research and theories on the subject of this book, especially about the sudden invention of the letter J in the English language, as fascinating and perfectly valid theories based on my own background in science.

Shortly before his death, he joked about having me act as his publisher since I had been handing out a previous version of his book at my Pow Wow stands. This is especially relevant since my dad had strong feelings about the poor treatment of native Americans, and included a section of his book detailing some of it. My mother was part native American, and I'm proud of that portion of my lineage. Dad also felt strongly about the terrible treatment of blacks, including those with whom he grew up in Alabama.

If one thing stands out from the reading of his book, it is his conviction and loyalty to his faith and to the people in his life. He believed in standing up for what is right no matter what the consequences might be. It's the number one life lesson I learned from him and is the thing about him of which I am most proud.

I hope that somehow, wherever he is, he will be able to see that his wishes were met. If only he had lived long enough to see this book and hold it in his hands. He will be truly missed, and this project will just not be the same without him around to bring it to life.

~*~

Table of Contents

Dedication v

Forward vii

Introduction 3

Part 1 - Names and Titles
Question: *What's in a Name?* 17

Question: *Is Christ an Acceptable Appellation for Y'shua* 52

Question: *Is God an Acceptable Appellation for Y'HoVah?* 60

Question: *Is 'the LORD' or 'the Lord' an acceptable appellation for* הוהי *(YHVH or Y'HoVaH)?* 62

Question: *What does Y'HoVaH think about the Yisra'elim?* 66

Part 2 - History
Question: *What is the History of Christianity's Treatment of the Y'hudim?* 77

The Ill-Treatment of Blacks in America 151

The Ill-Treatment of Native Americans 159

The History and Treatment of Native Americans, Something About Which My Father had Strong Feelings (by Laura Dobbs Pemberton) 160

Wounded Knee I (1890) and Wounded Knee II on

Pine Ridge Reservation (1970)	161
The Saga of Leonard Peltier	163
The Illegal Extradition	168
The Keystone Pipeline	179
The Indian Boarding Schools and Tribunals of 2014	184
Genocide Against Native Americans By Abducting Their Children	194
What Most People Don't Know About Homeland Security (by Laura Dobbs Pemberton)	203

Part 3 – Shabbat
  Question: *Which Day of the Week is a Kodesh Day of Elohim?*   220

Part 4 – Diet
  Question: *Is It A Sin To Eat Food that Y'HoVah Declares Unclean?*   233

About the Author	251
Afterword from a Grandchild	255

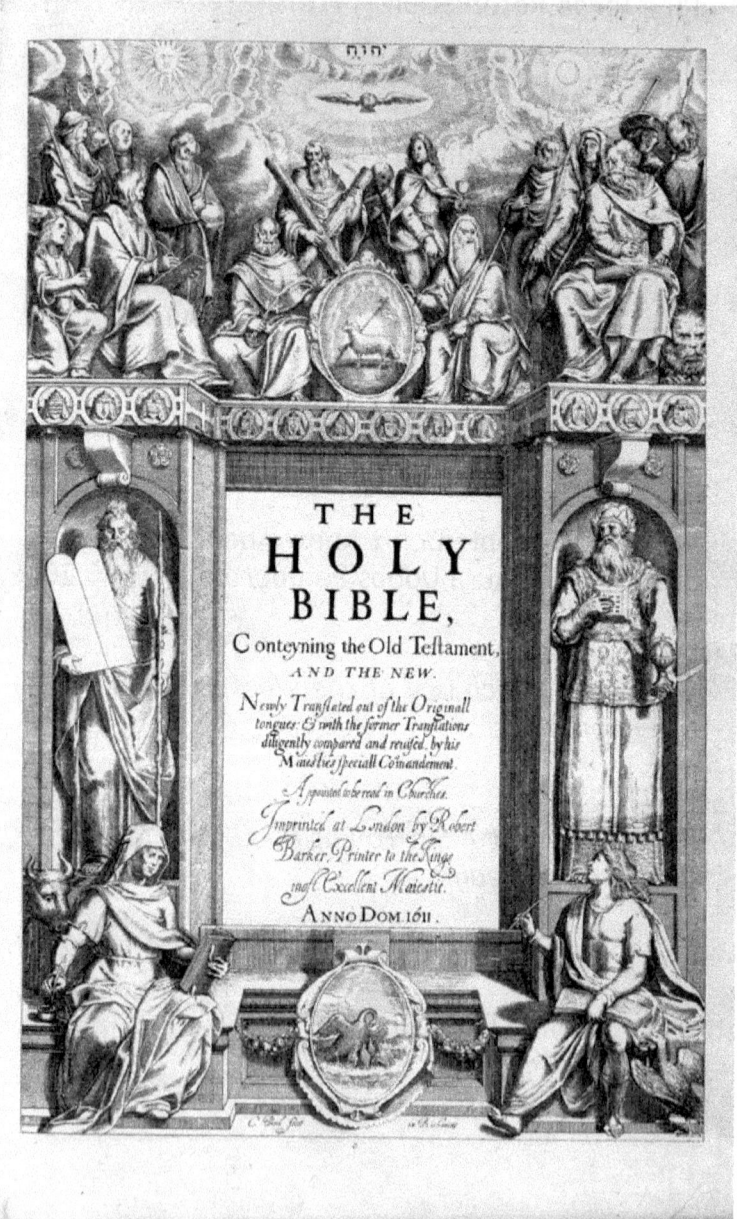

Cover of the 1611 English Bible.

Introduction

About My Book

My wife and I both had a Church of Christ upbringing, and we drifted along with fairly regular, back-pew attendance at Sunday school and Sunday worship services at various types and sizes of Churches of Christ. All of them were more moderate in their dogma and larger in membership than those I attended growing up.

The last stop for us in our Church of Christ odyssey was a 500-plus member church in Marietta, Georgia. This denomination didn't encourage members to study the Bible on their own, a practice similar to the Mother Roman Catholic Church. If you had questions, the priests, or elders as they were designated in the C of C, would answer your questions with denominational church-approved orthodoxy, rather than something from the Bible.

The problem with this approach was twofold: Their answers were primarily concerned with perpetuating their theological doctrines rather than telling the truth, and certain questions could result in having your name added to a "to be watched list."

The primary purpose of denominational doctrine, orthodoxy, and by-laws is to defend the beliefs or creed—written or unwritten—which give them a unique identity. Otherwise there would be just one large church with no need for a hundred different denominations and a thousand different sects ranging from extremely conservative to extremely liberal.

The position on this imaginary conservative-liberal scale is of the utmost importance to people in the C of C churches. Those congregations like yours, or more conservative than yours, are considered "okay," and can be recognized or "fellowshipped." Those to the left of your church, or more liberal, are doomed for hell-fire and brimstone, and can't be acknowledged *or* fellowshipped by your church. While this sounds crazy to people who have never been in the C of C, it's the truth.

The C of C's unique doctrine consists of the following basics:

1.) We are the only church—they hate the word denomination—from which the saved will come.

2.) Our church name is the only approved name because we have the correct surname for Jesus which is Christ.

3.) You must be completely immersed in a tank of warm water, preferably in a C of C baptistery by a certified C of C preacher when you are old enough to know what you're doing and can understand his incantation of "I baptize you in the name of God the Father, Jesus Christ the Son, and the Holy Ghost." No infant baptisms are allowed.

4.) If you've been baptized, you must partake of the communion, also called the Lord's supper, every Sunday morning or Sunday night. The communion consists of unleavened bread—usually in the form of crackers or wafers—and a small glass of Welch's Concord grape juice. No red or white grape juice is allowed, and for sure no wine is allowed.

5.) You must believe that the C of C can be traced back to the 1st century. This is similar to the Roman Catholic assertion that their popes can be traced back to the 1st century even though the 'seating' of the first pope was in 325 C.E. The first C of C was established circa 1840.

6.) You must tithe each Sunday morning, usually in conjunction with the Lord's Supper, after drinking the grape juice. The collection plate is passed around the congregation so people can see if you donate. After all, bills must be paid: church mortgage, preacher's salary, preacher's home mortgage, church utilities, preacher's home utilities, church cleaning and maintenance, etc. Some Christian denominations also pay their song leaders, youth directors, elders, etc.

7.) The hymnal must be approved by the C of C even though there is no central governing body, or synod, or written statement of doctrine. There is also an ironclad, unwritten creed that is similarly unenforceable.

8.) The worship ritual must conform to an opening hymn, an opening prayer, the Lord's Supper, and a sermon, usually by a paid preacher (I see them as salesmen). They hate the term "pastor" because it's used by the despised Baptists. Then comes the invitation hymn, after which the preacher faces the congregation and welcomes the penitent sinners to "come forward" and seat themselves on the front pew. I've seen a half dozen come forward at the same time.

Sometimes they will repeat the invitation hymn during a mass movement of parishioners surging forward. Once the invitation song is finished, the preacher approaches each person sitting in the front pew, and the person whispers in his ear his or her transgressions. The preacher then relays his sanitized version to the assembly. In other words, there are usually no specifics like, "Brother Jones says he is sorry he committed adultery with sister Smith."

The only time I ever said I was sorry was right before I resigned. I went to the podium to defend myself, and a young black member told me privately afterwards I had offended him. So that night I stood before the congregation and said I had acted out of order.

I recall an earlier incident at a previous C of C where a man had been caught by his wife in bed with her mother who suffered from Alzheimer's disease, and nobody reported him to the police. The following Sunday, the rapist went forward at church and whispered nonsense in the preacher's ear, and the preacher repeated the weasel words that the "brother" was sorry for something he might have done. No mention of the atrocity he had committed. The preacher knew what he had done because the wife had run crying to him right after it happened.

Needless to say, that terminated my membership

in that C of C, but only one other family left when we did. It's disgusting what some Christians will do and condone. I used this confessional method of coming forward during the invitation hymn to gain access to the lectern to address the congregation and bid them adieu since the elders wouldn't give me permission outright. It once again proved the verity of the old saying, "It's easier to get forgiveness than permission."

So, I secretly defied the elders at that C of C and began a serious, studious reading of the entire New King James English Version of the Bible. By reading a prescribed portion of scripture each day, in one year I read the entire book of the so-called Old and New Testaments.

The C of C especially ignored the Old Testament books because, as part of their dogma, they argued that it had been abrogated—that's a convenient lie if you don't want to obey the commands. Anyway, here I had been a dues-paying member of the C of C for about 62 years, and I had never read the entire instruction book—the Bible which the C of C piously claims is their source of guidance.

After a year of reading the Bible, I concluded the Old Testament had not been nullified by the New, and the Ten Commandments were still just as valid today as when they were written down by Moshe about 3,300 years ago, and would continue to be valid for eternity.

"The main thing about your word is that it's true, and all your just rulings last forever." Tehillim 119:160. This is the reason the elders of the C of C discourage reading of the Old Testament, as they erroneously call it. When the elders heard I planned to obey all the commandments in the Torah, they began to consider my

excommunication. I was already on thin ice with them because of my refusal to eat their ham during fellowship hall dinners once a month, and for my refusal to believe that only people in the C of C would be saved.

I was not yet obeying the fourth commandment—resting on the seventh day of the week which is the weekly Shabbat, which means simply that: rest—but the clever elders surmised it would only be a short time before I did. So, as crazy as it sounds, I got in trouble with the elders because I wanted to obey more, not less, of YaH's commandments.

I resigned our membership in that C o C in 2002. This was the first miracle for me, my escape from the clutches of the Christian Church of Christ which I had been attending for 64 years. I made a promise to the Creator of the Universe that I would start over with a clean slate and an open mind, and that whatever He revealed to me, I would accept and obey, starting with the basic Ten Commandments as given in Sh'mot (Words) chapter 20.

Things soon began to snowball, or rather, like an avalanche of snowballs. The truth piled up faster than I could assimilate it. I learned from a Messianic congregation in Atlanta about a fairly new English version of the Bible titled **Complete Jewish Bible** by a Y'hudi scholar named David H. Stern. The publisher was Messianic Jewish Resources. I ordered a paperback copy, and my life was suddenly transformed. This book was the second miracle for me in my quest for the truth.

When I first opened this book I was stunned to find names I had never seen before in the King James or New King James Bibles I had used all my life. The Y'hudi names in this Y'hudi book written by Y'hudim about

Y'hudim for Y'hudim were completely different than the English names I was accustomed to seeing. It was Yeshua instead of Jesus, Mashiach instead of Christ, Mattitiyahu not Matthew, Kifa instead of Peter, Yochanan instead of John, Yesha'yahu instead of Isaiah, Yirmeyahu instead of Jeremiah, Moshe instead of Moses, etc. I learned a rudimentary fact about translating from one language to another language: You never translate proper nouns such as people's names, cities, states, countries, rivers, mountains, etc.—you *transliterate* them! This is a very, very important point.

A person's name doesn't change. The pronunciation of a person's name stays the same regardless of the person's location in the world. If you can't get close to writing the correct pronunciation in language #2, then you simply transcribe it in its original #1 language. You don't Anglicize it or use so-called equivalent names in language #2 unless you intend to hide the identity of the people and places of language #1.

I studied the weekly Shabbat using my newfound Bible, and my wife and I commenced resting on the Seventh Day—a "day" in HaBook is defined as sundown Friday to sundown Saturday—as clearly laid out by the fourth commandment. The weekly Shabbat is discussed in detail in Part 3 of this book. This was miracle number three.

We initially attended worship services on Saturday morning with a small group meeting in a mobile home in Hiram, Georgia. They were called Seventh Day Baptists, which I had never heard of before. They were basically a Christian church that met on Saturday instead of Sunday, similar to the Seventh Day Adventists. We eventually left that church because they insisted on following their charter and using Jesus and Christ and all the other phony English names.

Like the Hank Williams song which asks the question, "Hank, why do you drink, why do you smoke dope, why do you live out the songs that you wrote?"

Hank answers, "Because it's a family tradition." Well, I aver that's the same reason most Christians are Christians, just as I was for 62 years; it's family tradition.

We then visited a few Messianic congregations which met on Friday night or Saturday morning. But still, authenticity was missing, and they used Christian Bibles and God and Lord but mostly did use Yeshua for HaBen (The Son). Also they would read from the Torah, and they wouldn't eat scavengers such as pigs and shellfish.

They mostly seemed afraid to tell Christians the truth about their beliefs. I suppose it was justified considering all the atrocities dealt the Y'hudim by the Christian Crusades, Inquisitions, and the Holocaust—I discuss these horrors in detail in Part 2 of this book. The Messianics were more into peddling their wares than peddling the truth. I once offered to furnish the pews at Congregation Beth Hallel in Roswell, Georgia, with copies of the **Complete Jewish**

The author, James Dobbs, and his wife, Joyce. [Dobbs family photo]

Bible instead of their Christian Bibles, but they declined.

So we simply started reading the Torah each weekly Shabbat at home. The Orthodox Y'hudim all read this same portion of the Torah every Seventh Day; it's called the Parashah, And we continued to study Christianity and the Y'hudim. The more I studied, the more I believed that the Christian religion is nothing but lies and deception. This was miracle number 4.

Miracle number 5 occurred in 2011, while I was visiting the campus of Kennesaw State University in Kennesaw, Georgia, in an unsuccessful effort to monitor a Hebrew language class. An aide working at the school mentioned the university had set up a display of the 1611 English Bible on the second floor of the school library in observance of the book's 400th anniversary. (See graphic on page 2) I decided to go have a look.

Large, color posters arrayed around the room portrayed English kings, queens, and Protestant reformers. In the center of the room stood an open book, approximately 8" X 10", inside a glass enclosure. The book was an original version of the 1611 English Bible erroneously called the "King James Version," and from which 95% of all Christian Bibles are derived today. I peered intently at the book, trying to read the old English text which had Vs for Us and Us for Vs. The first character of the first word in a sentence, and the first character of all the proper nouns, was done in fancy scroll lettering I found very hard to read.

But I noticed at the top of the page, the plain print name of Iohn. I then found Iohn in the text and noticed what the fancy capital *I* letter followed by *ohn* looked like. I noticed the same fancy capital *I* letter in the text followed by the letters *efus*. So it was Iefus.

I asked the young lady in charge of the display about the fancy capital I letter and the lower case f-looking letter. She confirmed my suspicions that the fancy scroll letter was indeed an Old English capital I, and the lower case f was a long s. So the name written was Iefus in Old English, which is actually Iesus—Ee-eh-soos like in the Greek language—in modern English.

She also said, "There was no J letter in the English language in 1611." *Therefore, there was no person named Jesus in the English Bible of 1611. Also there was no English king named James; his name was Iames. So even the king's name had been retroactively changed, too.*

In my 66 years of membership in Christian Churches of Christ and the Seventh Day Baptist Church, nobody ever took the time to tell me the little Christian secret that there was no Jesus in the 1611 English Version Bible, nor was there even a letter J in the Old English language of 1611.

The J letter eventually wormed its way into the English language sometime later in the 17th century as a co-letter of the I letter. After all, the lower case *j* and lower case *i* are the same except for the direction of their little tails.

The intentional name and title changes to the 1611 English Version of the Bible were driven by Roman Catholic clerics in order to disguise the identities of the Y'hudi people of the Y'hudi Book of Words of Elohim called the Bible. This is discussed in detail in Part 1 of my book.

Names are very, very important, especially the names of HaAbbas (The Father) and HaBen (The Son).

So, I beseech you to read Part 1 very slowly and deliberately and then reread it as many times as needed to grasp its significance.

Also discussed in detail in Part 1 is Miracle #6, which is the even more important fact that *there is no English J-type letter in the Hebrew language*. You can't spell Jesus in Hebrew, so HABen's name could not have been Jesus.

Part 4 of the book deals with diet. Y'HoVah—HaAbbas' only correct name—describes in detail in the Torah what is permissible for humans to eat. Basically, we're forbidden to eat scavengers. Of course, the Christian religion puts no restrictions on man's diet. As far as they are concerned, you can gorge yourself on pigs, horses, dogs, cats, rats, bats, shrimp, lobster, catfish, sharks etc. Once again, this goes counter to the precepts and instructions of the Torah. As with all the commandments of Y'HoVah, the prescribed diet has proven beneficial to our health.

So, this book is like a legal indictment of Christianity. It presents the facts, and the reader can act as the jury as they consider the evidence, hopefully in an objective fashion. My definition of fact is truth, or things that have actually happened and which can be verified by various sources, or things that are predicted to happen by the prophets of Y'HoVah as written in the Hebrew Tanakh and the English versions that have correctly transliterated all the proper nouns such as the English *Complete Jewish Bible* and *The Scriptures* Bible.

To me, the primary source of truth is the 10th century Hebrew Aleppo Codex Text with vowel markings—initially the Tanakh and only consonants. I trust the righteous Y'hudim to have received HaWords from Y'HoVah and to have written them down exactly and then preserved them exactly as they received them.

Y'shua HaMashiach stated in Yochanan 4:22, "Salvation is from the Y'hudim." Not the Greeks, not the Romans, and certainly not the English. In Romayin chapter 11, Shaul stated that the salvation tree like a Y'hudi domestic olive tree comprised of righteous Y'hudi branches with Y'shua HaMashiach as the root. The righteous Goyim are branches on a wild olive which must be cut off the wild tree and grafted onto the Y'hudi domestic olive tree to be saved.

I've been asked why I wrote this book. My answer is that I wanted to go on record with the many things Y'HoVah has revealed to me about the evils of Christianity during my reading and research over some 15 years. Y'shua states in Mattitiyahu chapter 7: "Good trees produce good fruit and bad trees produce bad fruit. Good trees cannot produce bad fruit and bad trees cannot produce good fruit."

The original Roman Catholic Christian Church—the only Christian church for 1200 years—has produced more bad fruit than any other organization of any kind and is not capable of producing good fruit.

This book serves a dual purpose: both to inform and to warn Christians to flee their religion and connect with the righteous Y'hudim which is the source of all salvation. Start by obtaining a copy of the *Complete Jewish Bible* and then obtain a copy of the Y'hudi Hebrew Bible with vowel markings. Then, at the least, learn the Hebrew alphabet so you can look up words in the Hebrew Bible to verify the instructions and correct pronunciation of proper nouns. Better still, become fluent in Hebrew so you can read the Hebrew Bible for yourself. The more you learn of Yiera'el and the Y'hudi people, the closer you will move towards YaH.

Quoting Yechezk'el, a prophet of Y'HoVah in chapter 3, verse 17-21, YaH tells the prophet, "When you hear a word from my mouth you are to warn them for me. If I say to a wicked person, 'You will certainly die' ; and you fail to warn him, to speak to warn the wicked person to leave his wicked ways and save his life; then that wicked person will die guilty; and I will hold you responsible for his death. On the other hand, if you warn the wicked person and he doesn't turn from his wickedness or his wicked way, then he will still die guilty; but you will have saved your own life. Similarly, when a righteous person turns away from his righteousness and commits wickedness, I will place a stumbling block before him—he will die; because you failed to warn him, he will die in his sin; his righteous acts which he did will not be remembered; and I will hold you responsible for his death. But if you warn the righteous person that a righteous person should not sin, and he doesn't sin; then he will certainly live, because he took the warning; and you too will have saved your life."

The author, James W. Dobbs Jr.
[Dobbs family photo]

So this book is official warning from me to those deceived by the Christian religion. I don't want their blood on my hands.

I'm not selling anything, and I'm not trying to convert anybody to anything, I could care less about the money from the sale of this book. I realize this book is not fun to read, but I believe anything worthwhile in life requires hard work. People who win with gambling and lotteries acquire ill-gotten gains which are soon squandered, and the person becomes depressed.

Steven Paddock, the shooter in Las Vegas, is a recent example of a high stakes poker player who won a lot of money but was very unhappy.

True happiness only comes from obedience to YaH, and as stated in D'varim 30:20 by Moshe, "Obeying Y'HoVah your Elohim, paying attention to what He says and clinging to Him—for this is the purpose of your life!"

James Dobbs

November, 2017

Part 1 - Names and Titles

Question: What's in a name?
Answer: Eternal life!

Proof #1:

[Mattityahu 1:18-22, 24, 25] "Here is how the birth of Y'shua HaMashiach took place. When his mother Miryam was engaged to Yosef, before they were married, she was found to be pregnant from the Ruach HaKodesh. Her husband-to-be, Yosef, was a man who did what was right so he made plans to break the engagement quietly, rather than put her to public shame. But while he was thinking about this, an angel of Y'HoVah appeared to him in a dream and said, 'Yosef, son of David, do not be afraid to take Miryam home with you as your wife for what has been conceived in her is from the Ruach HaKodesh. She will give birth to a son, and you are to name him Y'shua, (which means, salvation) because he will save his people from their sins.' All this happened in order to fulfill what Y'HoVah had said through the prophet, ''The young woman will conceive and bear a son, and they will call him Immanu El'.... When Yosef awoke he did what the angel of Y'HoVah had told him to do—he took Miryam home to be his wife, but he did not have sexual relations with her until she had given birth to a son, and he named him Y'shua."

Proof #2:

[Lukem 2:21-32] "On the eighth day, when it was time for his b'rit-milah, he was given the name Y'shua, which is what the angel had called him before his conception. When the time came for their purification according to the Torah of Moshe, they took him up to Yerushalayim to present him to Y'HoVah (as it is written in the Torah of Y'HoVah, 'Every firstborn male is to be consecrated to Y'HoVah) and also to offer a sacrifice of a pair of doves or two young pigeons, as required by the Torah of Y'HoVah. There was in Yerushalayim a man named Shim'on. This man was a tzaddik, he was devout, he waited eagerly for Elohim to comfort Yisra'el and the Ruach HaKodesh was upon him. It had been revealed to him by the Ruach HaKodesh that he would not die before he had seen HaMashiach of Y'HoVah. Prompted by HaRuach, he went into the Temple court and when the parents brought in the child to do for him what the Torah required, Shim'on took him in his arms, made a b'rakhah to Elohim, and said, 'Now, Y'HoVah, according to your word, your servant is at peace as you let him go, for I have seen with my own eyes your yeshu'ah (salvation), which you prepared in the presence of all peoples—a light that will bring revelation to the Goyim and glory to your people Yisra'el.'"

Proof #3:

[B'Filim (Phillipians) 2:9] "Therefore Elohim raised him to the highest place and gave him the name above every name that in honor of the name given Y'shua, every knee will bow—in heaven, on earth and under the earth—and every tongue will acknowledge that Y'shua HaMashiach is Y'HoVah to the glory of Elohim the Father."

Proof #4:

[Ma'asheh (Action) 4:11-12] "This Y'shua is the stone rejected by you builders which has become the cornerstone. There is salvation in no one else! For there is no other name under heaven given to mankind by whom we must be saved!"

Proof #5:

[Ma'asheh 3:1-8, 16] "One afternoon at three o'clock, the hour of minchah prayers, as Kifa and Yochanan were going up to the Temple, a man crippled since birth was being carried in. Every day people used to put him at the Beautiful Gate of the Temple, so that he could beg from those going into the Temple court. When he saw Kifa and Yochanan about to enter, he asked them for some money. But they stared straight at him and Kifa said, 'Look at us!' The crippled man fixed his attention on them, expecting to receive something from them. Kifa said, 'I don't have silver, and I don't have gold, but what I do have I give to you: in the name of HaMashiach, Y'shua of Natzeret, walk!' And taking hold of him by his right hand, Kifa pulled him up. Instantly his feet and ankles became strong, so that he sprung up, stood a moment, and began walking. Then he entered the Temple court with them, walking and leaping and praising Elohim! …'And it is through putting trust in his name that his name has given strength to this man whom you see and know. Yes, it is the trust that comes through Y'shua which has given him this perfect healing in the presence of you all.'"

Proof #6:

[Ma'asheh 5:25-29, 32, 40-42] "Then someone came and reported to them, 'Listen! The men you ordered put in prison are standing in the Temple court, teaching the **people!**' The captain and his officers went and brought them, but not with force; because they were afraid of being stoned by the people. They conducted them to the Sanhedrin, where the cohen hagadol demanded of them, 'We gave you strict orders not to teach in this name! Look here! You have filled Yerushalayim with your teaching; moreover, you are determined to make us responsible for this man's death!' Kifa and the other emissaries answered, 'We must obey Elohim, not men....We are witnesses to these things; so is the Ruach HaKodesh, whom Elohim has given to those who obey him.' ...After summoning the emissaries and flogging them, they commanded them not to speak in the name of Y'shua, and let them go. The emissaries left the Sanhedrin overjoyed at having been considered worthy of suffering disgrace on account of him. And not for a single day, either in the Temple court or in private homes, did they stop teaching and proclaiming the Good News that Y'shua is HaMashiach."

Proof #7:

[Ma'asheh 10:42-43, 48] "Then he (Kifa) commanded us to proclaim and attest to the Y'hudi people that this man has been appointed by Elohim to judge the living and the dead. All the prophets bear witness to him, that everyone who puts his trust in him receives forgiveness of sins through his name....And he ordered that they be immersed in the name of Y'shua HaMashiach."

Proof #8:

[Ma'asheh 16:16-18] "Once when we were going to the place where the minyan gathered, we were met by a slave girl who had in her a snake-spirit that enabled her to predict the future. She earned a lot of money for her owners by telling fortunes. The girl followed behind

Sha'ul and the rest of us and kept screaming, 'These men are servants of Elohim Ha'Elyon. They're telling you how to be saved!' She kept this up day after day, until Sha'ul, greatly disturbed, turned and said to the spirit, 'In the name of Y'shua HaMashiach, I order you to come out of her!' And the spirit did come out, at that very moment."

Proof #9:

[Mattityahu 18:1-5, 19, 20] "At that moment the talmidim came to Y'shua and asked, 'Who is the greatest in the Kingdom of Heaven?' he called a child to him, stood him among them, and said, 'Yes! I tell you that unless you change and become like little children, you won't even enter the Kingdom of Heaven! So the greatest in the Kingdom is whoever makes himself as humble as this child. Whoever welcomes one such child in my name welcomes me; ... To repeat, I tell you that if two of you here on earth agree about anything people ask, it will be for them from my Father in heaven. For wherever two or three are assembled in my name, I am there with them'"

Proof #10:

[Yochanan 14:12-17, 21, 25, 26] "Yes, indeed! I tell you that whoever trusts in me will also do the works I do! Indeed, he will do greater ones, because I am going to the Father. In fact, whatever you ask for in my name, I will do; so that the Father may be glorified in the Son. If you ask me for something in my name, I will do it. If you care for me, you will keep my commands; and I will ask the Father, and he will give you another comforting Counselor like me, the Ruach of Truth, to be with you forever. The world cannot receive him, because it neither sees nor knows him.... Whoever has my commands and keeps them is the one who cares for me, and the one who cares for me will be cared for by the Father, and I will take care of him and reveal myself to him.... I have told you these things while I am still with you. But the Counselor, the Ruach HaKodesh, whom my Father will send in my name, will teach you everything; that is, he will remind you of everything I have said to you."

Proof #11:

[Ma'asheh 21:12,13] "When we heard this, both we and the people there begged him not to go up to Yerushalayim; but Sha'ul answered, 'What are you doing, crying and trying to weaken my resolve? I am prepared not only to be tied up, but even to die in Yerushalayim for the name of HaAdonay Y'shua.'"

Please take special note of the names in Proof #1 which have been properly transliterated into English. The first two of these names listed below are *the* most important names in the Ha'Olam (Hah-oh-lahm, the universe or cosmos) and they are as Echad (Eh-**chad**, One):

1.) Y'HoVah, incorrectly known as [i.k.a.] god, God, GOD, Lord, LORD, Lord God, LORD GOD, the Lord, THE LORD, the Lord God, THE LORD GOD, Allah, etc.)—written in Ivrit as הוהי yood-hey-vav-hey (YHVH) from right to left, with no vowel marks on the four consonants of YHVH.

This is my best guess at the pronunciation of the Father's or Abba's (Ah-**bah**) name based mainly on the shortened or contracted version of His name of הי (YaH) with an "ah" vowel mark of a small tee sign below the Y or yood letter. This contracted version of His name is used in a number of places in the Tanakh (Tah-nakh, I.k.a. The Old Testament) such as Yesha'yahu 26:4; 38;11 and Tehillim 68:5, 19. Testament).

The last syllable is assumed to be an "ah" vowel also so it becomes Y'HoVah. I must reemphasize that Y'HoVah is my best guess and there are other possibilities such as YaHVeh, YeHVaH, YeHVeH, YeHoVaH, Y'HoVaH, etc.

The original Tanakh scrolls had only consonants. Even today Ivrit (Eev-**reet**, i.k.a. Hebrew language) copies of the Bible which have vowel points still do not put them on the Father's name. This tradition is born out of extreme respect for His name and is rumored to have originated with the Babylonians who had a superstitious fear of pronouncing the names of their Gods.

Personally, although I have the utmost respect for His name, I don't think Moshe (Moh-**sheh**, i.k.a. Moses) would have written יהוה over 2000 times in the Torah alone if הוהי, YHVH, Y'HoVah, did not want his name written or pronounced—there again this is just an opinion of a lowly Ger Tzdek (Gehr Zee-**deck**, Gentile righteous) who has become part of Yahadut (Yah-hah-**doot**), i.k.a. Judaism).

His name appears almost 7000 times total in the entire Bible. "I am הוהי, that is my name." Ref Yesha'yahu (Yeh-shah-**yah**-hoo, i.k.a. Isaiah) 42:8. Note: The spelling in English of Y'HoVah is my own personal variation of using all caps of YHVH to represent the four consonant letters of His name and then inserting lower case a's for vowel sounds on the y o o d (Y) a n d   and the vav (V).

2.) Y'shua (Yuh-**shoo**-ah, i.k.a. Jesus, Iesus, Iesou, Iesous, etc.)—written in Ivrit as עוש which is yood-shin-vav-ayin reading from right to left with two vertical dots below the yood indicating a sheva or rapid contraction-like pronunciation of the yood (y), then an oo sound for the shin (sh) letter indicated by the vav (v) with a dot to the left side of it, and an ah sound for the guttural letter ayin (a) indicated by the dash below the ayin—being the most important male child who was given his name by an angel of Elohim while still in his mother's womb.

3.) The Ruach HaKodesh (**Roo**-ach Hah-**Koh**-desh, i.k.a. Holy Spirit, Holy Ghost)—written in Ivrit as חר שדוקה which is reish-chet hey-koof-vav-dalet-shin reading from right to left with three diagonal dots below the reish (r) letter indicating an oo sound for the rolled and guttural R letter and a chet (guttural h) letter which is written in English as ch and has a dash below it indicating an ah sound, then the hey (h) letter with a dash below indicating an ah sound, a koof (k) letter with a vav with a dot above indicating an oh sound for the koof (k), then a dalet (d) letter with two horizontal dots below it indicating an eh sound, and finally a shin (sh) letter on the end. So Ruach means Spirit, Ha means The, and Kodesh is similar to the English word Holy, so it's Spirit The Holy.

4.) Mattityahu (Maht-teet-**yah**-hoo, i.k.a. Matthew) is a select talmidi of Y'shua who wrote the Scriptural verses quoted in Proof #1.

5.) Yosef (Yoh-**sef**, i.k.a. Joseph) is the father of Y'shua;

6.) Miryam (Meer-**yahm**, i.k.a. Mary), with a rolled and guttural r also, is the mother of Y'shua.

7.) Immanu El (Ee-**mah**-noo Ehl) which means "with us Elohim" and although mentioned as his name in Yesha'yahu 7:14 and in Proof #1 is, in my opinion, actually more of an aspect of Y'shua—he has many titles or descriptions but like HaAbbas has only one name. Y'HoVah, Y'shua, Ruach HaKodesh, Mattityahu, Yosef, and Miryam all have Ivri (Eev-**ree**, i.k.a. Hebrew) person singular names. Why? Because Y'shua, Mattityahu, Yosef and Miryam, were all Yisra'elim (Yees-rah-**ehl** -eem), with the r-letter rolled and grunted once again, and their Aba was Y'hovah and His Spirit was called Ruach Hakodesh. The angel of Elohim told Yosef that Y'shua will save *his* people from their sins. His people are the Yisra'elim! Sha'ul (Shah-**ool**, i.k.a. Paul) says in HaRomayim (i.k.a. Romans) 1:3 that Y'shua is descended from the Y'hudim (Yuh-hoo-**deem**, i.k.a. Jews), quote: "It concerns his Son—he is descended from David (Dah-**veed**) physically."

The name Y'shua, which was used as a name for nine men and one city in the Tanakh but never for the prophesied HaMashiach was, in my opinion, indirectly determined from the Greek name Iesous in the Greek manuscripts of the B'rit HaDashah compared to the Greek name of Iesoun of a man named Y'shua in the Septuagint which is a Greek version of the Tanakh plus some extra books not in the Tanakh. This is necessary because the original Ivrit manuscripts of the B'rit HaDashah are all either hidden away or destroyed, except for two Ivrit manuscripts of Mattitiyahu.

The first manuscript, called the Shem-Tov Manuscript, was included in a polemical work against Christianity entitled *Eben Bohan* in 1385 by a Y'hudi physician named Shem-Tov Shaprut who was living in Castille, España (i.k.a. Spain) at the time.

The second manuscript of Mattitiyahu was discovered by a French Bishop named Jean du Tillet in

Roma in 1553. Both the Shem-Tov and the Jean du Tillet manuscripts have ישוע (yood-shin-vav-ayin), which is transliterated into English using vowel points as Yeshua (Yeh-**shoo**-ah). Both manuscripts also use ה (hey, sof**t h**) as a circumlocution or abbreviation for the Father's name of יהוה and both manuscripts, according to scholars, appear to be taken from original Ivrit writings and not Greek translations.

Iesoun or Iesous was the rather inadequate attempt by the ancient Greeks at pronouncing the Ivri name of Y'shua. The Greek language is ill-equipped for transliterating Ivrit nouns, as will be explained later. Y'shua is the masculine form of the Ivri word yeshu'ah as given in Proof #2 which means "salvation." Also, Y'shua is a contraction of the Ivri name Y'hoshua which means "Y'HoVah saves." So it really has a double meaning of "Y'HoVah saves" and "salvation" in Ivrit. Jesus is a meaningless name of a person who never existed—at least never in Yisra'el.

The written Word of Elohim (Eh-loh-**heem**, i.k.a. God) is a completely Y'hudi (Yuh-**hoo**-dee, i.k.a. Jewish) book from B'resheet (Buh-reh-**sheet**, i.k.a. Genesis) through Hit'gelut (means be revealed, i.k.a. Revelation). The first part of this Y'hudi book is called the Tanakh which is an acronym formed from the first letters of the three parts of this portion of the Bible: **T**orah (Toh-**rah**) comprise the first five books written by Moshe, **N**evi'im (Neh-vee-**eem**) or Prophets constitute the next six books, and **K**'tuvim (Kuh-too-**veem**) or Writings are the final eleven books.

The last part of this Y'hudi book is the B'rit HaDashah (Buh-**reet** Hah-dah-**shah**) which means, Covenant The New, i.k.a. New Testament. The entire Book was written by Y'hudim, about Y'hudim (except for B'resheet 1-11), and preserved by Y'hudim for about 3300 years. Therefore, all the names of the books in both the Tanakh and B'rit HaDashah are Y'hudi names that must be transliterated into English for English Bibles, not translated into "equivalent" English names which may or may not be something similar.

So ask yourself, why have *all* the Y'hudi proper nouns of books, people, places and things—including one of the two most important names in the Ha'Olam—in this Y'hudi book been changed in 99% of the English translations? The phony name Jesus (**Jee**-sus) is simply an English-sounding invention of haSatan via the Christian Church!

As is the Y'hudi custom, he was officially named by his Ivri father Yosef on the eighth day subsequent to his b'rit milah **(buh-reet mee-lah),** or covenant circumcision)— Y'shua was obedient to every mishpatim (meesh-pah-**teem**), eternal moral commands, in the Torah of Moshe.

One could say he was very "legal" when it came to obedience to Y'HoVah. Therefore, his professed followers today who loudly sing the hymn, "Oh To Be Like Him," are lying because, as Christians, they are nothing like him and make no effort to be like Him. I don't think anyone will be chastised by Y'shua in the final judgment for being 'too obedient' to Elohim's commandments. Yosef then, in obedience to the angel of Y'HoVah, gave the Ivri child the Y'hudi name of Y'shua.

Please note in the Scripture quoted in proof #3 from B'Filim 2:9 that Elohim gave him the name Y'shua that is above every name and that in honor of the name Y'shua every knee will bow and acknowledge that Y'shua

HaMashiach (Hah Mah-**shee**-ach, i.k.a. Christ), is Adonay (Ah-doh **nahy,** Master) to the glory of Elohim the Father. Amen! Adonay Elohim, named his Son Y'shua as shown in the Scripture in Proof #1. Every knee, in heaven, on earth, and under the earth will bow and verbally acknowledge that Y'shua—not Jesus—is HaMashiach or The Anointed One of Elohim.

Also pay special attention to the following portion of Scripture which is quoted in Proof #4 from Ma'asheh (i.k.a. Acts) 4:11,12: "For there is no other name than Y'shua by whom we must be saved." It is not a question of which is more accurate or what do we prefer, it is simply a question of what is his name? There is only **one** correct name for The Anointed One of Elohim, and it isn't Jesus. There is no salvation in the name Jesus.

The Yisra'eli scholar, David H. Stem, says in the Introduction to his **Complete Jewish Bible** *(CJB)* translation/transliteration, "you might as well call him George as to call him Jesus."

I'm from Alabama, so suppose I wanted to call him Bubba, which is a popular name in Alabama; is that okay, too? These very same Christians who lie and tell you, "It don't matter what you call him; he's got lots of names; he knows who you're talking about, so you can call him anything you want to," would not take kindly to a person coming into their church on Sunday and reading, singing, praying, and being baptized, in the name of a person called Bubba, or George, or for that matter, Y'shua. They also would strongly disapprove of you referring to them as, "my brother or sister in Bubba?"

Y'shua is the three syllable Ivrit name of HaMashiach and is properly pronounced Yuh-**shoo**-ah and means 'salvation."

In my opinion, the Ivnt name of Y'shua—using the modern English alphabet letters of y-s-h-u-a—was poorly transliterated into Greek as ιησουζ (Iota-eta-sigma-omicron-upsilon-sigma) because of the limitations of going from Ivrit to Greek, and not to intentionally mislead. The Greeks don't have a yood or y type letter or sound and they don't have a shin (sh) or shoo sounding letter. So Iota-eta said fast, Ee-eh, is their feeble attempt at a y-sound and sigma-omicron-upsilon-sigma, sous or soos is their best attempt at shoo—I don't know why they didn't put an alpha letter at the end for the ah sound; that appears suspect.

So it's transliterated from Greek into English as Iesous (Ee-eh-soos). As mentioned earlier, the Y'hudi name of Y'shua was spelled as ιησου (transliterated into English as Iesou) in the Septuagint. Then it went from the very poor Greek transliteration of the New Testament Greek Manuscript directly into the Latin Vulgate New Testament Bible of 600 C.E. as Jesus (Ye-eh-sus).

The Latin language was the beginning of the abcdef...xyz alphabet that the Europeans and Americans use today. The Latin language, initially called classical Latin, had no j letter in it's alphabet but had a long i vowel which was pronounced as ee, similar to the Greek iota, and a short vowel i pronounced as ih. The new j letter was later added to what's commonly called Ecclesiastical Latin in about the third century C.E. by curving the tail of the i to the left. The j letter in Latin was pronounced as a y like the German and Scandinavian j is pronounced today.

The Latin language has an sh combo letter with a shoo sound just like the English language, so why didn't they go back to the original Ivrit, instead of using the poor Greek transliteration of Iesous and spell his name Jeshua (Ye-shoo-ah) which would be pretty close to exactly right?

After all, Y'shua was a Y'hudi with a Y'hudi name, not a Greek with a Greek name, nor a Roman with a Latin name, nor an Englishman with an English name. Why, why, why indeed? Anyway, the official Christian Bible is in Latin with all the proper nouns mistransliterated, and only the clergy were allowed to own or read from the few copies available prior to the advent of the printing press.

The invention of the printing press using replaceable metal letters by Yohannes Gutenberg in the mid-15th century was the beginning of the end of the Christian church's strict efforts, for the previous 1150 years, to keep Bibles out of the hands of the ordinary or laity Christians—both Catholic and Protestant varieties.

Copies of the Bible began to be translated into English and printed in large numbers early in the 16th century and smuggled into England illegally—it was a death sentence for anyone found in possession of a Bible printed in olde English as late as 1523 under Catholic King Henry VIII of England.

After ten years of pursuit by the Christian Inquisitors, English scholar William Tyndale, born in 1492, was burned alive by the authority of the Church in Belgium in 1536 for smuggling Bibles into England that he had translated into English and had printed in Germany and Belgium. The Church especially hated Tyndale because he had the audacity to attempt to translate/transliterate from the original Ivrit manuscripts of the Tanakh directly into English.

Tyndale would be the first to print an English translation of the New Testament based on Greek and Hebrew texts, and the first to be executed for this heresy.

Has the import of what I've just written registered in

your brain yet? It was illegal for non-clerical members of this religion, called Christianity, to read from their purported instruction book, viz. the Bible for over 1200 years, and even longer in some European countries such as Italia, where, I've been told, it was illegal to own a Bible or read from a Bible as late as the mid 19th century.

The possession or reading of religious works in the vernacular was declared illegal by the Constitution of Oxford in 1408. Those found guilty were burned alive at the stake. The Act of Six Articles in 1539 confirmed fundamental Catholic practices and doctrines in the Church of England. The act for the Advancement of True Religion In 1543 restricted Bible reading to the educated clergy and the wealthy, making it illegal for 90% of the population to read the Scriptures. (Copied from the exhibit of the 1611 English Bible exhibit on display at Kennesaw State University Library in 2011 commemorating its 400th anniversary).

The Catholic Church conducted their Sunday mass services in Latin—which only the clergy understood—in every country, including America, well into the 1960's. Today, the new strategy of the Christian churches is: it's okay to own Bibles, just don't read them; they are only for show, for outward appearance, like stage props. Just become a dues-paying member of a local church—religious social club—of your choice, most of whom employ a highly paid—overpaid for the work they do—smooth talking, salesman-type pastor, who can tickle your ears and entertain you while you warm a pew spot once a week and feel good about yourself. And if you have a question, just ask the clergy.

Whatever you do, don't dust off your Bible and try to read it yourself; that's why they have a multi-billion dollar industry of Christian elementary and high schools,

Christian colleges, Christian churches and Sunday schools, Christian publishers of denominational propaganda literature in books, booklets, tracts, and leaflets, Christian book stores, Christian professional priests, preachers, and pastors, and highly paid Christian "rock stars" called television evangelists.

But it provides haSatan with his same desired result as not even owning a Bible: disobedience to Y'HoVah. The constant overriding message of the entire Bible, from B'resheet through Hitg'lut, is: obey, obey, obey, obey, obey, obey! "If the righteous are barely delivered, where will the unrighteous and sinful end up?" Ref. 1 Kifa 4:18. And the righteous are defined as those who keep on doing what is right, i.e., they don't sin by violating Torah (Ref. 1 Yochanan 3:3-10). HaSatan never gives up, he just changes his tactics to keep people from knowing and doing the will of Y'HoVah.

Welcome to the Christian fantasy world of "once-saved—just say Lord, Lord, I believe!—always-saved." Just do anything your little heart desires; lie, steal, fornicate, adulterate, murder, engage in homosexual acts, kill your unborn baby, divorce your wife or husband, profane the weekly seventh day Shabbat, worship idols, eat pig meat, shrimp, oysters, catfish, eels, octopi, reptiles, rats, rabbits, squirrels, horses, dogs, cats, etc., celebrate pagan-based holidays, etc. It doesn't matter what you do as long as your "heart" is right.

There are no rules anymore; all the rules for right-living have been "nailed to the cross." There is no such thing as sin anymore. You're saved by grace regardless of how wicked you are; you're locked-in for heaven and your ticket is punched. This doctrine is, of course, very popular and fills the mega-churches, but it is an evil lie and is contradictory to everything written in the Bible.

I was surprised in 2011 to discover—quite by accident, or perhaps not—another truth Christianity keeps hidden, during a very careful examination of a 400th anniversary exhibit of the original 1611 Authorized Version (AV) of the King James Bible at a local college library: There are no J or j letters in the entire text of the 1611 Old and New Testament Bible!

This is the source from which all the Christian Bibles of today have emanated. It was Iohn instead of John, Iames instead of James and Iefus instead of Jesus (the f-looking letter with a short serif in Iefus actually was a long s). So, assumedly, the 1611 English I/i letter was pronounced similar to the Greek iota and Latin I/i letter, i.e. as an ee sound. So John would be Ee-ohn, and Iames would be Ee-aims or Ee-ahms (maybe similar to the pronunciation of the pet food brand, Iams), and Iefus would be Ee-eh-soos just as in the Greek and Latin.

Not only is the King of Kings name wrong in the modern-day English Bibles, but the king of England's name is wrong also, or at least it's wrong today.

Questions: When did the modern day English J-letter come into existence and why? How did it manage, like a cancerous letter, to replace all the I-names of 1611? Why does almost nobody today know these facts? My suspicion is that the J-letter with it's jay, jah, juh, jee, and joe sounds was invented for the express purpose of further disguising the identity of the men, women, cities, nations, rivers, and mountains of the Bible. All the modern day English Christian Bibles such as the KJV, NKJV, NIV, ESV, etc. with their Jesus (**Jee**-sus) are further from his correct name than the earlier Bibles such as the 1611 AV with it's Iefus (Ee-**eh**-soos), the Vulgate Bible's Jesus (Yee-**eh**-sus) and the Greek Bible's Iesous (Ee-**eh**-soos).

This phony English name of Jesus (**Jee**-sus) bears no resemblance either in meaning, looks, or vocalization to the authentic Y'hudi name of Y'shua (Yuh-**shoo**-ah).

Mission accomplished once again by haAdversary via his Christian religion—with their clever Replacement Theology substitution of meaningful things Y'hudi with worthless things Goyim (Go-**yeem**, means non-Y'hudim, gentile, pagan, heathen). Here again if we were dealing with honest translators of Elohim's Word they would have simply transliterated the Y'hudi name, which is pronounced as Yuh-**shoo**-ah, directly from Ivrit into English as Y'shua, just as a single Y'hudi scholar, David H. Stem, did 387 years later with his English *CJB*. This is not brain surgery.

Why would these purportedly unbiased theological linguistic scholars deliberately mistransliterate an Ivri person's name of Y'shua, pronounced Yuh-**shoo**-ah, into modern English as Jesus pronounced **Jee-**sus, via a twisted trail from Ivrit (with y's and sh's but no i's or j's) > Greek (with i's but no j's, y's or sh's) > Latin (with i's, j's as y's and sh's) > 1611 Olde English (with i's, y's and sh's but no j's) > Modern English (with i's, j's, y's, and sh's); instead of simply going directly from Ivrit > English for the Tanakh and from Greek > Ivrit > English for the B'rit HaDashah? It's a no-brainer. They were not unbiased but very biased; they were influenced and controlled by Christians— mainly the Roman Catholic Church and the Church of England Protestants—and their Replacement Theology agenda based on a virulent hatred of everything Y'hudi.

Unfortunately the Catholic protestors, known as Protestants—Catholic sects without a pope, or more accurately, whore daughters of the mother whore Catholic

Church—have also embraced this mythical name of Jesus, along with other characteristics of their "mother," such as Sunday, Christ, churches, crosses, Christmas, Easter, Halloween, pig meat, etc. Hey, like mother, like daughter.

Consider the following inconsistencies and deception in the English Christian Bibles: In Nechemyah (Neh-chem-yah, i.k.a. Nehemiah) 3:19, the Y'hudi name of עשוי yood-shin-vav-ayin in the Ivrit Tanakh is transliterated correctly into English as Y' shua in the CJB but mistransliterated as Jeshua in the KJV, NKJV, RSV, NIV, ESV, etc., and Iefhua in the 1611 AV. Now the same Y'hudi name of yood-shin-vav-ayin given in the Ivrit B'rit HaDashah in Mattityahu 1:21, is transliterated correctly as Yeshua in the CJB, and mistransliterated as Jesus in the KJV, NKJV, RSV, NIV, ESV, etc., and Iefus in the 1611 AV. They are not even consistent with their own deceptions since it's Jeshua (Jesh-yoo-ah) in the OT and Jesus (Jee-sus) in the NT of all the Christian Bibles for the same Y'hudi name.

David Stern believes most of the B'rit HaDashah was originally written in Ivrit, specifically Mattityahu, Mark, Luke, Yochanan (Yoh-cha-nahn, i.k.a. John), Ma'asheh, i.k.a. Acts), Ivrim (Eev-reem, i.k.a. Hebrews, Ya'akov (Yah-ah kohv, i.k.a. James), l Kifa (Kee-fah, i.k.a. Peter), 2 Kifa, 1 Yochanan, 2 Yochanan, 3 Yochanan, Y'hudah (Yuh-hoo-dah, i.k.a. Jude), Hit'gelut (Hee-tuh-geh-loot, i.k.a. Revelation).

I disagree with Mr. Stern. I believe all of the B'rit HaDashah was originally written in Ivrit since that was the language of the Y'hudi authors and also the language of the people written to. The original Ivrit manuscripts are probably hidden away somewhere within the archival tunnels below the Vatican, with the possible exception of the two extant Ivrit manuscripts of Mattitiyahu mentioned earlier. Even if Sha'ul wrote some of his letters in Greek, he most likely would have written Y'shua in Ivrit as ישוע yood-shin-vav-ayin and Y'HoVaH as יהוה yood-hey-vav-hey. But even if he wrote Y'shua as Ιησους (Iota-eta-sigma-omicron-upsilon-sigma), it wouldn't change his name or its pronunciation as Y'shua.

A person's name doesn't change. It is an integral part of their identity. No matter where I travel or what is written about me in any language, my first name is still James; that's what my parents named me, and it is written on my certificate of birth. If I moved to Yisra'el, my name wouldn't suddenly become the so-called "equivalent" of Ya'akov. Conversely if an Yisra'eli named Ya'akov moved to America he wouldn't suddenly become James or Jacob. Likewise, a Yhudi named Sha'ul wouldn't be called the so-called "equivalent" name of Paul in America, England, and Australia nor would he suddenly become Pablo if he moved to Central or South America—unless, of course, he wanted to blend in and be accepted in his new Christian environment by his new Protestant and Catholic friends.

Even if you have trouble pronouncing a person's name, have enough respect for the individual to make every effort to pronounce it correctly—and that includes guttural sounds and rolling of r- sounds, when required. I worked with some Asian and Indian (from India) men when I was employed by Lockheed Aircraft Corporation, and some of their names were difficult for me to pronounce, but I always tried to say their names correctly, and I asked for patience and help from the individual until I learned.

Many of my American co-workers were just too lazy,

stubborn, or arrogant to try and say their Asian or Indian names correctly, so they would just call them Jim or Joe. This, to me, is disrespectful and wrong. It is the height of arrogance, this type of Anglomania, to think that an upstart language called English is so superior to every other language that all proper nouns, such as peoples names from other cultures and languages must be Anglicized-even the names of the Yisra'eli people and places of the Bible.

Elohim spoke and wrote exclusively in Ivrit to his people. The Ten Mitzvot were actually inscribed in Ivrit—not English, Greek, or Latin, none of which even existed at the time—by Y'hovah's finger on the front and back of the two stone tablets. The English language is, after all, a relatively new language as languages go; it has only been around for about 600 years in anything close to its present form. The first English dictionary, Johnson's Dictionary, wasn't published until 1755, and it had an i/j combo heading for both i and j words since the j letter, which evolved from the older i letter, began to replace the i letter when followed by a vowel sometime in the late 17th century.

English uses the Latin alphabet with variations in pronunciation for some letters and I've noticed that about 90% of the words in an English dictionary are derived from Latin words, which are mostly based on Greek words. Unfortunately, English has been the lingua franca of the world for the past century or so, and there have probably been more perverted English Bibles printed than in any other language.

The English language also has some major flaws, the worst being that it has a one-word-fits-all called "love."

The most important commandment originally stated by Moshe in D'varim 6:5 and repeated by Y'shua in Mattityahu 22:37-39: "You are to obey Y'hovah Elohekha with all your heart and with all your soul and with all your strength. This is the greatest and most important mitzvah. And a second is similar to it, "You are to care about your neighbor as yourself." If you obey Y'hovah then by definition you are obedient to his mitzvot. Everything else is taken care of, including the second most important commandment involving proper treatment of your fellow man—agape in Greek, meaning doing what's best for them, instead of what's best for you—because you will treat your neighbor rightly, i.e., you won't lie, steal, envy, despise, slander, murder, gossip, or commit adultery against them. Christians invariably will reply that they "love God" but then in the next breath they will contradict themselves by telling you that they don't have to "obey God."

They are ignorant of what it means to love Him. To them it's the same love as loving a pet, loving chocolate cake, "making" love, "falling" in love, etc., just something they like, enjoy, or feel warm and fuzzy in their heart about. If I were to write an English Bible, the four-letter word "love" with it's many and varied meanings would not be in my translation/transliteration, not once. I would use other English verbs, nouns and adjectives to be specific.

I believe it is just plain wrong—evil—to rename and rearrange the Y'hudi books of the Y'hudi Bible, rename the Y'hudi people of the Y'hudi Bible, and rename the Y'hudi places, nations, towns, cities, rivers, lakes, mountains, etc. of the land of Yisra'el; especially since the English language is so well suited, unlike the Greek language, to transliterate the Y'hudi names correctly into English. This makes it even more diabolical to assign phony or fictitious names to all the

Y'hudi people of the Bible, most egregiously, Ben (Son of) Y'HoVaH! I believe it is blasphemy against HaAdonay as a violation of the third commandment of Elohim; it's also a blatant and deliberate lie, and therefore it is sin! Remember, there is salvation in no other name than Y'shua ImmanuEl; not Jimmy, not Joey, not Jerry, not Johnny, not Jeffrey, not Jasper, not Jason, not Jesse not Justin, not Josh, not Julius, and not Jesus.

All the other Y'hudi proper names and places should be transliterated and pronounced correctly also, including rolled and guttural r's (reish), guttural h's (hecht and khat) which are usually denoted as ch and kh respectively in English and the guttural a (ayin)—at least try.

If this redneck Southern boy, born and raised in Alabama who has lived most of his life in Georgia, can get it close to right, anybody can. It is Mashiach (Mah-shee-ach) not Christ (Creist), Mattityahu (Maht-teet-yah-hoo) not Matthew (Mat-thew), Yochanan (Yoh-cha-nahn) not John (Jahn), Kifa (Kee-fah) not Peter (Pee-ter), Sha'ul (Shah-ool) not Paul (Pahl), Ya'akov (Yah-ah-kohv) not James (Jayms) or Jacob (Jay-cub), Avraham (Ahv-rah-hahm) not Abraham (Ay-bra-ham), Sarah (Sah-rah) not Sara (Say-ra), Rachel (Rah-chehl) not Rachel (Ray-chul), Rivkah (Reev-kah) not Rebecca (Ree-beck-ah), Leah (Leh-ah) not Leah (Lee-ah), Moshe (Moh-sheh) not Moses (Mo-ses), Shim'on (Sheem-on) not Simon (Sigh-mon), Yosef (Yoh-sef) not Joseph (Jo-seph), Miryam (Meer-yahm) not Mary (Mare-ee), Yesha'yahu (Yeh-shah-yah-hoo) not Isaiah (Eye-zay-ah), Yitz' chak (Yeetz-chahk) not Isaac (Eye-zeck), Shimshon (Sheem-shon) not Samson (Sam-son), Yirmeyahu (Yeer-mee-yah-hoo) not Jeremiah (Jehr-eh-my-ah), Adam (Ah-dahm) not Adam (Add-ehm), Havah (Hah-vah) not Eve, Y'hudah (Yuh-hoo-dah) not Judah (Joo-dah), Levi (Leh-vee) not Levi (Lee-vie), Eliyahu (Eh-lee-yah-hoo) not Elijah (Ee-lye-jah), David (Dah-veed) not David (Day-vid), Yisra'el (Yees-rah-ehl) not Israel (**Is**-ray-ehl), Yerushalayim (Yeh-roo-shah-**lah**-yeem) not Jerusalem (**Jee**-ru-sah-lem), Kena'an (Kee-nah-**ahn**) not Canaan (**Cay**-nan), etc.

By the way, you should also make an effort to roll the r's and grunt the j's (pronounced as an h) of Spanish names also. Be humble, respectful, and right; don't be a typical haughty, disrespectful, lying, and wrong, ugly American. The old adage, "Lies are still lies even when widely accepted and truth is still truth even when it stands alone," is very applicable to all the incorrect proper nouns used in the Christian vernacular.

Please notice that the correct Ivri names are mostly (90%), like French words, pronounced with stress on the last syllable; the fictitious English replacement names are mostly stressed on the first syllable. Also note that most of the nom de guerre are unrecognizable in print or sound from their real Ivri names, e.g. Y'shua and Jesus, Kifa and Peter, Ya'akov and James or Jacob, Yesha'yahu and Isaiah, Yitz'chak and Isaac, Yirmeyahu and Jeremiah, Yochanan and John.

Y'shua is quoted in Mattityahu 5:17, 18: "Don't think that I come to abolish the Torah or the Prophets. I have come not to abolish but to complete. Yes indeed! I tell you that until heaven and earth pass away, not so much as a yood or stroke will pass from the Torah—not until everything that must happen has happened."

It's rather ironic, but telling, that every Ivrit yood (y) letter has been removed from all the many Y'hudi names that begin with the yood letter, including the two most important names, Y'hovah and Y'shua—in all the Christian Bibles—and replaced by the late 17th century made-up English letter called a jay.

Guess what? There are no j's or j-sounds or j-letters in the 26 characters of the Ivrit alphabet. No words with a j or J—zero! But there are a plethora of Ivri names that begin with the yood (y) letter. It is impossible to write the English name Jesus in Ivrit! It is also impossible to write the phony English word Jew in Ivrit! A good rule-of-thumb for those who are still using Christian Bibles with literally hundreds of thousands of incorrectly transliterated proper nouns is simply to replace the erroneous and odious J with a Y for all Ivrit nouns that start with the English letter J. So it becomes Yesus, Yoshua, Yeremiah, Yohn, Yacob, Yoseph, Yew, Yewish, Yudah, Yude, Yerusalem, etc. This Y-for-J substitution method, while not being a completely accurate transliteration of the Ivrit word is, nevertheless, far, far better than using J words.

Try to use some common sense and get it right, especially when transliterating non-English names into English. Why are the names of Scandinavian people, such as the Swedish golfer Yesper Parnevik, always written as Jesper in American newspapers and golf magazines but invariably correctly pronounced as Yes-per, not Jes-per, by informed TV golf announcers who know he is from Sweden and know that names that start with a J in Sweden are pronounced as an English Y?

Why not just correctly transliterate his name into English print as Yesper and remove any possibility of error by people who don't know his origins, or if they do know are just too dumb or too arrogant to pronounce it right? It's almost like they can't bear to see a name that starts with a Y in English print. If you see Juden written in a German publication, how would you say it? If you're an average uninformed American you would likely mispronounce the word as Joo-den, instead of the correct Yoo-den. So why not just simply transliterate it into English as Yuden, not Juden or Jew, if you're printing the name for a mostly ignorant American audience?

I've noticed that the latter-day Y'hudim all have their names respectively transliterated correctly into English—even the names that begin with a Y, except for Yisra'el and Yerushalayim—and also pronounced correctly; but the men and women of the Bible have all undergone major name-change surgery and never have their names written or pronounced correctly by the news and entertainment media, books, newspapers, magazines, television, radio, computers, etc., and worst of all, the Christian religious industry.

For example: Why are the former Yisra'eli defense minister Moshe Dayan and the former Yisra'eli prime minister Yitzchak Rabin referred to in print and verbally in America as Moshe (Moh-sheh), not Moses (Moh-ses), and Yitzchak (Yeetz-chak), not Isaac (Eye-zeck), respectively? Is the former defense minister, Dayan, more respected than the man Elohim selected 3400 years ago to lead the Yisra'elim from Egypt to Kena'an for forty years and through whom Elohim talked to and dealt with directly as a friend during this time, thereby providing the Yisra'elim with written instructions and mitzvot (meetz-voht), or moral commands in the Torah, such as the Ten Commandments?

Is the former prime minister, Rabin (Rah-been, with a rolled r which is never rolled by Americans because they are just too arrogant, or stupid, or both to do it), more important than the son of Avraham, the father of Ya'akov and the grandfather of the twelve tribes of Yisra'el? HaSatan does not want you to know that the Bible is a completely Y'hudi book, from B'resheet through Hit'gelut. Most ignorant Christians think the Bible is an English book because of the English-only names in their Bibles.

Earlier I mentioned the Complete Jewish Bible (CJB) translation copyrighted in 1998, which I now mostly use, although it is a highly edited version since I have marked through ADONA! and God and replaced them with Y'HoVaH and Elohim. Also his constant use of, correct name (incorrect name), for the book names is very irritating. But it is still a far superior and more accurate transliteration than all of the many perverted English versions used by Christians.

The CJB is an English translation/transliteration with Y'hudi names for Y'hudi people, places and things such as Shabbat (Shah-baht), Ruach HaKodesh, Adonai, cohen hagadol (coh-een hah-gah-dohl), Torah (Toh-rah), talmidim (tahl-mee-deem, a.k.a. disciples) etc. It is a refreshingly accurate translation/transliteration with Y'hudi words such as Yeshua, Mashiach or Messiah, congregation or synagogue, execution stake, Torah, immersion or mikveh, etc., instead of the Catholic contaminated translations such as the King James, New King James, and American Standard, with their "replacement theology" Gentile words such as Jesus, Christ, church, cross, law, baptism, etc. respectively. As it's title indicates it is the complete Bible with both the Tanakh and the B'rit HaDashah. It is one continuous Y'hudi book from B'resheet through Hit'gelut, with no break in pagination. The books of the Tanakh are arranged in the same order and named the same as they are in the Ivrit original, which is totally different than in all the Christian English translations.

Another good English translation/transliteration of the Bible is **The Scriptures** (TS) First Edition 1993, Second Edition 1998, which is an earlier English Bible than the *CJB* and is published in South Africa. It is very similar to the *CJB* but much, much improved with regard to the exclusive use of the actual name of the Father written correctly in Ivrit as יהוה in all the approximately 7000 times His name appears throughout the Bible.

It also is vastly improved by eliminating the Pagan/Christian names of God and Lord and replacing them with correct English transliterations of Elohim and Adonay respectively. For the Son they use the Ivrit name of יהושע exclusively, which is pronounced more like Y'hoshua or Yehoshua rather than it's variant of Y'shua, or Yeshua as used in the CJB. These are huge, huge improvements over the CJB since these two names are the most important and must be right. A minor annoyance of this Bible is that they use a "w" instead of a "v" for the Ivrit vav letter, a "q" rather than a "k" for the Ivrit kaf letter, and a "b" rather than a "v" for the Ivrit vet letter. Obtaining and reading the CJB or TS Bible is the logical first step towards disconnecting from Christianity and connecting to the Y'hudi roots of your salvation.

As Y'hudi Yosef Shulam described it in a 2004 lecture in Atlanta: "Protestantism is still connected from its umbilical cord to Rome; to the creeds that were made by the Catholic Church in Nicea, in Chalcedon, in Trent and in Ephesus. Whether they have a written creed or don't have a written creed, you try to question one of the main tenants that these creeds bring and you'll find out immediately, you'll lose your favor with most of the church; even with things that are not written in the Bible at all. Because Protestantism is still basically Catholicism without a pope!"

Rabbi Milton Steinberg says pretty much the same thing in his book, **Basic Judaism**, p. 32, 33, 39: "There is no creed for Judaism like there is for Catholics and Protestants ...The Christian denominations are religious communities each of which is held together almost entirely by its special convictions (creeds, dogmas, etc.). Each then needs to be very careful about defining its beliefs, or it may lose its identity ... Judaism sets morality or obedience to God's mitzvot above logic and creeds. Religions put doctrine first and then ethics." I can only say, Amen! To what these two Y'hudim have said about Christianity.

Rabbi Y'shua bluntly told the Shomron woman at the well in Yochanan 4:22: "You people don't know what you are worshipping; we worship what we do know, because salvation comes from the Y'hudim." Wow! A shot across the bow of the Romayim and European crewed pirate ship, SS Christianity, flying the Catholic/Protestant flag emblazoned with a large cross.

Sha'ul in Romans 11:13,16-24 states: "However, to those of you who are Gentiles (evidently some in Roma were Y'hudim) I say this: ...Now if the hallah (portion of dough set aside for the cohanim) offered as first fruits is kodesh, so is the whole loaf. And if the root is kodesh, so are the branches. But if some of the branches were broken off, and you—a wild olive—were grafted in among them and have become equal sharers in the rich root of the olive tree, then don't boast as if you were better than the branches! However, if you do boast, remember that you are not supporting the root, the root is supporting you. So you will say, 'Branches were broken off so that I might be grafted in.' True, but so what? They were broken off because of their lack of trust. However, you keep your place only because of your trust. So don't be arrogant; on the contrary, be terrified! For if Elohim did not spare the natural branches, he certainly won't spare you! So take a good look at Elohim's kindness and his severity: on the one hand, severity on those who fell off; but, on the other hand, Elohim's kindness toward you—provided you maintain yourself in that kindness! Otherwise, you too will be cut off!

Moreover, the others, if they do not persist in their lack of trust, will be grafted in; because Elohim is able to graft them back in. For if you were cut out of what is by nature a wild olive tree and grafted, contrary to nature, into a cultivated olive tree, how much more will these natural branches be grafted back into their own olive tree!" This is a direct torpedo hit amidships below the water line of the evil Vatican pirate ship. I believe the attempt to replace Elohim's Mashiachim Yisra'elim with haSatan's Christian Gentiles had already begun in Roma and Sha'ul was trying to nip it in the bud with what he wrote in Romayim chapter 11. He starts with a rhetorical question in verse 1: "In that case, I say, isn't it that Elohim has repudiated his people?" and emphatically follows with the answer: "Heaven forbid!"

Some important things to consider in Sha'ul's olive tree analogy quoted above:

1.) The salvation tree planted and cultivated by Elohim

is a Y'hudi tree!

2.) The natural branches are all Y'hudim, therefore the tree, root, trunk, bark, sap, natural limbs, leaves, and fruit are all Y'hudi, it's "their own olive tree."

3.) By the grace of Adonay, the Gehr Tzdek believers are taken from a wild, uncultivated, scraggly, diseased, unfruitful, olive tree and grafted onto Elohim's domestic Y'hudi tree—against nature.

4.) Gehr salvation is against nature; that is a humbling thought.

5.) We get our sustenance from the Y'hudim, just as Y'shua said in Yochanan 4:22.

6.) How can a Gentile who trusts in Y'shua be anything but humble and thankful that Elohim has let us take the place of some of the Y'hudim—not all, as Christianity teaches—who didn't accept Y'shua as their Mashiach.

7.) The grafted Gentiles who become haughty and arrogant, no longer terrified, boast that they support the root, enviously rail against the natural branches, disrespect them by giving them Gentile names and bear no good fruit are not long for the tree, i.e. they are quickly and easily pruned and thrown into the fire—personally, I don't believe that Elohim grafts these types of Goyim onto the tree to begin with.

In Ephesians 2:19-22, Sha'ul says to the gentile believers: "So then, you are no longer foreigners and strangers. On the contrary, you are fellow-citizens with Elohim's people (Y'hudim) and members of Elohim's family. You have been built on the foundation of the emissaries (all Y'hudim) and the prophets (all Y'hudim), with the cornerstone being Y'shua HaMashiach, (also a Y'hudi of the seed of Avraham, Yitz'chak, Ya'akov, Y'hudah and David). In union with him the whole building is held together, and it is growing into a kodesh temple in union with Adonay. Yes, in union with him, you yourselves are being built together into a spiritual dwelling place for Elohim!" Amen!

A few points to ponder in Sha'ul's letter to the mainly gentile believers in Ephesus:

1.) Gentiles are referred to as foreigners before joining the Y'hudim.

2.) After joining the Y'hudim we are called fellow citizens with Elohim's people, the Y'hudim.

3.) We must join the Y'hudim, not replace them— actually we should embrace them!

4.) We are Ger Tzdek to Mashiachi Yahadut.

5.) We become naturalized citizens of spiritual Yisra'el.

6.) As citizens of Yisra'el we must become like the native-born blood citizens as follows:

    a.) Their Elohim becomes our Elohim.

    b.) Their Mashiach becomes our Mashiach.

    c.) Their Bible becomes our Bible.

d.) Their diet becomes our diet—which means no unclean meat such as pig, catfish, and shellfish.

e.) Their weekly kodesh day of rest, devotion, and convocation to Elohim, the seventh day or weekly Shabbat, becomes our weekly kodesh day of rest, devotion, and convocation to Elohim.

f.) You show respect and propriety towards your native fellow citizens—past and present—by using their Y'hudi names, which means no demeaning Gentile renames.

g.) Our day begins and ends at sundown, not midnight to midnight—this is very important once you start keeping Shabbat, as will be explained later.

h.) We use their Y'hudi calendar with its year 5776 dating from creation and Biblical lunar month names not the Roman pagan calendar with its year 2015 and its days and months named after Greek and Roman G ods or Roman e m p e ro rs.

i.) We celebrate the Y'hudi festivals such as Rosh HaShanah, Pesach, Shavu'ot, Purim, Yom Kippur, Sukkot, Rosh Hodesh, etc. which are commanded by Elohim in the Torah of Moshe and therefore are all about praising Elohim.

j.) We cease participating in the Pagan/Papal/Protestant holidays, such as Halloween, All Saints Day or Day of the Dead, Christmass or Christmas, Saint Stephen's Day, Saint Valentine's Day (formerly known as Lupercalia Day), Saint Patrick's Day, Ash Wednesday, Holy Thursday, Good Friday, Easter Sunday, Easter Monday, April Fool's Day, Ascension Day, Mother's Day, Father's Day, etc., which are all rooted in Paganism and therefore involve praising haSatan's men and women—both real and mythical—God's and Goddesses with orgies, vulgar dancing, drunken revelry, debauchery, lies, threats, candy-filled stockings, pagan sex symbols such as eggs and bunny rabbits, decorated evergreen trees, holly, mistletoe, mythical all-knowing Saint Nicholas or Santa Claus who distributes gifts to children who have been "good." Sha'ul rebukes the Goyi brethren at Galatia for turning again to weak and miserable elemental spirits by observing special days, months, seasons and years. (Galatians 4:8-11).

k.) Their hygiene becomes our hygiene and a married woman who is still having her menstrual period should not engage in sexual activities during this time and for one week afterwards, because she is considered unclean. So she and her husband are limited to approximately two weeks out of each month for sexual intercourse.

l.) Their burial procedures become our burial procedures and when someone dies you clean them, wrap them in a white linen garment and bury them as soon as possible—just as was done with Y'shua's body. No draining of blood, no embalming, no cremations, no elaborate and expensive funerals with flowers and singing and ghoulish open caskets.

7.) Sha'ul also uses a salvation building analogy where Gentile Gehr Tzdeks who have joined the Mashiachi Y'hudim become a part of a kodesh building with a Y'hudi foundation composed of the Y'hudi emissaries (apostles) of Y'shua, the Y'hudi prophets of Elohim, and the Y'hudi chief foundational cornerstone—Y'shua ImmanuEl HaMashiach. You will discover that the closer you draw to Y'HoVaH's people—the Y'hudim—the closer you will draw to Y'HoVaH and the further you will move away from the religions of haSatan such as Christianity and Islam.

Besides our everlasting salvation that we receive *only* in the name of Y'shua HaMashiach and the fact that every knee will bow and every tongue will acknowledge that Y'shua HaMashiach is Y'HoVaH, we also do and receive the following blessings and assistance in the name of Y'shua HaMashiach while we are still living on earth, as evidenced in Proofs #5-11:

1.) Our sins are forgiven *only* in haname of Y'shua HaMashiach;

2.) We are immersed *only* in haname of Y'shua HaMashiach; we can teach *only* in haname of Y'shua HaMashiach;

3.) We can be healed and strengthened *only* in haname of Y'shua HaMashiach;

4.) We can expel evil spirits or demons *only* in haname of Y'shua HaMashiach;

5.) We welcome fellow talmidim *only* in ha name of Y'shua HaMashiach;

6.) We assemble together to praise Ha Aba *only* in haname of Y'shua HaMashiach;

7.) We ask for physical or spiritual help and give thanks for physical or spiritual blessings, i.e. pray, *only* in haname of Y'shua HaMashiach;

8.) We receive the gift of Ruach HaKodesh from HaAba *only* in haname of Y'shua HaMashiach;

9.) We must be willing to suffer, and even die, *only* in haname of Y'shua HaMashiach. In fact, our whole lives and everything we do should be done *only* in haname of Y'shua HaMashiach. So you'd better get this most important and most powerful of names right!

But everything done and received in haname of Y'shua HaMashiach is contingent on one thing as plainly stated in Proof #10: We must obey Y'shua HaMashiach, which means we must obey *all* the commands of HaBen Elohim Y'shua, which are the exact same commands as those of HaAba Elohim Y'HoVaH.

Question: Is Christ an acceptable substitute for HaMashiach?
Answer: No!

Proof #1:

[Dani'el 9:25-26] "Seventy weeks have been decreed for your people and for your holy city for putting an end to the transgression, for making an end of sin, for forgiving iniquity, for bringing in everlasting justice, for setting the seal on vision and prophet, and for anointing the Especially Holy Place. Know, therefore, and discern that seven weeks [of years] will elapse between the issuing of the decree to restore and rebuild Yerushalayim until an anointed prince comes. It will remain built for sixty-two weeks [of years], with open spaces and moats; but these will be troubled times. Then after the sixty-two weeks, Mashiach will be cut off and have nothing. The people of a prince yet to come will destroy the city and the sanctuary, but his end will come with a flood, and desolations are decreed until the war is over. He will make a strong covenant with leaders for one week [of years]. For half of the week he will put a stop to the sacrifice and the grain offering. On the wing of detestable things the desolator will come and continue until the already decreed destruction is poured out on the desolator."

Proof #2:

[Mattityahu 16:13] "When Y'shua came into the territory around Caesarea Philippi, he asked his talmidim, 'Who are people saying the Son of Man is?' They said, 'Well some say Yochanan the Immerser, others Eliyahu, still others Yirmeyahu or one of the prophets.' 'But you,' he said to them, 'who do you say I am?' Shim'on Kefa answered, 'You are the Mashiach, the Son of the living Elohim.' 'Shim'on Bar-Yochanan,' Y'shua said to him, 'how blessed you are! For no human being revealed this to you, no, it was my Father in heaven.'"

Proof #3:

[Yochanan 1:35-42] "The next day, Yochanan was again standing with two of his talmidim. On seeing Y'shua walking by, he said, 'Look! Elohim's lamb!' His two talmidim heard him speaking, and they followed Y'shua. Y'shua turned and saw them following him, and he asked them 'What are you looking for?' They said to him, 'Rabbi!' (which means 'Teacher!') 'Where are you staying?' He said to them, 'Come and see.' So they went and saw where he was staying, and remained with him the rest of the day—it was about four o'clock in the afternoon. One of the two who had heard Yochanan and had followed Y'shua was Audrey the brother of Shim'on Kifa. The first thing he did was to find his brother Shim'on and tell him, 'We've found the *Mashiach!*' (The word means 'the One who has been anointed of Elohim') He took him to Y'shua. Looking at him, Y'shua said,

'You are Shim'on Bar-Yochanan; you will be known as Kifa.' (The name means 'rock.')"

Proof #4:

[Yochanan 4:5-10, 19-25] "He came to a town in Shomron called Sh'khem, near the field Ya'akov had given to his son Yosef. Ya'akov's well was there; so Y'shua, exhausted from his travel, sat down by the well; it was about noon. A woman from Shomron came to draw some water; and Y'shua said to her, 'Give me a drink of water.' (His talmidim had gone into town to buy food.) The woman from Shomron said to him, 'How is it that you, a Y'hudim, ask for water from me, a woman of Shomron?' (For Y'hudim don't associate with people from Shomron.) Y'shua answered her, 'If you knew Elohim's gift, that is, who it is saying to you, Give me a drink of water, then you would have asked him; and he would have given you living water.' ... 'Sir, I can see that you are a prophet,' the woman replied. 'Our fathers worshipped on this mountain, but you people say that the place where one has to worship is in Yerushalayim.' Y'shua said, 'Lady, believe me, the time is coming when you will worship the Father neither on this mountain nor in Yerushalayim. You people don't know what you are worshipping; we worship what we do know, because salvation comes from the Y'hudim. But the time is coming—indeed, it's here now—when the true worshippers will worship the Father spiritually and truly, for these are the kind of people the Father wants worshipping him. Elohim is spirit; and worshippers must worship him spiritually and truly.' The woman replied, 'I know that Mashiach is coming' (that is, 'the One who has been anointed by Elohim'). 'When he comes, he will tell us everything.' Y'shua said to her, 'I the person speaking to you am he.'"

Proof #5:

[Ma'asheh 10:36-38] "Here is the message that he sent to the sons of Yisra'el announcing shalom through Y'shua HaMashiach, who is Lord of everything. You know what has been going on throughout Y'hudah, starting from the Galil after the immersion that Yochanan proclaimed; how Elohim anointed Y'shua from Natzeret with the Ruach HaKodesh and with power; how Y'shua went about doing good and healing all the people oppressed by haAdversary, because Elohim was with him."

The Ivrit word maschiach which means "anointed of Elohim" consists of the four Hebrew letters משיח (mem-shin-yood-chet, reading right to left) with the mem (m) letter having a small tee vowel sign below it indicating an ah sound and the shin (sh) letter with a dot below it and a yood letter to its left indicating an ee pronunciation and the chet (h) letter with a dash below it indicating an ah sound for this guttural h letter represented by ch. Therefore it is correctly transliterated into English as mashiach (mah-shee-**ach**).

Elohim's cohen, prophets, and kings were anointed or ordained by him and were therefore considered cohen (coh-hehn, i.k.a. priest) mashiach or anointed cohen. However there is only one 'Anointed One of Elohim' and he is Y'shua HaMashiach. Mashiach was purposely mistransliterated from Ivrit into Greek using the Greek word of χριστοζ (chi rho iota sigma tau omicron sigma) which is transliterated into English as the two syllable Greek word cristos (crees-tos) which means to rub, smear or anoint with oil as in a body massage. Y'shua was not rubbed or smeared with oil but was anointed by Elohim with the Ruach HaKodesh and with power, as shown in Proof #5. The word christos, which is properly used as a verb, adjective, or participle was then improperly capitalized and made into the proper noun of Christos. This made-up word Christos (Crees-tos) was subsequently transliterated into Latin as Christi or Christus and from Latin into English as the one syllable word Christ (Creist, as in heist, except when used in Christian or Christmas—which means Christ-Mass).

Once again a twisted, torturous, roundabout trail of deception from Ivrit-to-Greek-to-Latin-to-English. Did you follow this? You're not supposed to. Christ, as you can obviously see, bears no resemblance to Mashiach in print, sound, or meaning. If Christ is fraudulent, then every word that is prefixed or suffixed with Christ is bogus also: Christian, Christianity, Christendom, Christology, Christianization, Christianize, Christlike, Christly, christen, Church of Christ, in-the-name-of-Christ, Christmas, etc. All come tumbling down with it, including Christian churches, Christian schools, Christian Bibles, Christian hymn books, Christian inquisitions, etc.

If the Bible translators and scholars had been honest and not influenced by the Christian establishment, then Mashiach would have simply been transliterated directly into English using the eight English letters of M-a-s-h-i-a-c-h which is pronounced Mah-shee-ach, just as it is in Ivrit, with the ch being a guttural h as explained earlier.

The transliteration from Ivrit to Greek uses the seven Greek letters of μεσσαψ (Mu epsilon sigma sigma alpha zeta) or Messias (Mes-see-ahs) or more commonly Messiah (Meh-sigh-ah) since, as mentioned earlier, the Greeks don't have a sh sound such as shoo or shee). Messiah at least sounds somewhat similar to the Ivrit Mashiach. My opinion is that the Ivrit-to-Greek transliterations were an honest effort but the Greek language, unlike the English, is severely handicapped because it doesn't have any "y" letters or sounds nor any "sh" or shoo sounding letters. However, the King James English translators/transliterators, who were a learned scholarly group of linguistical experts in the Ivrit, Greek, Latin, and English languages could have easily and correctly transliterated the Ivri names and places from Ivrit directly into English just as the CJB and TS Bible mostly did 387 years later. I'll let the reader speculate as to why they chose not to.

It gets worse. The Greek word christos which is derived from the Greek word chriein is actually associated with sexual stimulation by rubbing the body, usually in the genital area, using olive oil or some other mixture of oils and aromatics. In other words, it is a sexual, body massage parlor type rub-down. Remember, the Greeks were pagans and had a multitude of deities, many of which, such as Eros, were of a sexual or fertility nature. There is no equivalent to mashiach (anointed one of Elohim) or HaMashiach (The Anointed One of Elohim) in the Greek language because they didn't believe in Y'HoVaH the Elohim of the Y'hudim. Also there is no mention of a Christ character in the Tanakh, but HaMashiach is mentioned in the prophecy of Dani'el as given in Proof #1.

This fictional Gentile character with the first name Jesus and the last name Christ was an invention of haSatan to replace the true Y'hudi Mashiach. It is one of the primary foundational building blocks of haSatan's replacement theology "wall" which was erected by the Romans, Empire and Church, to accomplish two evil goals:

1.) To separate the Y'hudim from their own Y'hudi Mashiach by persecuting them in the name of the fictional Christian character known as Jesus Christ.

2.) To lead Gentiles astray with this Christian religion which doesn't require obedience to Elohim, only membership and attendance and monetary contributions, or dues, in a church and obeyance to church creeds and doctrines.

Dr. Raleigh Washington, the former chief executive of the Promise Keepers organization, says that 40% of pastors and 60% of members in Protestant denominations are involved in internet pornography. Also, it is rare to find an adult man or woman in any Christian church who hasn't been divorced—at least once. With the abetting of the Protestant churches, which are simply spin-offs or sects of the Roman and Orthodox Catholic Churches, haSatan has been very successful over the past 1700 years with his 'two-fer' strategy of "keeping the Y'hudim at bay" and "leading the Gentiles astray."

Can you blame the Y'hudim for fleeing from Christianity when a crucifix was the last thing that millions of their Y'hudi ancestors viewed before they were executed "In the Name of Christ." There has been more innocent blood, especially Y'hudi blood, shed "In the Name of Christ" than in any other name in history, including Islamic atrocities "In the Name of Allah."

But as the Bob Dylan song title says: "The Times, They are A-Changin." Catholicism, Protestantism, and Islamism are in decline and HaMashiachi Y'hudim or, "remnant" as Sha'ul calls them in Romayim 11:5, are growing in numbers and assuming their rightful leadership role that Elohim has always had for them. The Goyim that are true "followers of Adonay" are hungering and thirsting for the truth and are eagerly attaching themselves to Elohim's Y'hudi remnant who have accepted their Y'hudi Mashiach named Y'shua and have stepped forward to lead the way.

You must join the Mashiachi Y'hudim to be saved! The "salvation tree" that Rabbi Sha'ul speaks of in Romayim chapter 11 is a Y'hudi tree! Believing Gentiles are grafted onto the Y'hudi tree, against nature. Once you get on the Y'hudi tree, by the grace of Adonay, and begin to receive your sustenance from the Y'hudi roots, everything else will fall into place. The Mashiachi congregations are growing fast.

Just recently I learned from a publication I receive titled *Jewish Jewels*, written by a Mashiachi Y'hudi and his wife, Neil and Jamie Lash, that 90 Orthodox rabbis had accepted Y'shua as their Mashiach. That blew my mind. The Orthodox Y'hudi rabbis, essentially, have only to state: "I believe Y'shua is HaMashiach," just like Rabbi Sha'ul did. They supposedly have everything else right already, unlike someone like me who has been in the dark in a Christian denomination for over 60 years and must learn fast because my time is running out.

But Elohim has blessed me with the light of knowledge and understanding in my twilight years because I opened my heart and committed myself to making the necessary changes in my life in order to be obedient to Elohim.

Y'shua promised in Mattityahu 7:7,8: "Keep asking, and it will be given to you; keep seeking, and you will find; keep knocking, and the door will be opened to you. For everyone who keeps asking receives; he who keeps seeking finds; and to him who keeps knocking, the door will be opened." I politely and beggingly knocked on His door and the door was opened to me about ten years ago. I'm living proof that it's never too late to knock on His door and to enter when he opens it. You must humble yourself and put obedience to Y'HoVaH first in your life—ahead of family, friends, job, religious affiliations, popularity, money, etc.

I truly turned my life completely over to Y'HoVaH. I have joined his select people, and become his obedient servant—there's no other way to be saved. It's an amazing ongoing miraculous journey. It has worked for me and it will work for you, too. The very purpose of this little booklet is to share with others some of the many things I've learned in my search for the truth.

Question: Is God an acceptable appellation for הוהי (YHVH or Y'HoVaH)?
Answer: No!

Proof #1:

Definition from ***Webster's Twentieth-Century Dictionary of the English Language***, Unabridged, 1938. "god, n [M.E., god, godd; A.S., god; akin to L.G., god; M.H.G., got; Ice., godb; SW., gud; Goth, gudb, god.] The word is common to Teutonic tongues but not identified outside of them. It was generally in plural, and neuter. It was applied to heathen deities and later when the Teutonic peoples were converted to Christianity, the word was elevated to the Christian sense. There is no connection between god and good in form, nor was the conception of goodness prominent in the heathen conception of a deity."

Proof #2:

[B'resheet 30:10,11] "Zilpah, Le'ah's slave-girl, bore Ya'akov a son; and Le'ah said, 'Good fortune has come,' calling him Gad (good fortune).

Proof #3:

Nowhere in the Ivrit language Tanakh—the authentic, untampered with version of the Bible—is the word God (Gahd) used as a title, description, or designation for his name, Y'HoVaH.

It appears that the Christian English Bible scholars of 1611 simply took the pagan word god, (gahd) which they were all familiar with since it identified their heathen deities, as shown in Proof #1, capitalized it and, Bingo! the word God now becomes a new name or title for Y'HoVaH. Another example of mixing pagan ingredients into this new poisonous religious concoction called Christianity. But this one is especially horrid because they are assigning a title applied to their pagan deities to use as a name for Ha One True and Living Elohim named Y'HoVaH. Only followers of haSatan could devise this evil scheme of giving Y'HoVaH a pagan name.

The seventh of Ya'akov's twelve sons, whose mother was the slave girl to his first wife Le'ah, was named Gad (Gahd); which is written in Ivrit as גּד or gimmel-dalet reading from right to left with the gimmel (g) letter having a small tee below it indicating an ah vowel sound and the dalet (d) letter on the end. The Ivrit name transliterated into English as Gad sounds identical in pronunciation to the English word god or God. Ya'akov, a.k.a. Yisra'el, would never, ever, use a name for his seventh son which was identical in enunciation to an appellation for Y'HoVaH.

As stated in Proof #3, nowhere in the real authentic Bible, which is written in Ivrit, is there a title for Y'HoVaH that is anything remotely close to God or Gad. Some of the proper titles and attributes for Y'HoVaH are: Elohim (Judges), Adonay (Master), Elohei Tzva'ot (Elohim of Hosts), Eloheinu (our Elohim), Eloheikha (your Elohim), Yah (a shortened version of Y'HoVaH), Ha'Elyon (The Most High), HaG'dulah (The Greatness), HaG'dulah BaM'romim (The Greatness on High), HaG'vurah (The Power), and El Shaddai (Almighty).

The word God is used in Christian Bibles, starting with the 1611 AV, mostly as a substitute for the Ivrit Bible proper title of Elohim (plural for Judge). Even worse, God has become the more popular vernacular of Christian literature and churches, and by people in general as his actual name, rather than just a title. Unfortunately, the *CJB* uses God a lot of times instead of Elohim, so I have taken the liberty to substitute Elohim for God in my quotes from the *CJB*. I do not agree with David Stem that God is equivalent to Elohim and neither does the *TS* Bible, or more importantly, neither does the Masoretic Text Ivrit Bible.

Question: Is 'the LORD' or 'the Lord' an acceptable appellation for הוהי (YHVH or Y'HoVaH)?
Answer: No!

Proof #1:

Definition from ***Webster's Twentieth Century Dictionary of the English Language***, Unabridged, 1938. "lord, n. [M.E. lord, loverd, laferd; A.S. hlaford, a master of a house-hold, a lord.] 1. A master; a person possessing supreme power and authority; a ruler; a governor. 2. A title of respect; a title given to a husband with reference to his wife; often in a humorous sense. 3. A baron; the proprietor of a manor; a landlord; as the lord of a manor.

4. A noble man; a title of honor; in Great Britain, given to those who are noble by birth or creation; a peer of the realm, including dukes, marquises, earls, viscounts, and barons. Archbishops and bishops, also, as members of the House of Lords, are lords of parliaments. By courtesy, also the title is given to the sons of dukes, and marquises, and to the oldest sons of earls. 5. An honorary title bestowed on certain official personages; as lord advocate, lord chamberlain, lord chancellor, lord chief justice. 6. [L-] In Scripture, the Supreme Being; Jehovah; also applied to Jesus Christ, who is called the Lord, or our Lord. 7. In Hindustan, Buddha. lord'ly, a. 1. Becoming a lord; pertaining to lord; like a lord; noble; aristocratic. 2. Proud; haughty; imperious; insolent; arrogant; dictatorial; despotic; arbitrary; tyrannical; domineering.

Proof #2:

Copied directly from the Ivrit *Masoretic Text Aleppo Codex Tanakh* (*MTACT*) with English phonetic transliterations, using vowel pointers of *MTACT*, in parentheses to right of Ivrit word: היעשי 42:8 (yeh-shah-yah-hoo) "ינא (ah-nee), הוהי (yood-hey-vav-hey), אוה (hoo-eh), ימש (shuh-mee)"

Proof #3:

Translation and/or conventional transliteration into English on left of all phonetically transliterated Ivrit words given in Proof #2 which are repeated in parentheses on right: Yesha'yahu (yeh-shah-yah-hoo) 42:8 I (ah-nee), Y'HoVaH (yuh-hoh-vah, yood-hey-vav-hey), be (hoo-eh), name (shuh-mee)."

Proof #4:

Ifaiah XLII copied directly from the original olde English *Holy Bible, 1611 King Iames Version*, "I am the LORD, that is my name." (Note: the f-looking letter in Ifaiah, is actually an olde English long s-letter)

Proof #5:

Isaiah 42:8 copied directly from the later English edition of an undated *Holy Bible, King James Version*, "I *am* the LORD: that *is* my name."

Proof #6:

Yesha'yahu 42:8 copied verbatim from the English *Complete Jewish Bible*, dated 1998: "I am ADONAI, that is my name."

Proof #7:

Yeshayahu 42:8 copied verbatim from *The Scriptures English Bible*, dated 2012: "I am הוה, that is my name."

As shown in Proof #1, the word lord is an English invention and mainly pertains to English nobility and land owners who lorded over their poor slave-like serfs or servants. It was also used, and still is, for titles of rank and honor in their society and government. It's subsequent capitalization and use as a name for Y'HoVaH is typical to what they did with the conversion of their pagan deities, called gods, by capitalizing it and making it singular. Although the word Lord, whether with just a capital L or all caps and usually prefaced with the article the, as in, 'the LORD' or 'the Lord' as shown in Proofs. #4 and #5, does not have the pagan origins as God does—although the Hindu Buddha deity is referred to as Lord as shown in Proof #1—it is nonetheless wrong and improper because as plainly shown in Proofs #2 and #3, it is not his name! Also the fact that the negative characteristics associated with the word 'lordly,' such as proud, haughty, dictatorial, despotic, etc. are just additional reasons not to use the word Lord when referring to Y'HoVaH.

His name הוהי (yood-heh-vav-heh) in Ivrit or written YHVH in English, which I write and pronounce as Y'HoVaH as explained earlier, is used over 7000 times in the Ivrit Bible from B'resheet through Hitgelut, mostly in the Tanakh. The Christian Bibles, taking their cue from the *1611 AV*, have incorrectly substituted 'the LORD' or 'the Lord' for YHVH all 7000 times just as they did in Yesha'yahu 42:8 as shown in Proofs #4 and #5. That's 7000 blasphemous lies in their Bibles!

The name IEHOVAH is used a total of four times, out of 7000, in the OT of the *1611 AV* Bible; the first time it is used is in Exodus 3:15. Likewise, the name JEHOVAH is also used a total of four times, out of 7000, in the OT of the more modern English *KJV* Bible. Although the Greek and Latin derived word of IEHOVAH (Ee-eh-hoh-vah) is closer to YEHOVAH (Yeh-hoh-vah) than JEHOVAH (Gee-hoh-vah), neither is correct, and besides, they were only used 4 out of 7000 times. There is no excuse for this error in 1611 or anytime thereafter. The olde English of 1611 had a Y letter as have all the English versions since then.

It is just plain and simple premeditated deception. It seems the Christian scholars of 1611, and all subsequent, could just not bring themselves to use a proper noun name in the Bible—even one as important as the Aba's—that began with the English letter Y to represent the little, but powerful, Ivrit letter of י (yood). After all, a name, or especially many names, beginning with a Y just might tip-off the reader that the Bible is a Y'hudi book, not an

English book, wouldn't it? The fact that the mono-theistic religions of Christendom and Islam worship deities named God, GOD, Lord, LORD, the Lord, the LORD, Jehovah, IEHOVAH, Jehovah, JEHOVAH, Allah and ALLAH is just one more proof that they belong to haSatan.

The Ivrit words of adonay, or adony when used to show respect or deference, as a slave addressing his master or a young person addressing an older person as sir, is fine. However, capitalizing the first letter and defining Adonay as the Christian word Lord is bogus. It seems even worse to me to capitalize and italicize all six letters, as David Stern does in his *CJB*, and then try to pass *ADONAI* off as a proper euphemism for his correct name in English of YHVH, Yhvh, Yehovah, Y'HoVah, YaHoVaH, Y'HOVAH, Y'hovah, or Y'HoVaH as I prefer.

Question: What does Y'HoVaH think about the Yisra'elim?
Answer: They are His chosen people for eternity.

Proof #1:

"Now Y'HoVaH said to Avram, 'Get yourself out of your country, away from your kinsmen and away from your father's house, and go to the land that I will show you. I will make of you a great nation, I will bless you, and I will make your name great; and you are to be a blessing. I will bless those who bless you, but I will curse anyone who curses you; and by you all the families of the earth will be blessed.'" B'resheet 12:1-3

Proof #2:

Then you are to tell Pharaoh: 'Y'HoVaH says, "Yisra'el is my firstborn son. I have told you to let my son go in order to worship me, but you have refused to let him go. Well, then, I will kill your firstborn son!" Sh'mot 4:22,23

Proof #3:

Elohim spoke to Moshe; he said to him, "I am Y'HoVaH I appeared to Avraham, Yitz'chak and Ya'akov as El Shaddai, although I did make myself known to them by my name, הוהי [yood (y)-hey (h)-vav (v)-hey (h), YHVH or Y'HoVaH]. Also with them I established my covenant to give them the land of Kena'an, the land where they wandered about and lived as foreigners. Moreover, I have heard the groaning of the people of Yisra'el, whom the Egyptians are keeping in slavery; and I have remembered my covenant. Therefore, say to the people of Yisra'el: I am Y'HoVaH. I will free you from the forced labor of the Egyptians, rescue you from their oppression, and redeem you with an outstretched arm and with great judgments. I will take you as my people, and I will be your Elohim." Sh'mot 6:2-7

Proof #4:

"If a foreigner is staying with you and wants to observe Pesach for Y'HoVaH, he is to do it according to the regulations and rules of Pesach—you are to have the same law for the foreigner as for the citizen of the land." B'midbar 9:14

Proof #5:

"If a foreigner (Goyi or non-Y'hudi) stays with you—or whoever may be with you, through all your generations- and he wants to bring an offering made by fire as a fragrant aroma for Y'HoVaH, he is to do the same as you. For this community there will be the same law for you as for the foreigner living with you; this is a permanent regulation through all your generations; the foreigner is to be treated the same way before Y'HoVaH as yourselves. The same Torah and standard of judgment will apply to both you and the foreigner living with you." B'midbar 15:14-16

Proof #6:

"How lovely are your tents, Ya'akov; your encampments, Yisra'el! They spread out like valleys, like gardens by the riverside, like succulent aloes planted by Y'HoVaH, like cedar trees next to the water. Water will flow from their branches, their seed will have water aplenty. Their king will be higher than Agag and his kingdom lifted high. Elohim, who brought them out of Egypt, gives them the strength of a wild ox. They will devour the nations opposing them, break their bones, pierce them with their arrows. When they lie down they crouch like a lion, or like a lioness—who dares to rouse it? Blessed be all who bless you! Cursed be all who curse you!" B'midbar 24:5-9

Proof #7:

"For you are a people set apart as kodesh for Y'HoVaH Elohekha. Y'HoVaH Elohekha has chosen you out of all the peoples on the face of the earth to be his own unique treasure. Y'hovah didn't set his heart on you or choose you because you numbered more than any other people—on the contrary, you were the fewest of all peoples. Rather it was because Y'HoVaH liked you, and because he wanted to keep the oath which he had sworn to your ancestors, that Y'HoVaH brought you out with a strong hand and redeemed you from a life of slavery under the hand of Pharaoh king of Egypt. From this you can know that Y'HoVaH Elohekha, indeed Elohim, the faithful Elohim, who keeps his covenant and extends grace to those who obey him by observing his mitzvot, to a thousand generations. But he repays those who hate him to their face and destroys them." D'varim 7:6-10

Proof #8:

"You are the people of Y'HoVaH Elohekha. You are not to gash yourselves or shave the hair above your foreheads in mourning for the dead, because you are a people set apart as kodesh for Y'HoVaH Elohekha. Y'HoVaH Elohekha has chosen you to be his own unique treasure out of all the peoples on the face of the earth." D'varim 14:1-2

Proof #9:
"Today Y'HoVaH Elohekha orders you to obey these laws and rulings. Therefore, you are to observe and obey them with all your heart and all your being. You are agreeing today that Y'HoVaH is Elohekha and that you will follow his ways; observe his laws, mitzvot and rulings; and do what he says. In turn Y'HoVaH is agreeing today that you are his own unique treasure, as he promised you; that you are to observe all his mitzvot; and that he will raise you high above all the nations he has made, in praise, reputation and glory; and that, as he said, you will be a people for Y'HoVaH Elohekha.... Next Moshe and the cohanim, who are L'vi'im, spoke to all Yisrael. They said, 'Be quiet; and listen, Yisra'el! Today you have become the people of Y'HoVaH Elohekha. Therefore you are to listen to what Y'HoVaH Elohekha says and obey his mitzvot and laws, which I am giving you today.'" D'varim 26:16-19; 27:9,10

Proof #10:

"I, Y'HoVaH, called you righteously, I took hold of you by the hand, I shaped you and made you a covenant for the people, to be a light for the Goyim, so that you can open blind eyes, free the prisoners from the confinement, those living in darkness from the dungeon.... The wild animals will honor me, the jackals and the ostriches; because I put water in the desert, rivers in the wasteland, for my chosen people to drink, the people I formed for myself, so that they would proclaim my praise.... Now listen Ya'akov my servant, Yisra'el whom I have chosen: Thus says Y'HoVaH, who made you, formed you in the womb, and will help you: Don't be afraid, Ya'akov my servant, Yeshurun, whom I have chosen....

Thus says Y'HoVaH, Yisra'el's M'lakhi and Redeemer, Y'HoVaH-Tzva'ot: 'I am the first, and I am the last; besides me there is no Elohim. Who is like me? Let him speak out! Let him show me clearly what has been happening since I set up the eternal people; let him foretell future signs and events.... Keep these matters in mind, Ya'akov, for you, Yisra'el, are my servant; Yisra'el, don't forget me.... He said to me, 'You are my servant, Yisra'el, through whom I will show my glory'.... Sing, heaven! Rejoice, earth! Break out in song, you mountains! For Y'HoVaH is comforting his people, having mercy on his own who have suffered. But Tziyon says, 'Y'HoVaH has abandoned me, Y'HoVaH has forgotten me.' Can a woman forget her child at the breast, not show pity on the child from her womb? Even if these were to forget, I would not forget you. I have engraved you on the palms of my hands, your walls are always before me.... I will fight those who fight you, and I will save your children. I will feed those oppressing you with their own flesh; they will be drunk on their own blood as with wine. Then everyone will know that I, Y'HoVaH, am your Savior and your

Redeemer, the mighty one of Ya'akov." Yesha'yahu 42:6, 7; 43:20; 44:1, 2, 6, 7, 21; 49:3, 13, 14-16, 25-26

Proof #11:

"A foreigner joining Y'HoVaH should not say, 'Y'HoVaH will separate me from his people'; likewise the eunuch should not say, 'I am only a dried-up tree.' For here is what Y'HoVaH says: 'As for the eunuchs who keep my Shabbats, who choose what pleases me and hold fast to my covenant: in my house, within my walls, I will give them power and a name greater than sons and daughters; I will give him an everlasting name that will not be cut off. And the foreigners who join themselves to Y'HoVaH to serve him, to honor the name of Y'HoVaH, and to be his workers, all who keep Shabbat and do not profane it, and hold fast to my covenant, I will bring them to my holy mountain and make them joyful in my house of prayer; for my house will be called a house of prayer for all peoples.' Adonay Elohim says, he who gathers Yisra'el's exiles: 'There are yet others I will gather, besides those gathered already.'" Yesha'yahu 56:5-8

Proof #12:

"This is what Y'HoVaH says: 'If the sky above can be measured and the foundations of the earth be fathomed, then I will reject all the offspring of Yisra'el for all that they have done,' says, Y'HoVaH." Yirmeyahu 31:36

Proof #13:

"For Y'HoVaH-Tzva'ot has sent me on a glorious mission to the nations that plundered you, and this is what he says: 'Anyone who injures you injures the very pupil of my eye. But I will shake my hand over them and they will be plundered by those who were formerly their slaves.' Then you will know that Y'HoVaH-Tzva'ot sent me. 'Sing, daughter of Tziyon; rejoice! For, here, I am coming; and I will live among you,' says Y'HoVaH'.... Y'HoVaH will strike all the people who made war against Yerushalayim with a plague in which their flesh rots away while they are standing on their feet, their eyes rot away in their sockets, and their tongues rot away in their mouths." Z'kharyah 2:12-14; 14:12

Proof #14:

"But Rut said to Naomi (Yisra'eli mother-in-law), 'Don't press me to leave you and stop following you; for wherever you go, I will go; and wherever you stay, I will stay. Your people will be my people and your Elohim will be my Elohim. Where you die, I will die; and there I will be buried. May Y'HoVaH bring terrible curses on me, and worse ones as well, if anything but death separates you and me.'" Rut 1:16, 17

Proof #15:

"It was just before the festival of Pesach (Peh-**sach**), and Y'shua knew that the time had come for him to pass from this world to the Aba. Having cared for his own people in the world, he cared for them to the end." Yochanan 13:1

Proof #16:

"Then I saw a new heaven and a new earth (reference Yesha'yahu 65:17 and 66:22), for the old heaven and the old earth had passed away, and the sea was no longer there. Also I saw the kodesh city, New Yerushalayim, coming down out of heaven from Elohim, prepared like a bride beautifully dressed for her husband. I heard a loud voice from the throne say, 'See! Elohim's Sh'khinah (divine presence) is with mankind, and he will live with them. They will be his people, and he himself, Elohim-with-them (Immanu El), will be their Elohim (reference Vayikra 26:11-12). He will wipe away every tear from their eyes. There will no longer be any death; and there will no longer be any mourning, crying or pain; because the old order has passed away.' Then the One sitting on the throne said, 'Look! I am making everything new!' Also he said, 'Write, These words are true and trustworthy!' And he said to me, 'It is done! I am the Alef and the Tav, the Beginning and the End. To anyone who is thirsty I myself will give water free of charge from the Fountain of Life. He who wins the victory will receive these things, and I will be his Elohim, and he will be my son. But as for the cowardly, the untrustworthy, the vile, the murderers, the sexually immoral, those involved with the occult and with drugs, idol-worshippers, and all liars—their destiny is the lake burning with fire and sulfur, the second death.' One of the seven angels having the seven bowls full of the seven last plagues approached me and said, 'Come! I will show you the Bride, the Wife of the Lamb.' He carried me off in the Ruach to the top of a great, high mountain and showed me the kodesh city, Yerushalayim, coming down out of heaven from Elohim. It had the Sh'khinah of Elohim, so that its brilliance was like that of a priceless jewel, like a crystal-clear diamond. It had a great, high wall with twelve gates; at the gates were twelve angels; and inscribed on the gates were the names of the twelve tribes of Yisra'el. There were three gates to the east, three gates to the north, three gates to the south and three gates to the west. The wall of the city was built on twelve foundation stones, and these were the twelve names of the twelve emissaries of the Lamb." Hit'gelut 21: 1-14

As clearly shown in the above quotes in Proofs #I

and #2, Yisra'el is the first born son of Y'HoVaH who gets the special blessings and inheritance of the Aba. Elohim chose them and set them apart as kodesh to be a blessing to all the nations and promised to bless those Gentiles who bless and help the Y'hudim and curse the ones who curses them.

Elohim rescued his people from Pharaoh and punished the Egyptians severely for their harsh treatment of the Yisra'elim, who were their slaves, as shown in Proof #3.

In Proofs #4, #5 and #11 Y'HoVaH plainly says that the foreigners or Goyim living with the Y'hudim are to obey the same rules and regulations, such as the keeping of Shabbat as will be shown in Part 3, as his treasured people do. There are not two sets of mitzvot, or moral commands, one for Y'hudim and one for non-Y'hudim, as most Protestants argue. Elohim even promises more blessings on the obedient Gentiles who have joined the Y'hudim; probably because they are at such a disadvantage since they have been brought up in a Pagan/Christian anti-Y'hudi enviromnent.

In proofs #7, #8 and #9 the Yisraelim are called his unique treasure out of *all* the peoples on the earth and promised in Proof #9 that they will be raised high above all the nations in praise, reputation and glory, *if* they remain obedient to the mitzvot of Y'HoVaH their Elohim. They have become the people of Y'HoVaH, but as with all covenants with Y'HoVaH—including the one today involving Y'hudim who have recognized Y'shua as their Mashiach and the Gentiles who have joined themselves to these Y'hudi believers—it is conditional on obedience to Elohim's laws, rulings, regulations and mitzvot.

Y'hovah states in Proofs #10 and #12 that he will never abandon Yisra'el, the descendants of Avraham, Yitz'chak, and Ya'akov—they are his eternal people.

Y'shua says in Proof #15 that he loved his own people, the Yisra'elim, to the end. Y'shua never turned against the Y'hudim while sojourning on earth, even though some of them hated him enough to want him killed. Not only did Elohim create the chosen people starting with Avraham, then Yitz'chak, then Ya'akov, or Yisra'el, but he dealt directly and exclusively with them, both in oral and written Ivrit, and entrusted them to keep a written record of these communications, which they have done. Then when it was time for Ben Elohim to also become the Son of Man and to live on earth among men, his ancestry was miraculously traced from Y'hudah, the fourth son of Ya'akov and he was given the Y'hudi name of Y'shua which means salvation.

Think about that. Elohim became a Y'hudi. Y'shua, the Y'hudi Mashiach, dealt exclusively with his people, the Yisra'elim, or descendants of Yisra'el, during his short time on earth (Mattityahu 15:24) just as Elohim's Y'hudi prophets had done for the previous 2000 years. The Y'hudim were Elohim's light to the non-Y'hudim before Y'shua's time on earth, during Y'shua's time on earth, and after Y'shua's time on earth. The Y'hudi people represent Elohim. As Yosef Shulam said, "At the right hand of Elohim today sits a circumcised Y'hudi by the name of Y'shua." And Y'shua still loves his own people while sitting at Ha Aba's side in heaven where he is identical to Elohim. (Yochanan 1:18).

In Proof #16 we learn that the kodesh city in the new heaven and new earth is named New Yerushalayim; not New York, not New London, not New Paris, not New

Moscow, and certainly not New Roma; but the new Y'hudi city of New Yerushalayim!

Please take note of the names inscribed, in Ivrit, on the twelve gates of this kodesh city in the new heaven and new earth: Re'uven, Shim'on, Levi, Y'hudah, Yissakar, Z'vulun, Yosef, Binyamin, Dan, Asher, Gad, and Naphtali (B'resheet 35:22-26; Mattityahu 10:1-4; Lukem 6:14-16; Ma'asheh 1:26).

Also, the names on the twelve foundation stones of the holy city of New Yerushalayim coming down out of heaven from Elohim were Y'shua's chosen special emissaries: Kifa, Andrey (brother of Kifa), Ya'akov Ben-Zavday, Yochanan (brother of Ya'akov), Philip Bar-Talmai, T'oma, Mattityahu (tax collector), Ya'akov Bar-Halfai, Tadday, Shim'on the Zealot, Y'hudah Ben-Ya'akov, Mattityahu (replacement for Y'hudah from K'riot (Mattityahu 10:2-4; Mark 3:4-19; Luke 6:13-16).

Guess what? They are all Yisra'elim! All twenty-four of them! There won't be any Y'hudi-haters or anti-Semitic people on the kodesh mountain of Elohim mentioned in Proof #11 nor in the kodesh city of Eiohim mentioned in Proof #16. So make the vow that Rut did in Proof #14, because salvation is from the Y'hudim. (Yochanan 4:22)

Part 2 - History

Question: What is the history—the fruits—of Christianity, especially regarding their dealings with the Y'hudim?
Answer: Christians have hated and persecuted the Y'hudim unmercifully from the very beginning of their (Christian) existence.

Proofs:

The proof lies in the secular history of Christianity itself. This proof is readily available today in books and on the Internet if an individual has the will to search for it and the courage to use a little common sense and a little dot for connecting when they find it. A few historical examples of Christian atrocities against the Y'hudim are presented in the commentary that follows.

I believe that the religion called Christianity was officially inaugurated under the rule of Roman emperor

Flavius Valerius Aurelius Constantinus in the early part of the fourth century C.E.—F. V. A Constantinus ruled from 306 to his death in 337. By royal decree he declared Christianity to be the official religion of the entire Roman Empire, and he provided the first Cathedral "seat" at the Lateran Palace—later called St. John's Lateran Palace—for the first Roman Catholic pope, Sylvester I, in 325.

One can only speculate as to his motives for creating this Christian religion. He was just a typical evil, self-serving, clever, power-mad, vain, ruthless, megolamanical, autocratic, tyrannical, murderous Roman ruler. He murdered his eldest son, Crispus, and his second wife Fausta, who had previously resided in the Lateran Palace. He was a Roman soldier/politician who happened to be emperor and probably saw this new religion as a means to bring all the various and sundry religious beliefs in his vast realm under the control of one state-approved religion. However, I believe that in the big scheme of things, Constantinus and his minions were just pawns for their spiritual master haSatan who cleverly contrived to eliminate the Y'hudim, whom Elohim has entrusted with the salvation of mankind, and replace them with Gentiles, thereby eliminating salvation.

This new "witch's brew" of a religion named Christianity—it more appropriately should have been designated Constantinianity—would supposedly appeal to all Roman subjects since it was a "pork-barrel" religion which had something in it for everybody, pagans and non-pagans alike.

The supposed instruction book for this new religion was a plagiarized and perverted Gentile version of a Y'hudi book called the Bible. All the Y'hudi titles, names and places in the Bible, both Tanakh and B'rit Hadashah, were given Gentile-sounding titles, names and places as discussed earlier.

The books of the Tanakh were rearranged and renamed and called the Old Testament and then copied into Latin from the Septuagint, which was an earlier Greek translation of the Tanakh. The B'rit Hadashah or New Covenant Scriptures was renamed the New Testament and copied from the Ivrim and Greek original manuscripts into Latin.

The books of the New Covenant which were originally written in Ivrit were then either destroyed or hidden in the vast underground archives of the Vatican. The Empire and the Church then proceeded to make it illegal for the common people to own or read even these contaminated Latin versions of the Bible. Only the officials of the Church, called clergy, had access to its pages and these evil people were the final authority on Christian doctrinal matters. Disagreement with the Church and its evil practices and practitioners was not tolerated. Lies, and deception, perverted clerical employees such as homosexual priests and nuns, corruptions, papal edicts, rituals, chants, signs, sorceries, incantations, magic spells, exorcisms, sacraments, inquisitions, heinous murders such as being burned alive, imprisonments, tortures, artifacts, idols, crosses, rosary beads, trinkets, bones, shrouds, confiscations and lootings of property and valuables of those murdered and imprisoned, claims of papal infallibility, opulent cathedrals and palaces, vast holdings of Vatican wealth such as real estate, gold, silver, and precious gems, prohibitions of reading the Old or New Testaments and an irrational hatred of Elohim's chosen people—the Y'hudim—defined the Roman Catholic Christian religion.

Some other major deviations from Y'HoVaH's instructions to the Y'hudim in his Torah that occurred under this new Christian religion were:

a.) Elohim's weekly special day of rest, Shabbat, for man, which he clearly defined as the seventh day of the week, starting at sundown of the sixth day and going to sundown of the seventh day, was changed to Sunday.

Sunday was named after the Roman sun god—Sol Invictus—and is measured in Roman time from midnight Saturday—named after the Roman god Saturn—to midnight Sunday and is mostly part of the first day of the week. Shabbat is discussed in more detail later.

b.) The Y'hudi special days or celebrations which praise and honor Elohim such as Pesach, Rosh HaShanah, Purim, Shavu'ot, Yom Kippur, Sukkot, etc. that Elohim instituted in the Torah were replaced by the revelry of Pagan/Papal/Protestant holidays, which of course were not instituted by Elohim, such as Halloween, All Saints Day, All Souls Day, Christmas, Epiphany, Saint Valentines Day, Palm Sunday, Ash Wednesday, Holy Thursday, Good Friday, Easter Sunday, Easter Monday, April's Fool Day, Saint Patrick's Day, etc.

c.) Unclean meats from scavengers such as pigs, shellfish, catfish, etc. which Y'HoVaH strictly forbade his people, the Yisra'elim, from eating now became the meat of choice for Christians, especially ham on their most important holidays of Christmas and Easter; more about proper diet later.

Under this new Roman religion which was designed to replace both the Y'hudi theology and the Y'hudi people, the Y'hudim began to be severely discriminated against and persecuted; just as a hated cowbird takes over another bird's nest by laying her eggs in it and then the fledgling interloping cowbirds force out and kill the legitimate fledglings. The Y'hudim had to be silenced and eliminated.

Some examples of Y'hudi persecution which occurred during and shortly after the Christian rule of Constantinus I are as follows:

1.) On March 7, 321 Constantinus passed the first Sunday law which stated: "On the venerable Day of the Sun (Sunday) let the magistrates and people residing in cities rest, and let all workshops be closed."

2.) In the year 329, Y'hudim were forbidden to perform the act of circumcision on slaves who wished to embrace Y'hudi beliefs (Note: Y'hudi beliefs in this discussion refers to both Mashiachi and non-Mashiachi).

3.) Y'hudim were forbidden to own Christian slaves, although Christians were permitted to own both Christian and Y'hudi slaves.

4.) A year later, all people in the Roman Empire were forbidden to convert to the Y'hudi way of life; for any who did convert, the death penalty was prescribed.

5.) The death penalty was specified for all Y'hudim who taught the Torah to Gentiles or encouraged Gentiles to embrace Y'hudi beliefs specified in the Torah.

6.) Y'hudi converts to Christianity were promised certain privileges and rewards but they were never really trusted and were constantly being watched.

7.) All intermarriage between Y'hudim and Gentiles was forbidden, unless the Y'hudim converted to Christianity; the Y'hudi woman as well as the Y'hudi man would suffer death for intermarriage but not the Gentile man or woman.

8.) Y'hudi beliefs were referred to in imperial pronouncements as the *secta nefaria* or the *sectaferalis,* namely the "unspeakable religion" and the "bestial religion."

9.) Christianity was installed as the official religion of the Roman Empire.

10.) As a final touch, Constantinus reinstituted the ancient command of Emperor Hadrian, issued after the Y'hudi uprising of Bar Kochba, which forbade any Y'hudi to set foot in Yerushalayim.

11.) Later in 364, at the Council of Laodicea, during the reign of Pope Liberius, it was decreed: Christians are not allowed to be idle or to speak of their beliefs on a Shabbat, but instead must work. So it was done. Christianity was established in the Western World in the holy hatred of the Y'hudhim themselves and their practices—a hatred that would exact from the Y'hudim suffering beyond description, untold millions of lives, and a river of blood and burnt bodies." (Ref *The Jews, Story of a People* by Howard Fast, 1968, pg. 154, 155)

Another disciple of haSatan called Mohammed came along about 300 years after Constantinus I and started another replacement theology religion called Islam. Both Islam and Christianity are monotheistic—one worships a deity called God or Lord and the other a deity called God or

Allah—in nature and they both share a common irrational, almost insane, hatred for Elohim's people, the Y'hudim.

They also both preach a doctrine of hate and death to infidels and heretics. It's "convert or die." They differed, however, in their preferred method of punishment for heretics: Catholic Christians liked to tie their heretics to a stake and burn them alive, while the Muslims were a little more humane and would usually just slit the throats or behead their dissidents. Both religions are responsible for the shedding of a lot of innocent Y'hudi blood, as well as Gentile blood, but nobody is even close to the Catholic Church when it comes to total Y'hudi body count. The history of the Y'hudi Diaspora in Europe is simply the story of the Y'hudim trying to stay one step ahead of their Christian executioners who approached them holding a crucifix in their left hand and a sword in their right hand. A few historical examples of some of the more egregious atrocities or "bad fruit" which Christendom is responsible for are as follows:

A.) "The power and numbers of the Jews living in Alexandria, Egypt had shrunk subsequent to the overthrow of the Ptolemies by Rome in 180 B.C.E. but they managed to hold their own until the time of Christianity—when formal anti-Semitism replaced the intermittent anti-Semitism that they had combated for so long by the half-Hellenized pagan Egyptians. Yet they maintained themselves as an important community until the year 415 C.E. when Catholic Bishop Cyril instigated a brutal mob movement against them. Thousands of Jews were slaughtered by the Christian mobs, and thousands more were given the choice of baptism or death, watching their wives and children blinded. Some chose death, but many more gave in and accepted baptism. Subsequently, most of them who had been baptized fled from Egypt to begin life again as Jews in another land." (Fast, pg. 194,195).

B.) Consider over 200 years of Catholic Crusades atrocities from 1090-1320. The Crusades were primarily a campaign to brutally murder as many Y'hudim as possible—in the name of Christ, of course—under the guise of fighting the Muslim Turks or Ottomans.

"At the council of Clermont, France in 1096, Peter the Hermit preached to a great gathering of the 'flower of French chivalry,' with Pope Urban II listening approvingly in the background. Such was the chivalrous spirit of the 'flowers' that one, Godfrey of Bouillon, fired by the glory of the moment and the hope of redeeming Jerusalem, the city of Jesus, from the infidel, took a mighty oath: 'I will avenge the blood of little Iesus on the blood of the Iews—and God willing leave not one of the cursed lot alive.' ...

In Worms, Germany, all the Jews were killed. Killing the infants, the Crusaders cried out that they were saving the souls of the children for Christos. There as in most places, the Jewish houses, synagogues, and community buildings were burned.

In Neuss, Germany, the Crusaders were drunk, and in the spirit of good fun they threw more than twenty women and almost a hundred children into the river, seeing how far two men could fling a screaming child.

At Mors, Germany, almost a thousand Jewish bodies were observed floating in the Rhine.

In Regensburg, Germany, the Jews were cut down in

the streets. Count Agthar likened it to rabbit hunting. A great pile of Jewish bodies was dragged into the main square, and Crusaders amused themselves by beheading the dead. Over four thousand Jews were killed in this Rhine district alone." (Fast, p. 249, 250).

And it wasn't just German and French Christians who were busily and eagerly murdering Y'hudim during the Crusades in Europe. "Followers of Richard the Lion-Hearted turned their attention to the Jews of Lynne, England, killing all of them they could catch, stripping the bodies naked, and then pillaging the Jewish houses, they went on to Stamford.

Ten days later they were at Colchester—then Thetford, then Ospringe, where they got a bit out of hand and killed a dozen Christians.

In York, a half-insane mob, led by some drunken Crusaders, marched to attack the Jews. About five hundred of them fled to the Royal Keep, which at that moment was empty, the Royal Warder being away. The Jews took refuge there, barricaded the stout doors, and listened from behind them to the threats and infamies of the mob. Days passed. Weak from hunger, parched by thirst, the Jews chose an alternative to the torture and crucifixion that the mob promised. They killed each other, submitting willingly. Their gentle Rabbi Yomtov was the last, and he died by his own hand." (Fast, p. 251).

"So was Jesus honored in a mighty Christian effort called the Crusades. One could go on and on, detailing the horrors that occured in almost every community in Europe, not to mention those in Asia, and of course in Israel itself—when the Crusaders had captured Jerusalem in 1099, every Jew and Karaite in the city had been hunted down and murdered, often in a manner that beggars description.

"Indeed, a meticulous observer could have created an encyclopedia of bestiality out of that which history remembers as the 'Holy Crusades.' Western civilization has thrown up some odd specimens at times, but for sheer insane bloodlust and cruelty, the Crusaders are hard to match." (Fast, pg. 196, 251).

Unfortunately, most modern-day Christians seem to be proud of the Crusades. The athletic teams of Holy Cross University in Massachusetts are called the Crusaders. One of the larger Protestant groups even call themselves, the Billy Graham Crusade. Oh well, I guess it's just an inherited thing from the "mother-whore."

C.) After the Crusades, Catholic Germany became a place of unremitting horror for the Jew. Hatred for the Jew became a part of German being, of German culture—and even of German "excellence," as the German mind saw it. In 1298, Rindfleisch, a German knight, promoted a series of dreadful massacres in the district of Franconia, a great mob-army of Germans led by the Baron Rindfleisch, murdered the Jews in 146 communities.

As always in these grim German affairs, women and children were murdered along with the men. I cannot help noting that nowhere in ancient warfare, among so-called pagans and barbarians, do we find anything to match this Christian wrath.

In the 146 towns and villages, not a single Jew was left alive. In 1336, a movement arose in Germany that was based on the single fact of killing Jews. The members wore a short jacket of red leather and were called the

Armleder. Feeling themselves divinely motivated—within the German understanding of Christianity—they massacred the Jews in almost a hundred communities, most of them in Swabia and Alsace.

Twelve years later, Europe was scourged by the disease remembered as the Black Death." I believe it was Elohim's punishment on them for what they had done to the Y'hudi people. "Living under the strict regime of their dietary and lavatory laws, the Jews were to a very large extent exempt from the disease—which naturally led to the conclusion on the part of the Germans that the Jews had caused the disease by poisoning the wells. Over 210 communities of Jews were utterly annihilated.... and another 400 Jewish communities were attacked and suffered deaths. The toll of how many thousands of Jews were murdered by the Germans during this sad time has never been precisely calculated; but this was the worst holocaust of the Middle Ages, not to be equaled until Adolf Hitler turned the tools of modem science, in the hands of the capable citizen, to the same end." (Fast, pg. 257, 258).

D.) "By the end of the thirteenth century the Papal Inquisition had developed a system of records and officials, and its arm was notoriously long, so that the very name Inquisition started to strike terror into every heart. With complete independence, it possessed its own prisons and its activities were clothed in secrecy.

"Pope Innocent IV sanctioned the use of torture in 1252. The Inquisitor was to be maintained by the property of the victim—and his property was taken upon arrest. No defense was permitted, and the names of accusers were hidden. These were features that would also distinguish the Spanish Inquisition, though that institution developed them to a high pitch of sadistic perfection." (Ref. *The Most Evil Men and Women in History* by Miranda Twiss, p 52, 53).

"The Spanish Inquisition was officially born on September 7, 1480 when Pope Sixtus IV issued a Papal Bull (edict of the Pope) giving the Spanish sovereign, Queen Isabella, the right to appoint two Inquisitors from the Dominican Order to root out heresy in her Kingdom of Castille.

"A quemadero, or place of burning, was constructed just outside the Seville city walls. At the four corners, huge plaster figures of the four major prophets (Y'hudim) had been erected. To insure the maximum number of spectators for this horror show, the executions were performed on public holidays. The condemned Jews would be tied to a pyre of dry wood, located well above the crowd, to ensure a good view. When they were dead, the body was separated into pieces, the bones were broken and everything was thrown onto a fresh fire.

"The first Auto-de-fe (Act of faith) took place on February 6, 1481 at the newly constructed quemadero when six conversos, or Jewish men and women converts to Catholicism, were burned alive. Jews who fled Seville were mostly soon returned by neighboring communities out of fear of the Inquisitor's tribunals. By November 4, 1481, 290 Jews had been burned alive and 98 condemned to perpetual imprisonment. In February, 1482, Pope Sixtus IV appointed another seven Dominican friars, known as 'Hounds of the Lord,' as Inquisitors. One of them, the prior of a monastery in Segovia, was Tomas de Torquemada." (Twiss, p. 55, 60).

"Torquemada had previously been content with being

the power behind the throne of Queen Isabella, but his sadistic nature and fanatical devotion to his Christian religion made him the perfect candidate for the position of Inquisitor.

"He had found his calling—hunting down and murdering Jews. He was so good at his new job that in October, 1483, he was promoted to the new office of Inquisitor General who had ultimate authority in Spain to root out converso heretics.

"By then, the tribunals of the Inquisition were established in four other locations, and by 1492 tribunals were operating in eight major cities. When Torquemada's train of death appeared, city gates were flung open, the resources of the city were placed at his disposal and magistrates swore him their devotion.

"The Inquisition would descend on a town or village at regular intervals and present themselves to the local church and civic authorities. A day would be proclaimed and everyone would be compelled to attend a special Mass to hear the inquisitor's 'Edict' read in public.

"On the appointed day, at the end of the sermon, the inquisitor would raise a crucifix. Those in attendance would be required to raise their right hands, cross themselves and repeat an oath to support the Inquisition and its servants. In theory, each case was to be examined by a conclave of theologians—the visiting Inquisitor and at least one local, but in practice many people were arrested before their cases were assessed.

"The Inquisition's prisons were crammed with people waiting to hear the charges against them, and they might be kept for years without knowing why. In the meantime, they and their families would have been stripped of all their property, for an arrest was always accompanied by the immediate confiscation of all the accused's belongings— everything from the house down to pots and pans. Whilst in prison, the accused's property could be sold off to pay for his maintenance in captivity. When eventually released, he could find himself bankrupt or destitute.

"Children of prisoners are recorded as having died from starvation. The Jews who survived the prisons and tortures were usually those who had 'confessed' and would usually be required, as a form of penance, to wear a large saffron cross on the breast and back of all their garments for the rest of their lives and be exposed to constant social humiliation, ridicule and violence." (Twiss, p. 57, 58, 59).

The saffron or yellow cross, was the forerunner of the Nazi yellow Star of David patches that the Y'hudim, under Hitler's reign of terror, had to wear on the upper arms of all their shirt or coat sleeves to identify them as Y'hudim. The yellow color derived from the Y'hudim who dealt a lot with the saffron herb and therefore had yellow stains on their hands.

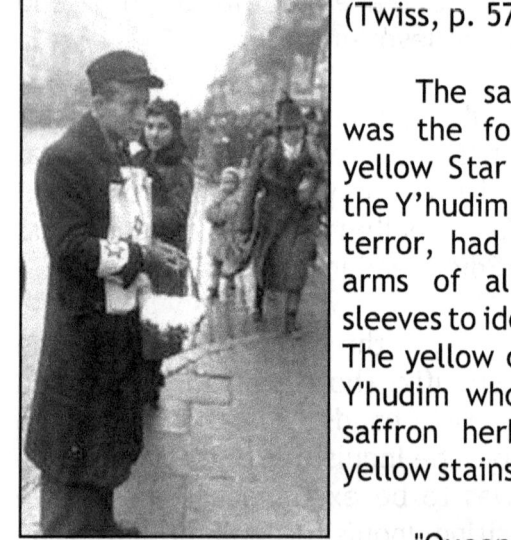

A young Jew selling Star of David armbands in the Warsaw ghetto. [New York Public Library Digital Collection]

"Queen Isabel de Castilla and King Fernando of Aragon had since married and combined the two large Spanish provinces into one. Tomas, whose zealous inquisitorial efforts were being hindered by the mix of converso and non-converso Jews in Spain—he legally only had authority to go after the conversos who easily could be accused of heresy if they were observed putting God's commands above the Papacy's commands—finally prevailed on Queen Isabella to expel all non converso Jews from Spain by August, 1492.

"There were around 300,000 Jews living in Spain at the time who had to do one of four things: become conversos by actually converting to Catholicism and taking a Spanish name; pretend to convert to Catholicism but secretly remain Jewish and become a marranos (means swine in Spanish); get out of Spain in the short time available; remain in Spain as a Jew and try to avoid the inquisitors.

"These were Jews who had lived and prospered under the previous 300 year rule of the Muslim Moorish Empire and had become an important and vital part of Spanish society just as they are in any society." (Twiss, p. 52, 60).

The Y'hudim are a civilizing influence on nations because they are Elohim's moral light to the Gentiles (Yesha'yahu 42:6, 7; Ma'asheh 13:47). Can you imagine uprooting your family from its property, livelihood, friends, and relatives, where they had lived for many generations? Their property and furnishings became worthless because the populace knew it would soon be theirs, free for the taking.

Remember, in 1492 there were no automobiles, trains, and planes. They could only take with them what they could carry or load on a donkey. Of course they were easy prey for thieves who had a free hand with them. And once you packed, where do you go? Neighboring Portugal, another

Catholic Christian country, didn't want them and would return them to España.

Many Y'hudim booked passage on sailing ships at high prices and were taken out to sea and dumped overboard.

In fact, Cristoforo Colombo's date for departing with his three ships from the port city of Palos de la Frontera, España bound for the West Indies just happened to coincide with the deadline date, August 2, 1492, that the Y'hudim had to be out of España.

Mr. Columbo was delayed because of the glut of boats in the harbor filled with Y'hudim trying to escape. Coincidence? I don't think so. I see the hand of Y'HoVaH at work providing a new safe haven for his people an ocean away from Y'hudi-hating Christian Europe. Most of the Y'hudim and their descendants—an estimated 30,000—who remained because they couldn't find a way to leave España and also the ones who chose to ride-it-out as conversos were eventually arrested and charged with heresy and burned alive at the local quemadero between 1493 and 1800.

If you didn't like your neighbor, or you owed him money, or he was a business rival, or you simply didn't like Y'hudim, you could anonymously lie to an inquisitor and say you saw them observing Pesach instead of Easter, observing Chanukkah instead of Christmas, washing their hands before eating or before prayer, resting on a weekly Shabbat, working on Sunday, eating kosher food or refusing to eat pig meat, etc. Arrest, imprisonment, torture, and most likely death by burning would quickly ensue. The inquisitors wouldn't get their grubby little hands dirty, they were the supervisors, witnesses, and clerks copying the victims last utterances—mostly screams and moans.

'The Church ruled that you could only torture someone once, but they easily got around that little minor restriction by saying they had only suspended the torture, not ended it. So the torture of the rack, thumbscrews, and white hot pincers—the hot pincers or pliers served a dual purpose of inflicting pain and also cauterizing the wound, since the Church wanted a minimum of bloodshed—would continue. They also used toca or water torture where water was forced down a victim's throat (sounds similar to our modern-day waterboarding). Also there was potro when a person is bound to a large wheel or circular rack by tight cords that could be tightened further and further. Then there was garrucha in which a heretic would be hung by the wrists from a pulley in the ceiling with weights fastened to his or her feet and then slowly raising the pulley, to maximize the pain, and then dropped abruptly a few feet, dislocating limbs.

"The Inquisition realized that confessions under torture did not carry a great deal of weight since under severe pain people will say anything. The victims were therefore made to confirm their statements a couple of days later so the confession could be labeled, 'not under duress." (Twiss, p. 59, 60).

Can you even begin to comprehend what these innocent Y'hudi people endured during the Church's Spanish Inquisition? Can you imagine the horror of being burned alive and seeing your flesh melt off your bones before you lose consciousness? This is the most depraved of wicked acts and to make it worse, they claimed to be doing it for God. There are still very few Y'hudim living in Espana today and Espana remains an insignificant nation even today.

E.) Also, lets not forget the Pogroms or organized massacres against Y'hudim in Russia, Ukraine, Latvia, Lithuania and Estonia under the auspices of the Eastern Catholic or Eastern Orthodox Christian Church—pretty much the same as the Western Catholic or Roman Catholic Church, except they don't have a Papacy with a Pope residing at the Vatican but instead have national Patriarchs or Archbishops.

About 500,000 Y'hudim were massacred by Ukranian Nationalist Bohdan Chelnitsky in the 1600's. These were mostly Y'hudim who had fled España in the late 15th century. (Ref. *Maoz Israel Report,* Dec. 2012)

"The year 1881 is rather sadly called 'the year the pogroms officially began.' In a town called Elisavetgrad in the Ukraine, an argument started in a tavern. A few drunken Russian soldiers and peasants began to elaborate on the sorry old saw of the ritual murder of Gentile children for their blood.

Jews present and listening took exception and a fight started. Three Jews were killed then and there, and the tavern fight boiled into a full scale riot. The rioters wrecked the Jewish quarter, set the Jewish houses aflame, and counted their loot.

Beer and vodka and vocal anti-Semitism spread the riot to Kherson and from there to Kiev. A week after it began, a whole garrison of soldiers was loosed into it, not to quell it but to join in the killing and looting.

The Russian officers stood by and the Czar and his advisors read the reports with delight. For them it was an opportunity to turn all the social unrest and revolutionary agitation aside and bury it under a national wave of anti-Semitism.

The Ukraine was a difficult and nationalistic place; the Czar decided to let Ukranians take out their frustration and hatred on the Jews. The riots spread to Odessa and to a thousand villages and hamlets between Kiev and Odessa.

Tens of thousands of Jews were robbed, beaten, and raped, poor people were burned in the shacks they lived in. Hundreds of them lay dead in the streets of their tiny villages. A group of edicts called the 'May Laws' were passed under the Czar's urging—expelling Jews by the thousands from the larger towns and cities." (Fast, p. 307-308). "Fiddler on the Roof" is an excellent movie depicting the struggles of Y'hudim living in nineteenth century Czarist Russia.

Thus the Y'hudi Pale of Settlement in Russia—an area of land where the Y'hudim had lived for centuries in their tiny hamlets and in the cities nearby—was destroyed, even as the Y'hudi will to live and work in Europe was broken.

The most intelligent, erudite, sophisticated, successful, hard-working, tolerant, patient, gentle, and peaceful people on earth had at last found their condition intolerable and the fortunate ones began to exodus, mostly they immigrated to another continent far away—America and its New York City—mostly between 1880 and 1920. By 1920 America was home to about six million Y'hudim, about half the total number of Y'hudim in the world. The anti-Y'hudi *Johnson Immigration Act* of 1921 and 1924 halted the influx of Y'hudim into the United States and subsequently resulted in untold millions dying at the hands of the Nazis and Nazi sympathizers in Europe, because no nation, including America, would give them refuge.

Just as earlier the Y'hudim of Europe had got along well with the Pagans until they were Christianized by the Roman Catholic Church, the Y'hudim remaining in the Soviet Union under the Bolshevik Communist rule fared much better than they had under the Czars and the Eastern or Russian Orthodox Church. In other words, paganistic, atheistic, polytheistic, idolatrous, non--monotheistic religions treated the Y'hudim better than the monotheistic Christians.

F.) HaSatan's crowning achievement in his quest to exterminate all of Elohim's chosen people off the face of the earth: the Nazi Holocaust, under the direction of Austrian Roman Catholic dictator Adolf Hitler—yes this monster was a Roman Catholic, as all Austrians are. The Nazis are responsible for the murders of over six million European and Soviet Y'hudim in a span of about twelve years between 1933-1945.

The Christians of Europe exterminated almost half of the total number of Y'hudim in existence at the time. It was a Satanic bloodlust frenzy which continued in the death camps even as the war was ending and American and Russian artillery could be heard in the distance. This is yet another example of hatred and evil that I have great trouble comprehending.

Adolfus Hitler was born in Brannau, Austria on April 20, 1889, to Alois and Klara Hitler and two days later was baptized in the local Catholic church by Father Ignaz Probst. By the time Adolf was eight years old he had become a Mutterssohnchen, or mother's boy, and was incurably devoted to his staunch Catholic mother with a latent and sometimes open hostility towards his father.

The family moved to Lambach, Austria, when Adolf was eight years old. "He was admitted to an elementary school which was attached to a Benedictine monastery, founded in the eleventh century, and was immediately fascinated by the new world of church ritual, the black robed monks, and the abbot ruling his flock with all the authority of an earthly king.

He did well in the school and was overwhelmed by the beauty of the services. Ecclesiastical music fascinated him, and in his spare time he took singing lessons so he could sing in the choir.

"Again and again I enjoyed the best possibility of intoxicating myself with the solemn splendor of the dazzling festivities of the Church," he wrote later. "It seemed to me perfectly natural to regard the abbot as the highest and most desirable ideal, just as my father regarded the village priest as his ideal." There was thus no trace of anticlericalism in the family.

For two years Adolf contemplated the possibility of one day joining the community of monks, eventually rising to the position of abbot, with supreme authority over all the monks. He enjoyed the church ceremonies and looked upon the abbot with awe and veneration. Visitors to the monastery have observed one curious and memorable detail. In six or seven places—over the ornamental gateway, over a stone well, and over some of the stalls in the abbey—a swastika appears.

The swastika was included in the coat of arms of abbot Theodorich von Hagen, who ruled the monastery in the 1750s and 60s. InGerman, a swastika is a *Hakenkreuz*, and evidently the abbot regarded it as a pun on his own name, the difference between Haken and Hagen being so small that it might pass unobserved.

Adolf, then living in a well-designed building at the corner of the Linzerstrasse and the Kirchengasse, could see the swastika from the window of his father's apartment, and he saw it more clearly when he went to school.

Abbot Theodorich von Hagen's swastika was probably the ancestor of the Nazi Hakenkreuz." (Ref. ***The Life and Death of Adolf Hitler*** by Robert Payne, pg. 15, 17, 20, 21). So the Catholic Church not only taught Adolf to hate Y'hudim, it also provided him with his hated Nazi symbol: the swastika or twisted cross.

Hitler greeting Catholic priests. [New York Public Library Digital Collection.]

Hitler is quoted as saying in a speech in 1926: "Christ was the greatest early fighter in the battle against the world enemy, the Juden (pronounced **Yoo**-dehn in German)... The work Christ started but could not finish, I, Adolf Hitler, will conclude."

In 1933, during a meeting with Catholic Church

officials, Hitler declared that he, "merely wanted to do more effectively what the church had attempted to accomplish for so long," maintaining that his actions—the attempt to exterminate all Juden on earth—"were service to a common cause."

The sign that greeted Y'hudim entering Dachau, one of the most infamous of the Nazi death camps, read: "You Are Here Because You Killed Our God." The belt buckles of SS soldiers, who just happened to be all Austrian, often read, "God With Us." (Ref. The Distortion by John and Patrice Fischer, p. 43).

This "murder for God" of Elohim's people was prophesied to occur by Y'shua in Yochanan 16:2 "...the time will come when anyone who kills you (Y'hudim) will think he is serving Elohim!"

Another person who had a bad influence on Adolf was the German Roman Catholic Christian monk, Martin Luther. Hitler revered Luther—as most Protestants do today—and his book, **Mein Kampf**, is full of references to his spiritual hero, Martin Luther.

Luther was a dyed-in-the-wool Yude hater as can be evidenced by some of his quotes regarding his own "final solution" to the Y'hudi problem: "First, their synagogues or churches should be set on fire. Secondly, their homes should likewise be broken down and destroyed. They ought to be put under one roof or in a stable, like Gypsies, in order that they may realize that they are not masters in our land, as they boast, but miserable captives. Thirdly, they should be deprived of their prayer books and Talmuds in which such idolatry, lies, cursing, and blasphemy are taught. Fourthly, their rabbis must be forbidden under threat of death to teach anymore. Fifthly, passport and traveling privileges should be absolutely forbidden to the Yuden. Sixthly, they ought to be stopped from usury. All their cash and valuables of silver and gold ought to be taken from them and put aside for safekeeping. For this reason, as said before, everything that they possess they stole and robbed from us through their usury, for they have no other means of support. Seventhly, let the young and strong Yuden and Yudenesses be given the flail, the ax, the hoe, the spade, the distaff, and spindle." (Ref. ***Chutzpah*** by Alan M. Dershowitz, p.106. 107).

Hitler followed Luther's advice and even added step number eight: Murder all who have one fourth or more Y'hudi blood or ancestry, including all women of all ages, all male infants and children, all older men, all the sick and infirmed men; and work the young healthy males to death on a starvation diet. I'm sure Martin would have hardly approved of step number eight.

My wife and I, along with one of our grandsons, recently visited the "Anne Frank in the World Exhibit, 1929-45" in Sandy Springs, Georgia. They have a plethora of photos regarding Miss Frank and the Holocaust in general, along with an excellent 30 minute video.

However, photo exhibit #23 titled "Church and Religion" especially caught my attention and is most revealing of the Christian connection to the Holocaust. I will quote some of what I read and describe a few of the photos: "Although the Nazi ideology is basically anti-Christian, from 1933 on, the Nazis can count on ample support from the German churches. With few exceptions, both the Protestant and Catholic churches endorse the racial and political principles of the Nazis. On March 28,

1933, the Catholic bishops declare their loyalty to Hitler. The next month the Protestant 'Altpreussische Union' also endorses Hitler. During elections in the Evangical Church on July 25, 1933, the anti-Semitic 'German Christians' capture a large majority. The official churches fail to protest against the persecution of the Jews, even Jews who had converted to Christianity."

Speech by Ludwig Müller after his formal inauguration as Bishop Reich in Berliner Dom, Sept. 23, 1934. [Bundesarchiv Bild 102-16219, Berlin, Dom, Einführung des Reichsbischofs]

One photo showed Bishop Muller speaking to a gathering of uniformed, Nazis in Berlin on Sept. 25, 1934.

Another showed an open-air church service at the opening of the "Reichstag" (Parliament) on Mar. 21, 1933.

In still another photo we see the baptism of an SS officer's child in what appears to be a Catholic church, one replete with swastikas hanging on the wall and even one next to the infant who

Bundesarchiv, Bild 146-1981-075-01 / CC-BY-SA 3.0 [CC BY-SA 3.0 de (https://creativecommons.org/licenses /by-sa/3.0/de/deed.en)]

Priests saluting Adolph Hitler [New York Public Library Digital Collection]

is lying on a pillow.

Still another photo reveals a Festival for Catholic Youth ceremony in Berlin in Aug. 1933, and shows seven black-robed Catholic clerics all with their right arms extended out at about 45 degrees in a Nazi salute and shouting, "Long live the Fuhrer."

The following information, about the Holocaust, where more than six million Y'hudim were brutally and methodically killed by the Nazis and their willing accomplices, the police, and the civilian population of Christian Europe, is taken from a book titled, **We Remember the Holocaust** by David A. Adler.

These atrocities, which were completely "legal" in Germany and its occupied countries, occurred over a twelve-year period starting in January 1933, and ending in May, 1945. But most of the mass murdering took place subsequent to the beginning of World War II, in September 1939, when the Germans invaded Poland and thereby took control of about two million Y'hudim living in western Poland. The remaining one million Polish Y'hudim living in eastern Poland fell into Nazi hands when Germany invaded the Soviet Union through Poland in June, 1941.

Like a shark in a feeding frenzy, the killing of Y'hudim started slowly but rapidly escalated as they refined their techniques while developing an insatiable lust for Y'hudi blood. Mr. Adler's book consists mainly of graphic personal eyewitness accounts of some of the few survivors. The Nazi Holocaust is an almost incomprehensible evil to me. The more you learn of what happened the worse it becomes.

"The Nazis wasted no time attacking the approximately seven hundred thousand Jews living in Germany once Hitler came to power as chancellor on January 30, 1933." (Adler, p. 105).

"The first concentration camp opened in Dachau, Germany on March 23, 1933. It was established by Heinrich Himmler, leader of the SS or *Schutzstaffel* (protection squad), as a 'model' camp. At the camp were thirty-two wooden barracks in two rows, all surrounded by an electric fence. Any prisoner caught walking toward the fence was shot. Camps such as Dachau, in which the enemies of Nazism were concentrated, became known as concentration camps. Labor and death camps set up later followed in many ways the brutal example set by Dachau and the other early concentration camps." (Adler, p. 12).

"On the Christian holiday of April Fool's Day, April 1, 1933, the Nazis encouraged a boycott of all Jewish owned stores and businesses and Jewish goods. The Christian German citizenry needed little encouragement to boycott Jewish stores.

"Officials throughout Germany, eager to show their support of Nazi policy, made their own decrees against Jews. They tried to force Jews out, so their towns could be made j*udenrein,* free of Juden. Any street named after a Jew was renamed. Monuments to Jews were destroyed. The names of Jewish soldiers were scratched off German memorials to the war dead.

"Tirzah Rothschild who lived in Hamburg, Germany, remembers: 'I saw Juden Unerwunscht—Jews Not Wanted—signs. They appeared all over, in food stores, clothing stores, and department stores, even though it wasn't the law yet.'" (Adler, p. 18, 21, 22).

"Jewish judges and lawyers were shut out of German courts and Jewish teachers, bankers, and railroad workers were fired in 1933." (Adler, p.l7).

"On May 10, 1933, the Nazis began an assault of a different kind. In Berlin, an estimated forty thousand people watched as five thousand German students marched behind cars and trucks loaded with books. The students carried lit torches, and they sang Nazi and college songs. The president of the student organization, wearing a Nazi uniform, declared that they had gathered to burn un-German books.

"As the books written by Jews and others were thrown into the fire, another student called out the names of the authors. 'Sigmund Freud! Erich Maria Remarque! Heinrich Heine! Thomas Mann! Emil Ludwig! Albert Einstein! Jack London! Ernest Hemingway! Stefan Zweig! Upton Sinclair! John Dos Passos! Theodore Dreiser! Sinclair Lewis! Helen Keller! Margaret Sanger!

"The crowd cheered. Dr. Joseph Goebbels, Nazi Minister of Popular Enlightenment and Propaganda declared, 'Jewish intellectualism is dead,' and again the crowd cheered. Millions of books were burned.

"A century before, Heinrich Heine, a German poet who was a Y'hudi, wrote: 'Where one burns books, one will, in the end, burn people.' How prophetic Mr. Heine was because eight years after the Nazi book burnings, Jews were burned to death.

"Only two youth groups were allowed—the Hitler Youth, for boys, and the League of German Girls. Both groups taught children to spy and report on enemies of Nazism, including their own parents." (Adler, p. 14).

"I must add that the previous Roman Catholic Pope Benedict—his real surname of Ratsinger is more descriptive of him—was a member of the Hitler Youth. The Nuremberg Laws were passed on September 15, 1935, which denied the Jews citizenship in Germany and prohibited them from flying a German flag, which was now a swastika or twisted cross symbol in a white circle on a red cloth.

"They were also prohibited from marrying a non-Jew. On March 3, 1936, Jewish doctors were prohibited from working in German hospitals. On July 16, 1937, the concentration camp of Buchenwald in central Germany was opened for "business." (Adler, p. 13, 108).

"On March 13, 1938, the German army marched unopposed into neighboring Austria to the cheers of the Austrian people. They greeted the German Army with their arms stretched out in the Nazi salute.

"Walter Strauss lived in Baden bei Wien, Austria. He remembers the very warm greeting many Austrians gave the invading Germans: 'We had a Jewish guest from Munich, Germany, the day the German Army marched into Austria. The next day my father had to go on a business trip. I was in the car when our guest drove Dad to the railway station in Vienna, about ten miles away. People must have assumed we were connected with the invasion. There we were, three Jews in a German car with German plates, and people all along our route to the station were smiling at us and giving us the Nazi salute.'

"Nazi police followed the German Army into Austria, and within days Jews lost their rights as citizens. German SS kicked and spit at Jews. They forced them to clean the streets and public toilets, to crawl on the ground and eat grass, to run in circles until they collapsed. Many Austrians watched the spectacle and laughed.

"Thea Sonnemark lived in Vienna. She remembers: 'At the end of March, 1938, as my father went to open his grocery store, the SA gave him a toothbrush and ordered him to scrub the street. Some of his non-Jewish customers came by, and when they saw my father there, they laughed and jeered. These were customers of long standing. He considered them to be friends.'" (Adler, p. 26-29).

Hitler enjoyed the support of many Catholic priests in Europe. [New York Public Library Digital Collection]

"The effects of the Nazi's anti-Jewish policies were felt beyond Germany and Austria. Anti-Semitic Christians all over the world were encouraged by them.

"In January of 1938, in Christian Romania, prior to the German occupation, there were anti-Jewish student riots. Jewish students were kept out of colleges. High taxes were imposed on Jewish businesses. Jews were physically assaulted. Anti-Jewish laws were passed in Christian Hungary in May, 1938, even before the Nazis took over their country. Jews lost their jobs, their homes, and their rights as citizens.

"Arthur Rubin lived in Derecske, Hungary, in the 1930s. 'I remember at the young age of six years walking to school or to synagogue, and all of a sudden kids in the courtyard would say, 'Hey, you're a Jude.' I remember being beaten and coming home with a bloody nose. It was particularly unwise to walk on the streets during Easter and Christmas holidays. On those holidays the name-calling and the Jew beatings were carried out with more zeal, with more passion than at other times.'

A hearty Christmas dinner with Der Führer. [New York Public Library Digital Collection]

"This hatred and hostility was a reflection, a mirror image of the adult population. In Christian Poland, before the German invasion on September 1, 1939, there were anti-Jewish boycotts and riots in the large cities, including such centers of Jewish life as Vilna and Warsaw.

"In small Polish towns and villages, peasants carrying clubs and rocks viciously attacked Jews just because they were Jews. Cecilia Bernstein was a young child in the 1930s and lived in a small town in Hungary. She remembers: 'Police with long black feathers in their hats rode on horses through the streets. We ran from them. They beat us, and no one could stop them.'

"Alfred Lipson lived in Radom, in central Poland, during the mid 1930s, prior to the German and Soviet invasion. He remembers: 'There were roving gangs in the streets. We were beaten many times. Once, I was in a movie theater with my mother. She was wearing a fur coat. When we left the theater, we found that anti-Semitic hoodlums sitting behind us in the theater had slit my mother's coat with razor blades.'" (Adler, p. 23, 24).

"On July 5, 1938 delegates from thirty-two countries met at Evian, France, not to discuss the problem of Jewish persecution but to discuss the problem of Jewish refugees. But delegates complained of unemployment and overpopulation in their countries. Large under-populated countries with no unemployment problems didn't want Jews either. Some said their countries could accept only agricultural workers, and Jews, denied the right to own land in Europe for hundreds of years were not farmers. No place was found for the hundreds of thousands of Jews who were desperate to escape persecution and death under the Nazis." (Adler, p. 42).

"This was a similar situation to the Y'hudim living in Spain about 450 years earlier. The Y'hudim of Germany, Austria, Poland, Italy, Hungary, and Romania had no place to go. The so-called civilized Christian and Muslim nations, including the United States, closed their doors to the doomed Y'hudim of Europe.

Anti-Semitism was also on the rise in other Christian countries such as Austria, Greece, Yugoslavia, Italy, and France; even in the United States. Cantor Moshe Ehrlich was born in Vienna, Austria. He remembers: "Anti-Semitism was rampant in Austria. Just as an example of it, on Good Friday, Holy Thursday, and Easter Sunday, I was warned by my parents not to go out, because Jews will be beaten up. This was before Hitler marched into Austria in March, 1938. The people would come home from church, and any Jew they could find, they would beat up. Seems they were getting a hate-filled sermon against the Jews at church."

"In the United States many anti-Jewish groups were formed, including the German-American Bund, the Silver Shirts, and the Christian Front. They published their views on radio, and in leaflets and magazines." (Adler, p. 23-25).

Then on November 9, 1938, along came a night of horror for the Jews of Germany and Austria: *Kristallnacht* or Night of Broken Glass where Germans and Austrians went on a murderous rampage against all Jews, burning their synagogues, breaking windows and looting their businesses and homes in revenge for the shooting on November 7, 1938, of a minor German official, Ernst vom Rath, in Paris, by a seventeen year old Jewish man by the name of Herschel Grynszpan. Herschel was angry because the Nazis had kicked his family out of Germany, and because he and his people were constantly being treated like animals. He said, "Being a Jew is not a crime. I am not a dog. I have a right to live and the Jewish people have a right to exist on this earth."

It's too bad there weren't millions more Y'hudim with the courage of Mr. Grynszpan.

Von Rath died two days after being shot, and the German Minister of Propaganda, Joseph Goebbels, naturally blamed all Jews for the shooting. Local citizens— not Nazis—broke into hundreds of synagogues throughout Germany and Austria. They poured gasoline on the seats and the holy arks and set them on fire. Fire brigades came to protect the nearby buildings, but they made no attempt to extinguish the fires in the synagogues. Vandals—not Nazi vandals, but local vandals—broke the windows of thousands of Jewish-owned shops.

In some cities, huge crowds of Germans and Austrians not involved in the attacks stood by and watched. Jews were forced to watch, too, as their homes and belongings were destroyed.

Many Jews, distressed by what was happening, committed suicide. Police kept onlookers from interfering with the vandals. They arrested Jews "for their own protection," as Jews could not defend themselves.

Heinrich Himmler, head of German police, issued an order that any Jew found with a weapon in his possession would be held in a concentration camp for a period of twenty years. (Good old reliable government gun-control).

"Thirty thousand Jewish men were arrested and taken to concentration camps. Julius Rosenzweig lived in Frankfurt am Main. He remembers *Kristallnacht*: 'I looked out my window and saw the regular policeman and two Brown Shirts, the SA, come into our building. My mother told me to take a walk. If I didn't, I might have been arrested like so many others. A day or two later I saw Jewish-owned department stores all with broken windows. None of the

German soldiers forcibly shaving off a Jewish man's beard.

stores reopened. They had no customers, no merchandise, no security. They were sold to Gentiles for almost nothing.'

"Shulamit Erlebacher lived in Karlsruhe, Germany. She remembers the morning after *Kristallnacht*: 'My uncle was the cantor in the great synagogue there. The next morning I came downstairs, and he was sitting there with tears flowing down. 'What's the matter?' I asked. 'They burned my synagogue,' he said. He couldn't stop crying. Then the doorbell rang. It was the SS. 'Where is he? Where is he?' They asked. They took him away to Dachau.'

"Cantor Ehrlich also remembers that the destruction and the beatings didn't end after *Kristallnacht*: 'The fear was constant. We had the same fear a week later and a month later.'

"Fred Erlacher was arrested on *Kristallnacht*. He remembers: 'They came to my store and told me to go to the city hall. When I got there, I saw every Jewish man from the village. It was a cold November night, but some of them were still in their pajamas. There was an American citizen, a tourist. He said, 'I'm an American citizen.' They said, 'You're a Jew,' and kicked him hard. The SS took us for a march of a couple of hours through the town, and the town residents looked at us as if we were criminals. They marched us to the next town and put us in a barn. The next morning they marched us to the railway station. They loaded us onto a freight train and took us to Dachau. When we got there, they opened the doors. 'Out!' they yelled at us, and knocked us with the butts of their guns. I was in Dachau for five weeks. My mother brought papers saying that I would leave Germany, so I was released. At that time it was enough if you just left.'

"Rabbi Dr. Manfred Fulda's father was arrested in Frankfurt am Main on the day after *Kristallnacht* and sent to Buchenwald concentration camp. He remembers: 'My mother had finally gotten a visa for him, and he was released after several weeks. He had lost eighty pounds. The Nazis had shaved off his entire beard. He had been severely beaten, and he was covered all over with bloody wounds. When I saw him lying on the couch in our living room, I turned to my mother and asked her, 'Who is that man?' I just did not recognize him. 'It's your father,' she answered me.'" (Adler, p. 33-40).

I believe that *Kristallnacht* was a defining moment regarding Y'hudi persecution during the twelve years of Nazi rule where government policy suddenly changed from one of exportation to one of extermination.

"On February 9, 1939, anti-Jewish laws were passed in Italy. On March 15, 1939 the Germans occupy Bohemia and Slovakia which were regions of Czechoslovakia. On September 1, 1939, the German Army invades Poland and occupies western Poland three weeks later. On September 27, 1939, German orders are issued to establish ghettos in Poland.

"The Polish ghettos were quickly set up in the larger cities near railway lines and the Jews were gathered (herded) from the small towns and villages into central locations. Throughout Poland and the rest of Nazi-controlled Europe, Jews were forced to leave their homes, taking along only as much as they could carry and move into ghettos which were walled-in sections of the cities.

"The possessions they left behind, their furniture, clothing, homes and businesses, became Nazi property.

The ghettos were terribly crowded. Each apartment was shared by many families. Each room was shared by six to seven people with no running water and with outside toilets. Thousands more lived in the streets.

"The Jews in Poland were all required to wear armbands with yellow stars of David in public at all times. There was very little food in the ghettos. Children searched the streets, the garbage for something to eat.

"Jews died of disease. They died of hunger. Ghetto gates were guarded. Jews caught outside the ghetto were killed. Erwin Bawn lived in the Warsaw ghetto. He remembers: 'There was no food, no clothes, just pure hunger and starvation. Children died in the streets. Every morning I climbed over the wall. I bent down and waited for a car to pass, and then I ran alongside it. I went to the market. There were all kinds of goodies there—food and bread. I bought as many loaves of bread as I could carry. One day a Polish policeman—not a Nazi policeman—caught me with the bread, and with his club he beat me over the head, over my body, over my hands, and he took all the bread from me, all six loaves.'

"Hirsh Altusky remembers: 'At night children were crying and begging, 'Throw down a piece of bread. Give us a piece of bread.' Everyday when you walked out of the house, you saw dead bodies, skin and bones covered with newspaper.' By the middle of 1941 as many as twenty thousand Jews had starved to death in the ghettos and ten thousand more had been murdered.'" (Adler, p. 52-61, 110, 111).

The Nazi methods of slaughtering Y'hudim were seemingly patterned after the slaughter of livestock: ghettos served as holding pens, freight train boxcars, or cattle cars, were used for transportation from the ghettos to the camps, and concentration camps became the slaughter houses. Except that cattle were treated much more humanely—they were fed well, not beaten, and had much roomier train rides—than these poor innocent Y'hudi men, women and children.

There were a total of 3.5 million Y'hudim living in Poland at the beginning of WW II. These were mostly Ashkenazi Y'hudim who had fled the massacres in Germany after the Crusades in the fourteenth century. Although Poland was Christianized by the Catholic Church in the tenth century, they never seemed to have the rabid bloodlust for Y'hudim that the more warlike Germans had. So Y'hudim had been living in Poland for centuries without any organized persecution by the Polish govermnent. In fact, they were an integral, and vital, part of Polish society which flourished as a great power during the fourteenth to seventeenth centuries. The Y'hudi Poles had fought alongside the mostly Catholic Gentile Poles in many wars.

After the Nazi and Russian conquest of Poland in Sept. 1939—I believe that Poland was Hitler's primary target in WW II because of its large Y'hudi population—the largest Nazi death camp of Auschwitz-Birkeneau, which was opened for business in April 1940, along with the smaller death camps of Treblinka and Chelmno, were constructed in western Poland.

The remaining three death camps of Belzec, Maidanek, and Sobibor were set up in eastern Poland shortly after the Germans took control of it from the Soviet Union in June-July of 1941. A total of 3.5 million Polish Y'hudim were systematically rounded-up and murdered in a five year period mostly at these six death factories in Poland. (Ref. *Chutzpah* by Alan Dershowitz, p. 139, 140).

"On May 10, 1940, the German Army began its invasion of Holland, Belgium, and France. France was the last to surrender only four months later. The German Army invaded the Soviet Union on June 22, 1941 and the Einsatzgruppen death squads immediately began mass killings of Soviet Jews. Typically they would order the Jews to gather for 'resettlement.' Then the Nazis took their valuables and forced them to march to barren areas, dig, undress, and wait. The victims did not know what was about to happen until they saw the Nazis raise their machine guns and fire. Many fell into the holes they had just finished digging. Some were only wounded but most were killed. With shovels and bulldozers, the dirt was pushed back into the holes. The Nazis buried them all, the living and the dead." (Adler, p. 62, 112).

"As the Wehrmacht rapidly advanced eastward, the slaughter of Jews, mostly by mass shootings, was the first order of business. About 1.4 million of the Soviet Ukraine's 2.4 million Jews were executed by mass shootings, gassings, starvation, and disease. Another 600,000 were murdered in Soviet Belarus and up to 140,000 in Soviet Russia." (Ref. *Marietta Daily Journal* newspaper, Marietta, Georgia, Feb. 1, 2009).

At Odessa, Ukraine, the Nazis and their collaborators destroyed 19,000 Jews in a single night in retaliation for a partisan bombing that had killed a dozen Romanian soldiers. Axis troops rounded up another 40,000 Jews and executed them during the following week.

The SS used gas wagons, disguised as Red Cross vans, to kill about 7,000 Jewish women and children near

Krasnodar, Ukraine. At least 33,000 Jews were slain in a single two-day massacre at Bibi-Yar, Ukraine, in September 1941, near the capital city of Kiev, and so on, and on, and on.

Hitler's high command carefully planned the extermination of Jews on the eastern front, drawing up directions for mass killings and distributing them to Wehrmacht and SS commanders. They established special SS teams devoted exclusively to mass murder—the Einsatzgruppen and their subgroups, the Sonderkommandos and Einsatzkommandos—and set up liaison between the killing teams and their army commanders at the front to ensure that the killing teams received the necessary intelligence and logistical support.

The SS carefully tabulated the results of the carnage as it took place, wrote it up, and sent word back to Berlin. Teams of inspectors and experts—among them men who were later employed as experts on Soviet affairs by U.S. intelligence agencies—traveled the eastern front throughout the war to make sure the exterminations and confiscations of food were going properly and being carried out.... Native collaborators and defectors became key to the German political warfare group's plans.

In the course of the war, the Nazis enlisted about a million such collaborators, including Ukranians, Azerbaijanis, Cossacks, and of course large numbers of Russians. The Osttruppen (eastern troops) Program, commanded by Kostring and Herwarth, embraced all eastern collaborationist troops under German army administration, while the SS recruited its own defectors into units that eventually became part of the Waffen SS. A variety of auxiliary police, militia, and other anti-partisan formations organized directly by the Nazis or by collaborationist local administrations under Nazi control filled out the picture.

The jobs assigned to these collaborators ranged from hauling ammunition for front line troops to mass executions of Jews—the dirty work, in short, that the Nazis often did not want to do for themselves. For the Germans, these units became a living laboratory for the development of sophisticated propaganda, guerilla warfare, and intelligence techniques for use against the Soviet government. After the war was over, they became raw material from which the new U.S. political warfare capability was built.

"The importance of these auxiliaries should not be underestimated," notes internationally recognized expert Raul Hilberg. "Roundups by local inhabitants who spoke the language resulted in higher percentages of Jewish dead. This fact is clearly indicated by the statistics of the Kommandos which made use of local help."

In Lithuania, municipal killing squads employing Lithuanian Nazi collaborators eliminated 46,692 Jews in fewer than three months, according to their own reports, mainly by clock-like liquidations of 500 Jews per day in the capital city of Vilnius with mobile 'cleanup' sweeps through the surrounding countryside." (Ref. ***Blowback*** by Christopher Simpson, p. 15, 17, 18, 24, 25).

"Germany and Italy declared war on the United States four days after Japan attacked Pearl Harbor on December 7, 1941. On December 8, 1941, mass killings began at the Chelmno death camp in Poland. Many thousands of Jews were loaded into trucks, which were sealed shut. The trucks were filled with exhaust smoke as they drove towards the open pits. By the time they arrived, the Jews were dead. Their bodies dropped into the pits and covered with dirt. The gas chambers at the Sobibor death camp began operations on March 1, 1942, the same day trains began arriving with Jews at the super death camp of Auschwitz-Birkeneau. Killings began at the Belzec, Poland, death camp on March 17, 1942. The Treblinka death camp opened on June 1, 1942." (Adler, p. 112-114).

"Leo Machtinger lived in Kielce, Poland. At four thirty one morning he was told to get up and get out, or he would be shot. As Jews ran to the square, the Germans separated those with jobs from the others. Leo was lucky to have a job and was one of those spared. After the roundup he walked through the town. 'There were so many dead. They forced some of us to dig a big grave and drop the dead in. There were five hundred, maybe six hundred, laid out like herring.'

Jewish pauper from the Warsaw ghetto. [New York Public Library Digital Collection]

"Alfred Lipson was in a ghetto in Radom, Poland. In August, 1942, many of the Jews there were deported. Alfred Lipson was spared. He remembers: 'A few days later, a young man came back. He had found a hiding place after the train had stopped at Treblinka. He hid under the train, by the wheels. He grabbed my coat by the lapels, and with a frightened look in his eyes he said, 'I was there, I was there. They were all gassed!' I wouldn't listen. I interrupted him several times. I tried to get away from him. What he was telling me was completely unbelievable. It couldn't penetrate my mind. The man ran to other people. We didn't want to listen.'

"In 1942, Leo Fischelberg was in the Bochnia ghetto in the Krakow district of Poland. He was just twelve years old. From a hideout he shared with many others, he witnessed a roundup of children. 'First they took the older children and then the younger ones. I saw mothers holding onto their children's clothing and begging, begging the Nazis, 'Please, please, don't take my child.' By the time the children were loaded into open trucks, the mothers were exhausted from crying. Then, while everyone watched, one of the Nazis took a machine gun and shot a few of the grieving mothers.'

Herding captured Jews from a Ghetto. [New York Public Library Digital Collection]

"Mendy Berger was seventeen years old when he was taken from Munkacs, Hungary. He remembers going to the train that took him to Auschwitz: 'We were chased from the ghetto to the train station. As we ran, and some of us were killed, the Christian people of the community were watching as if it were a parade, applauding, laughing. One man whom my father and uncle had helped many times smiled and yelled at us in Hungarian, '*Shoha vissa—You* will never return.' And he remembers the train ride: 'One hundred people standing in a locked railroad car, no food, no water, people dying, the smell of the dead, and we had no toilets. We did it right where we were standing, and we couldn't move from it.'" (Adler, p. 65-67).

"The Nazis were killing Jews in huge numbers, but it wasn't until January 20, 1942, that they devised their 'Final Solution' to the Jewish 'problem'—the existence of Jews. That day, sixteen Nazi leaders met just outside Berlin, at Wannsee. According to their notes at the meeting, 'Europe is to be combed through from West to East in the course of the practical implementation of the final solution.... The evacuated Jews will be taken, group by group, to the so-called transit ghettos, in order to be transported further east from there.' Their 'Final Solution' was the planned destruction of all eleven million Jews in the countries Germany already controlled and the ones they expected to conquer. Jews in the ghettos were told they were being taken to labor camps or just that they were being 'resettled' farther east. Many were already starving, too sick, too weak, even to question what was happening. Their organizations had been broken up long ago. They were mostly cut-off from people outside their ghettos.

"The Jews were herded into freight trains—cattle cars bound for one of the twelve camps in Auschwitz-Birkenau, Maidanek, Treblinka, Sobibor, Chelnmo, and Belzec in Poland; Bergen-Belsen, Ravensbruck, Terezin, Buchenwald, and Dachau in Germany; Mauthausen in Austria. Some had heard rumors about these camps. But who could believe such gruesome stories?" (Adler, p. 64, 65).

"Arthur Rubin and his family were in a ghetto for just ten days. Then they were taken by train, in cattle cars, to Auschwitz. ' The thirst on that trip was unbearable. Children were crying for water, and mothers' hearts were tom because they were unable to help them. I remember traveling through Poland (not Germany or Austria). The train stopped at various stations. There were women standing near the railroad tracks with buckets of water, and they would hand us cups of water through the small opening in exchange for something like a shirt or blouse. When we had nothing left to exchange they spitefully spilled the water on the ground. I remember this very clearly.'

"Hirsh Altusky was on a train destined for Maidanek. He remembers: ' It was hot. Everyone was thirsty. When the train was stopped at a siding, Polish (not German or Austrian) train workers traded us something to drink. They wanted gold, watches, anything. They wanted big money. I gave five hundred zlotys for a flask of vodka, and I slept, drunk, until we came to Maidanek.'" (Adler, p. 67, 68).

"Leo Fischelberg remembers: 'In Bergen-Belsen my job was to take out the ones who died on the trains. We carried them by their legs and arms and had to throw them onto a wagon, then bring them to an open pit and drop them in. I did this for five months. I was fifteen…. We once tried to take someone not completely dead and put him on top of the wagon so he could breathe. The Nazis beat us. We wanted to save a life, and they yelled at us, 'Schnell! Schnell! Macht los!—Quick! Quick! Get going!' To them, to save a life was a waste of time.'

"Ernest Honig remembers when he arrived at Auschwitz: 'We saw huge chimneys, and smoke, and there was a terrible smell. My brother and I were standing next to each other. We wondered what that could be. One of us said, 'Maybe a factory. Maybe they're making rubber. Maybe that's where we'll be working.' But it occurred to me, as it must have to my brother, that maybe they were burning people.'" (Adler, p. 70).

"At the camps the Jews were divided. First the men were separated from the women. Then those who were chosen to work as slave laborers were sent to one side, those who were to be killed to the other. Lena Mandelbaum remembers: 'I was sent to the right, with my sister. My mother and my two brothers, my aunt, uncles, and grandparents were sent to the left. We never saw them again. They were killed in Auschwitz.'" (Adler, p. 73, 74).

"Carol Frenkel Lipson remembers how she felt during the three months she was at Auschwitz: 'We had to undress in front of thousands of people. I remember being ashamed, embarrassed, and at the same time frightened and worried. There were beautiful women, but when their heads were shaved, they looked ugly. This was one way our oppressors found to dehumanize and degrade all of us, especially women. They gave us a rag of a dress and no underwear. It was unbearable for us women to stand for hours in the wind and cold and I can tell you that Auschwitz had terrible weather. We could go to the 'toilet' only at prescribed times, twice a day, and in a great hurry. Imagine rows of women sitting in public over a hole in the ground. For anyone who had come from reasonably human circumstances, the daily routine in Auschwitz had a dehumanizing effect at every step.' Carol remembers when the number A-24742 was tattooed on her arm: 'We were worried when we weren't given numbers right away. We knew if we didn't get a number, we were destined for the crematorium. In Auschwitz a number meant life.'" (Adler, p. 76, 77).

"Those selected for work built roads and dug ditches.

They sewed uniforms. They worked in factories set up near the camps, making ammunition and parts for airplanes. Many of the factories were run by some of Germany's largest industrial companies. The prisoners worked from morning until night and were hardly fed. Most died within a few months. The dead workers were replaced by others.

"The Jews not selected for work were told they needed to be cleaned of lice. They were led to a waiting area made to look like the hall of a bathhouse. Attendants, often dressed in white, distributed towels and pieces of soap. The prisoners were told to undress and to fold their clothes neatly. And they were told to remember where they left their clothes so that after the showers they could reclaim them.

"The Jews were crowded into the 'bathhouses.' There were shower heads and fake drains in the bathhouses, but no water. The 'attendants' often shot bullets into the room to force the prisoners closer together. The doors were locked. SS guards wearing gas masks dropped poison pellets of Zyklon B through an opening in the ceiling. Poison fumes filled the room. At times Nazi guards watched through peepholes as innocent men, women, and children gasped and struggled for air in their last moments of life. When the screaming stopped, the Nazis knew the Jews were dead.

"The gassings took from three to fifteen minutes. The doors were opened. The bodies were dragged out with metal hooks. Wedding rings were pulled off. Mouths were pried open in search of gold-filled teeth. The gold was sent to the *Reichsbank*, the German national bank. The dead women's hair was used to fill pillows and mattresses. Then the bodies were taken to crematoriums, ovens, where they were burned." (Adler, p. 77-79).

"Horrible medical experiments were performed on some prisoners. Jews were put into pressure chambers until they stopped breathing. They were placed naked in ice water until they froze to death. They were kept in a vacuum until their lungs burst.

A Jewish street scribe in the Warsaw ghetto, waiting to write letters for illiterate Jews. [New York Public Library Digital Collection]

"At Auschwitz the Nazi doctor Josef Mengele was especially brutal. Some three thousand twins suffered through his painful and often deadly experiments. Only 157 survived. Irene Hizme and her twin brother, Rene Slotkin were among the survivors. Irene Hizme remembers: 'I was a young child then, just five, and he was a doctor. I trusted him. The first time, he took blood from my neck. It was very scary and very painful. But I didn't dare make a sound. If I did, I knew it would be worse. He gave me shots in my back and in my arm, and X-rays. Each time I left his laboratory, I was sick, very sick.'"

"Esther Himmelfarb Peterseil remembers: 'We had to stay a certain time under quarantine. After that, at least twice a week, we had selections. That's when I first recognized Josef Mengele, when I first knew who he was. He was tall, slim, and always carried a riding crop. We had to stand straight, with our arms held so our numbers were showing. He walked behind us and selected people for the gas. He would point, and someone wrote the numbers down. A day later they would call the numbers. There was screaming, crying, praying. We could even hear them when they were taken to the gas chambers. The noise was so loud, it was impossible not to hear it.'" (Adler, p. 81, 82).

"By late 1942 reports of the death camps reached England, the United States, and elsewhere. But the media—newspapers, magazines, radio, and newsreels—did little to spread the news of the killings. Early in 1944, two Jewish engineers, Walter Rosenberg and Alfred Wetzler, escaped Auschwitz and reported in detail about the gas chambers and the ovens. They had secretly kept records of everything they had witnessed in their administrative jobs since 1942. Their detailed account of the horrors of Auschwitz was called the Auschwitz Protocol and was translated and distributed to Hungarian authorities as well as Swiss, British, and Swedish by the summer of 1944, but it received the usual "ho-hum" Christian reaction.

"Allied government officials seemed almost indifferent to the suffering. In 1944, Allied bombers were active just a few miles from Auschwitz. There were many appeals made to Allied leaders, to bomb the railroad tracks leading to the death camp and stop the deportations, even to bomb the camp itself. But the Allied leaders refused. They claimed they could not spare the few bombs and the few hours of flying time it would take to save Jewish lives.

"This refusal of the Christian nations of England and the United States to act against Auschwitz was costly to the Jews. An additional estimated 400,000 Hungarian Jews were murdered at Auschwitz during May and June of 1944." (Adler, p. 83, 115 and *Dangerous Diplomacy* by Theo Tschuy, pg. 75).

It seems that as the war was rapidly coming to an end, the Nazis and their collaborators and sympathizers, especially after the Allied D-Day invasion on June 6, 1944, became almost frenzied in their efforts to kill Y'hudim.

Just a couple more sickening examples of the thousands upon thousands of heinous atrocities against the Y'hudim by non-Nazi Christians who were more than eager to do the dirty work of their occupiers: "In Hungary, one day in 1944, a Catholic chaplain in full clerical garb appeared at the crowded Jewish hospital in Budapest and ordered all the patients into the courtyard. He held up a crucifix and shouted to the Hungarian Nazi Youth organization mob with him: 'In the name of Jesus, shoot!' Only two Jews survived." (Re£ *The Distortion* by John and Patrice Fischer, p. 43).

"For a few terrible weeks, Budapest belonged to the rampaging Arrow Cross hoodlums plus such freelance fanatics as Mrs. Wilmos Salzer, a society lady who liked to burn naked Jewesses with candles... Kurt Rettman, a former telephone company official who believed in shooting Jews on sight... and Father Andras Kun, a Minorite monk clad in black cape and carrying a giant crucifix in one hand, snub-nosed revolver in the other, and hate-literature in his robes. All three practiced what they preached—and so did their followers.

"As his executioners aimed their rifles at Jews they had tortured within an inch of their lives, Father Kun would give the command: 'In the holy name of Jesus, fire!' At dawn, on the banks of the Danube River, Father Kun's teenage Sunday-schoolers waited for their mentor to come and bless them before pushing the 'Christ-killers'—already packaged in bundles of three—into the river." (Ref. *Nazi Hunter, The Wiesenthal File* by Alan Levy, pg. 192, 193).

"The Maidanek death camp in eastern Poland was the first camp liberated on July 24, 1944, but was found to be abandoned. The SS guards had forced the few skin-and-bones surviving Jewish inmates to march to their deaths rather than be liberated. Bergen-Belsen in northern Germany was liberated by the British on April 15, 1945.

"Dachau in southern Germany was liberated by the Americans on April 29, 1945. Abel Jack Schwartz was a first sergeant with General Patton's Third Army. He was among the first soldiers to liberate the Buchenwald camp in central Germany. He remembers: 'The barracks were inhabited by pitiful, starved prisoners, too weak to move, just skin and bones, living skeletons, and many were already dead. The barracks reeked with the scent of human waste and death. Outside were heaps of naked bodies like stacks of logs.... I had witnessed many battlefield deaths. I considered myself to be tough, and inured to the sight and smell of

Jews replace horses as Nazi means of transportation in Warsaw. [New York Public Library Digital Collection]

death. However, at this sight, I just cried and cried. I laid down my pistols, carbine and grenades out of respect for the dead, and recited the *kaddish.*'

"Arthur Federman was an American soldier fighting in Europe. He entered Dachau which is located in southern Germany near Munich in early May of 1945. 'You could smell the camp from at least five miles away. Until then we didn't even know it was ahead. What we saw was horrifying. The Jews were emaciated. You could see their bones. There were bodies piled up in tremendous mounds. Practically all the soldiers became nauseous and threw up.'" (Adler, p. 89-91, 116).

"As Allied forces advanced toward the camps, many prisoners were forced by Nazi guards to march, sometimes for hundreds of miles, to territory firmly within control of the German Army. The Nazis were eager to escape, but not without their emaciated prisoners. Those who fell or sat to rest along the way were shot.

"Leo Machtingier was in seven different camps. In January, 1945, he was forced to march from one camp to another. 'There were ten thousand of us when we started. Only about two thousand of us made it. The others were either shot or froze. One night I slept in the middle of five men. Two on the outside never woke up.' Leo Fischelberg was on a thirteen-day march when he was liberated. 'A Russian major came riding on horseback along with a lieutenant and a sergeant. They saw men dying from typhoid, with their tongues hanging out. It was not a pretty sight. The lieutenant threw up. The major cried. We tried to comfort them.'

"After Leo Fischelberg was liberated, he felt lonely, 'I was alive, but so many of my friends were gone. I felt like the walking dead. I felt emptiness, nothing else.'" (Adler, p. 91, 92).

"On May 8, 1945, Germany surrenders to the Allies. After liberation, Judy Schonfeld Schabes traveled back to her hometown in Hungary. She remembers the train ride: 'Whenever someone new came aboard, or I saw someone standing on a platform, I asked, 'Do you know? Did you see? Did you hear? Were you together with so and so?' I hoped to hear about my father. He was only forty-three. Or my mother, she was only thirty-nine. Maybe they were separated out again, before the gas chambers. But they weren't. Of one hundred people in my extended family, just twelve survived.'

"After the war Esther Himmelfarb Peterseil returned to her hometown in Poland. 'I took a trolley to go back to the Jewish community to look for my brother. Then, while I was riding, I saw someone who looked like him. Remember, I hadn't seen him for five years. I called to him. It *was* my brother. He jumped onto the trolley. I don't have to tell you about the reunion. We were both crying, and so was everyone on the trolley. We returned to our apartment. The building superintendent lived there and wouldn't let us into our own apartment. My brother gave me money to buy some bread, and at the market I saw someone who used to work for my father. It was a thrill for me to see her, but she said, 'Are you still alive?' She wasn't pleased to see me.'

"Two hundred Jews had returned either from hiding or from concentration camps to rebuild the Jewish community in Kielce, Poland. On July 3, 1946. Polish police took away their weapons. The next day—over a year after Germany surrendered—Polish citizens attacked the Jews. They pelted the Jews with stones and shot at them. They clubbed Jews to death. Forty-two were killed. Many others were wounded. When news of this attack became known, thousands of Jewish survivors fled from towns and villages throughout Poland to Displaced Persons camps." (Adler, p. 93, 94, 116).

"The Jews of Europe who survived the Holocaust were labeled as Displaced Persons and no country wanted them. Camps for these displaced persons were set up in Germany, Austria, and Italy. The camps were guarded and surrounded with barbed wire. Many Jews still wore their prisoner uniforms. Some were given abandoned SS uniforms to wear. In August, 1945, the American representative on a refugee committee, Earl G. Harrison, inspected the camps. He reported, 'As matters now stand, we appear to be treating the Jews as the Nazis treated them, except that we do not exterminate them.' After reading this report, President Truman of the United States ordered that treatment of the Jews in the camps be improved.

By 1947 there were two hundred and fifty thousand Jews in these camps. Most of the survivors in the camps wanted to leave quickly, to resettle outside Europe. And people who lived near the camps were eager to have the Jews leave.

"Leah Goldberg was in a camp in Germany and heard one of the local citizens say, 'where did all these Jews come from? I thought we killed them all.'" (Adler, p. 94, 95).

Only a fraction of the many who wanted to enter the United States, Britain, and Palestine were allowed in. It was only in 1948, with the establishment of the state of Yisra'el—which I believe was a fulfillment of prophecy and a miracle of Y'HoVaH, that many of these Y'hudi refugees found a home.

The typical attitude of the European Christian populace to the Holocaust is best illustrated by Simon Wiesenthal's brief encounter with an Austrian farm woman shortly after the end of the war: "Wiesenthal often remembers his first walk as a free man into the outside world, after living four years behind barbed-wire fences. It was about ten days after his liberation from the Mauthausen concentration camp, in upper Austria, on a warm spring day in May 1945.

"Still weak and a little dizzy from unaccustomed exertion, he walked to the nearby village. Farmers worked in the fields, children played, the birds were singing. Less than a mile from the horrors of the gas chambers the countryside seemed a peaceful bucolic idyll. The people he met glanced briefly at his emaciated face, at the clothes hanging loosely from his shoulders. They showed no trace of either curiosity or sympathy.

"Wiesenthal suddenly felt terribly tired. He stepped up to a farm house and asked for a drink of water. A sturdy, well-fed Austrian peasant woman brought him a glass of grape juice. 'Was it bad over there?' she asked, pointing vaguely in the direction of the low gray buildings across the fields. 'Be glad you didn't see the camp from the inside,' said Wiesenthal. 'Why should I see it?' the woman indignantly replied, 'I am not a Juden.'" (Ref. *The Murderers Among Us*, by Simon Wiesenthal, p. 8, 9)

Alan Dershowitz's paternal great-grandfather wisely fled the Galician city of Pilsner, Poland in 1888 and immigrated to New York City; his maternal grandfather wisely fled the Galician city of Przemysl, Poland, in 1907 and immigrated to Scranton, Pennsylvania. All of Mr.

Dershowitz's relatives who stayed in Poland were never heard from again. There is no record today that his relatives or any Y'hudim had ever lived in Pilsner or Przemysl, Poland. Just like the other six million Y'hudim... vanished, gone, no trace, no graves, no markers, nothing. (Ref *Chutzpah* by Alan Dershowitz, p. 21, 26, 27).

People who say the Holocaust never happened should be put in prisons or mental hospitals. Even the Holocaust museums are still in denial about who the actual victims of the Holocaust were. Mr. Dershowitz relates a story in his book about a visit he and his son made to a museum at the Polish death camp of Auschwitz-Birkenau—the site of the largest murder camp.

They decided not to go on an "American" or "Jewish" tour but instead decided to tag along with some Polish school children on their tour. The following story is Mr. Dershowitz's thoughts and observations during this tour: "We simply followed a group of Polish school children in order to find out what *they* are told about this museum and what it represents to *them*.

"Their teacher spoke some English and translated for us. It was a shocking and infuriating experience. The children—indeed typical Eastern European visitors—are not told, as the Jewish visitor is, that nearly all of the three million people murdered in the various camps were Jews who were gassed solely because they were Jews.

"The Polish visitor is told that the victims were Polish citizens: intellectuals, priests, soldiers, journalists, resistance members. He is shown the wall of death, where hundreds of political prisoners were shot, but not the remnants of the gas chambers where millions of Jews were murdered.

"Indeed, the Birkenau part of the complex is not even on the tour. It was to the Birkenau portion that the Jewish women, children, and men were taken to be gassed and burned.

"The tour only includes the Auschwitz camp where Polish prisoners—all of them adults—were kept, and where many perished. It is true, of course, that a considerable number of Polish adults were individually murdered for inexcusable reasons—their politics, their participation in the resistance, their religious activities, their work as journalists, and so forth. But the Polish people, as such, were not marked for genocidal extermination as were the Jews and the Gypsies—approximately one-half million Gypsies were murdered by the Nazis.

"It in no way diminishes the horrors inflicted on these Polish adults, who were subjected to the camps, to point out that there is an enormous difference between what the Nazis did to individual Polish adults and what they did to *all* Jews—babies and adults—whom they managed to ingather to the extermination camps. And that distinction is quite deliberately blurred for the Eastern European visitor to the Auschwitz Museum.

"For example, in one room in the Polish pavilion—each country occupied by the Nazis has a pavilion—there are hundreds of pictures of the dead martyrs. My son and I gasped in shock as we passed the photographs and read the names under each of them: there was not a single Jewish name; every one was Polish.

"In the adjoining room, there is a display of photographs of babies and children gassed in the camps. Beneath their pictures there are no names, only numbers. The reason is apparent: to list their names would make it clear that Polish children were not murdered at Auschwitz-Birkenau; only Jewish and Gypsy babies and children were gassed as part of the Nazi genocide.

"Each of the Eastern European national pavilions goes out of its way to downplay the uniquely Jewish nature of the Holocaust. None mentions the fact that entire Jewish populations were transported to Auschwitz-Birkenau from the far-flung corners of the Nazi empire for systematic genocide. The reality of the words stated so eloquently by Nobel laureate Elie Wiesel: 'Not all the intended victims were Jews. But all the Jews were intended victims,' is lost on the typical visitor to Auschwitz.

"To be sure, there is a Jewish pavilion at the Auschwitz museum, but it is not a regular part of the tour. Only Jewish visitors, Americans, and other 'special groups' are even told about the Jewish pavilion. It is the last pavilion—number 27—and it is a dark, out-of-the-way house with no guide. When I found it, the lights were turned off. The caretaker, who spoke no English, Hebrew, or Yiddish, seemed almost reluctant to open it up. Walking along with my son through the Jewish pavilion, I felt my fists unclench and my eyes tear. But my fists quickly clenched again as I realized that those who most need to see what happened to the Jews were not even aware of the pavilion and what it represents." (Dershowitz, p. 140, 141, 144).

H.) The Roman Catholic Christian Church, under the leadership of Y'hudi-hating, Nazi sympathizer, Pope Pius XII, also helped many thousands of Nazis to escape the Allies after WW II through the aptly named Rat Line.

The Rat Line was an underground network that aided the escape of sixty thousand, or almost half, of the Nazi war criminals fleeing Allied occupied Europe at the end of the War. Dr. Yosef Mengele, the infamous "Angel of Death" who liked to experiment on Y'hudi children, was one of the more notorious of the sixty thousand Nazis who utilized the Catholic Church's Rat Line to escape Europe in 1948.

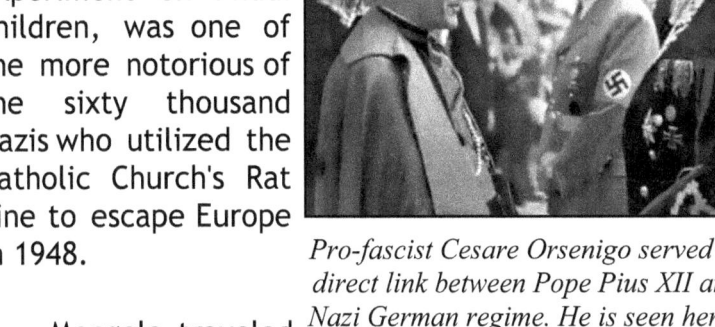

Pro-fascist Cesare Orsenigo served as the direct link between Pope Pius XII and the Nazi German regime. He is seen here with Hitler and his Foreign Minister, Joachim von Ribbentrop. [Bundesarchiv]

Mengele traveled to Italy where he was hidden in a Franciscan convent near the Vatican until he received a falsified Red Cross passport. With his fake passport in-hand he set sail in 1949 for South America—Catholic South America was a safe haven destination for most of the Nazis—where he lived relatively well in Brazil and Paraguay until his natural death in 1978. (Ref. ***The Manhunter*** by John Pascucci, p. 283, 308). The Catholic Church knew full well what Mengele had done and what all the other Nazi monsters had done but helped them escape anyway.

It is also disgraceful what the Allied governments have done, or more accurately not done, regarding justice or accountability for the cold-blooded murders of over seven million innocent Y'hudi and Gypsy civilians. I agree with the following statements by Alan Dershowitz regarding punishment of Germany and Austria after the war: "I do believe that the German (and Austrian) people—those who did not actively oppose Nazism—bear considerable *moral* responsibility for the Holocaust. Certainly every willing supporter of Nazism deserves some blame for its entirely predictable—indeed promised—genocidal outcome. Just as the vast majority of German people expected to reap material benefits from Hitler's aggression, so too they should have reaped the bitter fruit of defeat. They should have suffered—as a *people*—*after* the Holocaust. Individuals who actively resisted should have been individually rewarded. But those who went along with Hitler's genocidal program, even passively so as to live the good life, should have been made to suffer in rough proportion to their complicity and culpability.

"That is why the rebuilding of postwar Germany into one of the world's most affluent nations is a moral disgrace. A minimal appropriate response to the collective responsibility of the German people for the crimes of their leaders whom they elected and enthusiastically supported and whose mass murders were carried out with the assistance and knowledge of so many citizens should have been a generation of poverty, for most Germans, coupled with rewards for those who opposed Nazism.

"Henry Morgenthau, Jr. secretary of the U.S. Treasury during World War II wrote a book called **Germany Is Our Problem** (1945), in which he urged that postwar Germany be portioned and transformed into an agrarian society. Morgenthau called for the transfer of equipment and factories from Germany to the Allied nations as war reparations. But instead of requiring the German people to live at subsistence level for twenty or thirty years, we immediately rewarded them with the Marshall Plan.

"We also pardoned convicted Nazi criminals who could help rebuild West Germany. We rewarded the evils of the past to confront the more "pressing" concerns of the future. The most pressing of these concerns—the so-called "Cold War" against communism—certainly did not justify the rewards we heaped upon West Germany, Austria, and numerous individual Nazis whom we recruited in the name of our holy war against communism.

"The ultimate reward—the reunification of the Germanys and the establishment of the most powerful nation in Europe less than a half century after the destruction of Nazism—did not even claim a pressing international need. It was simply the natural consequence of refusing to recognize the responsibility of the German nation for the incalculable evil it wrought.

"In one respect, the success of postwar Germany marks the belated completion of Hitler's twin goals in starting World War II: The destruction of European Jewry, which he accomplished before his death; and the reemergence of Germany as the most powerful nation in Europe, which has now been accomplished with the aid of the United States and the other victorious survivors of World War II." (Dershowitz, 137, 138).

Knowing what I now know, I wish that the USSR had gotten all of Germany. At least they punished the East Germans by keeping them in an impoverished state for 45 years.

The Berlin airlift that the US is so proud of was stupid and wrong. Most Nazis went back home to Germany or Austria after the war and simply removed their uniforms, put on their civilian clothes, and resumed their lives right where they left off a few years earlier.

Ten thousand former Nazis were even allowed into

the US after WW II. The German rocket scientists and engineers, with plenty of Nazi's mingled in, were even put in charge of our missile and space programs—I have first hand knowledge of this because, as a young engineer, I worked for some of them at the Marshall Space Flight Center (MSFC) in Huntsville, Alabama, during the early 1960's. Infact, the director of the MSFC, Vernher von Braun, was a member of the Nazi SS.

My department head was an arrogant little middle-aged German named Willy Prasthofer. The Germans and Austrians were forgiven, pardoned, and even rewarded for their murderous deeds. The Christian world didn't really give a damn that almost half of the Y'hudim in the world had just been murdered. The Germans, Austrians, Poles, Hungarians, Romanians, French, Ukranians and other Christian Europeans once again got away with the mass murders of Y'hudim, but this time on a scale never seen before.

The show trials, at Nuremburg, Germany, in November, 1945, of a handful of old Nazis was just that: a trial for show, a cruel joke. Only 21 leaders out of a total of 140,000 Nazis were tried by an International Military Tribunal which was composed of sixteen judges, four from each of the main Allied powers of the United States, Great Britain, France, and the Soviet Union. Only 10 of the 21 were executed by hanging. Hermann Goering cheated the hangman by committing suicide with a cyanide capsule.

A photo in a book I have of the Nazis on trial at Nuremburg shows them smiling and laughing during their trial. Rarely in the seventy years since the end of WW II has a Nazi murderer been exposed and even more rarely have they been punished for their atrocities. They are unrepentant for their evil deeds; I've never heard one say he was sorry for his or her part in the Holocaust. They still believe what they did was right, and that they were simply doing what their Christian religion, whether Roman Catholic, Eastern Orthodox, or Protestant, wanted done—in the name of Christ of course.

Why, even a recent pope, Benedict, is a former member of the Nazi Youth, and he has bishops serving under him who deny the Holocaust ever occurred.

An old Nazi "reptile" was recently discovered "under a rock" in the United States where he had been living the good American life for the past 50 years or so. Germany asked for his extradition to stand "trial" for the personal murders of 29,000 Y'hudim in the Ukraine. The US, finally and reluctantly, sent him back to Germany where he undoubtedly will get a good wrist-slapping before he dies a natural death.

Adolf Eichmann is the only Nazi who has been executed, subsequent to the Nuremburg trials. Yisra'el hanged him after having to kidnap him from his "safe haven" in Catholic Christian Argentina. But even Yisra'el lost interest in justice a long time ago and wouldn't execute an SS murderer today if they had one presented to them on a silver platter because they don't have capital punishment any longer.

Let's be generous and say a thousand former Nazis, Gestapo, SA, and SS have been arrested, charged, tried and either found not guilty or given light sentences: what about the other 139,000? It is truly sickening at the lack of justice for the cold-blooded, pre-meditated murders of all those Y'hudim, not to mention the theft of all their properties which has never been returned to the survivors or their relatives. I only wish that Britain had developed the atomic bomb before Germany surrendered and British Air Marshall Arthur Harris, who ordered the firebombing of German cities such as Dresden, had dropped a few dozen 20 kiloton bombs on selected German and Austrian population centers. He would have had the guts to do it. I don't think the Christian United States would have. I believe the "blackest darkness" punishment mentioned in 2 Kifa 2:17 is reserved for those directly or indirectly involved in the Holocaust.

The role of the Roman Catholic Christian Church in the persecution and attempted annihilation of the Y'hudim is best summarized by the Y'hudi author, Howard Fast, in his book, **The Jews, Story of a People** on pages 271 and 365: "While many forces joined together throughout European history to use and promote anti-Semitism, the fact must be faced and stated bluntly; that anti-Semitism in the European Diaspora of the Jew was the child and the ideology of the Roman Catholic Church.

"In the ecumenical spirit of today, many Jews feel it is best to tone down such matters and forget; but history cannot be both written and forgotten; and still others, sensitive Christians, say, 'But surely you cannot blame the Nazi murder of six million Jews upon the Church. Surely the Church never countenanced it.' Far worse; the Church from its very inception organized anti-Semitism in modern clerical guise, spared no effort to inoculate the entire Catholic population with it, and gave it to the German pagans along with Christianity—as if to provide a perennial outlet for a blood and murder sickness that has been a part of Germany as long as Germany was a part of history.... The murder of six million Jews by Europe was the final hideous outcome of a Christian theology that had spent sixteen-hundred years teaching mankind to hate the Jews."

Amen! Needless to say, I don't purchase any German or Austrian products: no automobiles or motorcycles made by BMW, Audi, Volkswagen, or Mercedes Benz; no Beck beers; no Wolfgang Puck soups; no Vienna sausages; no Bayer aspirins; no Siemens electrical equipment; no Glock handguns; no Mauser rifles; no tourist travel to Germany, Austria, or Poland. In fact, I really have no desire to visit anywhere in Europe, period.

Think about the following fact: There has never been anyone, Y'hudi or Goyi, taunted, ridiculed, dehumanized, cursed, spat upon, beaten, robbed, raped, arrested, imprisoned in jails and ghettos, tortured, starved, crammed into railroad cattle cars, or murdered in the most cruel and sadistic fashion, such as being burned alive, in the name of Y'shua Immanu El HaMashiach! Contrast this with the millions upon millions, mostly Y'hudim, who have been taunted, ridiculed, dehumanized, cursed, spat upon, beaten, robbed, raped, arrested, imprisoned, in jails and ghettos, tortured, starved, crammed into railroad cattle cars, or murdered in the most cruel and sadistic fashion, in the name of Jesus Christ!

Y'shua says in Mattityahu 7:15-20: "Beware of the false prophets! (or false religions) They come to you wearing sheep's clothing (or clerical garb), but underneath they are hungry wolves! You will recognize them by their fruit. Can people pick grapes from thorn bushes, or figs from thistles? Likewise, every healthy tree produces good fruit, but a poor tree produces bad fruit. A healthy tree cannot bear bad fruit, or a poor tree good fruit. Any tree that does not produce good fruit is cut down and thrown in the fire! So you will recognize them by their fruit."

I don't know of any institution or organization that has produced more bad fruit than the Roman Catholic Christian

Church! It is a very unhealthy tree—especially for the Y'hudim—that is incapable of producing anything good! It is of haSatan, and its Christian offshoots called Protestant churches are also of haSatan! Rabbi Sha'ul also aptly describes the Catholic Christian Church in Romayim 3:13-18 when he quotes King David (Dah-**veed**): "Their throats are open graves, they use their tongues to deceive. Vipers' venom is under their lips. Their mouths are full of curses and bitterness. Their feet rush to shed blood (especially Y'hudi blood), in their ways are ruin and misery, and the way of shalom they do not know. There is no fear of Elohim before their eyes."

Sometimes when I tell people these things about the Catholic Church they reply: "But I have known some good people who were Catholics or Lutherans." I usually respond with something like: "Yes, and there were probably plenty of 'good' Nazis too; they came home every evening after a hard day at the local death camp to a nice little warm and cozy haus on a quiet tree-lined street, a loving frau who has just cooked a supper of hot knockwurst pork sausage and kraut, three well-behaved little blond-headed Teutonic kinder in knickers and leiderhose with a snappy 'heil Hitler!' salute greeting to their father, and a German shepherd dog slobbering on his face—after a long hard day at the 'office'... murdering Yuden.

They were faithful dues-paying members of their local Catholic, Lutheran or Evangical church where they regularly attended Sunday mass and were held in high esteem by the clergy, their fellow members, and their 'good' Christian neighbors. 'Why, old Klaus wouldn't hurt a fly. He even helps coach the little league soccer team, and his children are members of the Hitler Youth and the

Women's League;' just a typical German or Austrian Christian family. Truth of the matter: Righteous people aren't members of evil organizations and Christianity is the most evil of organizations!

Since joining the Y'hudim, I now view events and people through a Y'hudi lens. How does this affect Yisra'el and the Y'hudim? Yisra'el and the Y'hudi people are my prime concern, not the United States of America or any other Goyi nation; the USA is of secondary importance to me. The notable Goyim people I now admire are the ones who were and are friends with the descendants of Yisra'el, such as: Cornelius (Cornelius was a Roman army officer in the Italian Regiment who was stationed in Caesarea [Kah-sah-*ree*-ah], Yisra'el around the middle of the first century. He was a devout, upright, Elohim-fearing man, a man highly regarded by the whole Y'hudi nation; he gave generously to help the Y'hudi poor and prayed regularly to Elohim and in fact was praying minchah prayers in his house when an angel of Elohim appeared to him.

After hearing about Y'shua HaMashiach from Kifa, Cornelius immediately put his trust in Y'shua and received forgiveness of his sins through the name of Y'shua HaMashiach and then the Ruach HaKodesh fell on him and his household and they praised Elohim by speaking in tongues. Cornelius, along with the other Goyim believers in his house were then immersed in water in the name of Y'shua HaMashiach. Ref Ma'asheh 10:1, 2, 22, 43-48.).

Alexander the Great, liked and respected the Y'hudim during his reign and even dismounted and walked to meet the cohen hagadol or high priest upon his triumphal entry into Yerushalayim. He remarked to his troops who complained about his deference to the

Y'hudi cohen, "I didn't greet the arch priest but the Deity he represents."

The city of Alexandria, Egypt, which was named for Alexander, was a safe haven for many Y'hudim and their intellectual pursuits for centuries.).

Rembrandt van Riyn used Y'hudi models in his paintings who were residents of Holland at the time. He depicted the Y'hudim in his paintings, such as 'The Synagogue' in 1648, 'The Great Jude Bride' in 1653, and 'Portrait of a Rabbi' in 1657, with both fidelity and concern rather than the typical ugly Christian stereotype.

Blaise Pascal, the great philosopher and mathematician, was asked by King Louis XIV of France for proof that there is some kind of supernatural force in the world. Pascal simply replied, "Why the Y'hudim, your majesty, the Y'hudim."

Napoleon Bonaparte, in 1802, proclaimed freedom of worship in the territory he controlled and was quoted as saying, "A wise government protects all religions." In 1811, Napoleon emancipated the Y'hudim who were living in the newly created Confederation of the Rhine, making them full citizens. He also freed all the many Y'hudi and Goyi prisoners of the Catholic Inquisition.

Mark Twain, in 1889, observed: "The Jews constitute but one percent of the human race. It suggests a nebulous dim puff of stardust lost in the blaze of the Milky Way. Properly the Jew ought hardly to be heard of; but he is heard of, has always been heard of, he is as prominent on the planet as any other people, and his commercial importance is extravagantly out of proportion to the smallness of his bulk. His contributions to the world's list of great names in literature, science, art, music, finance, medicine, and abstruse learning are also way out of proportion to the weakness of his numbers. He has made a marvelous fight in this world, in all the ages, and has done it with his hands tied behind him.

"He could be vain of himself, and be excused for it. The Egyptian, the Babylonian, and the Persian rose, filled the planet with sound and splendor, then faded to dream stuff and passed away; the Greek and the Roman followed, and made a vast noise, and they are gone; other peoples have sprung up and held their torch high for a time, but it burned out, and they sit in twilight now, or have vanished.

"The Jew saw them all, beat them all, and is now what he always was, exhibiting no decadence, no infirmities of age, no weakening of his parts, no slowing of his energies, no dulling of his alert and aggressive mind.

"All things are mortal but the Jew; all other forces pass, but he remains. What is the secret of his immortality?" Ref **Why Marry Jewish** by Doron Kornbluth, p. 78,79.

Lev Nikolaevich Tolstoy wrote, "The Jew is the emblem of eternity. He whom neither slaughter nor torture of thousands of years could destroy. He whom neither fire nor sword nor inquisition was able to wipe off the face of the earth. He who was the only one to produce the oracles of God. He who has been for so long the guardian of prophecy, and who transmitted it to the rest of world—such a nation cannot be destroyed. The Jew is as everlasting as eternity itself." Kornbluth, p. 82, 83)

Raoul Wallenberg, a Swedish diplomat in Hungary during Nazi occupation risked his life numerous times to rescue thousands of Y'hudim by issuing them Swedish passports. Ref *Righteous Gentile*, by John Bierman)

Carl Lutz, Consul of the Swiss Legation in Budapest, Hungary during the Nazi control of Hungary, starting in the spring of 1944, provided Shutzbriefs or letters of protection to thousands of the approximately 762,000 Y'hudim living in Hungary at the time of the Nazi takeover—440,000 were sent to Auschwitz by the Nazi's under Adolph Eichmann, 100,000 were murdered by the Hungarian Christian group called Arrow Cross, and 222,000 survived, of which 72,000 of those were due to the efforts of Carl Lutz and his Swiss Legation. Eichmann was obsessed with trying to murder as many Y'hudim as he could during the last year of the war. Ref. ***Dangerous Diplomacy*** by Theo Tschuy.

Dirk Boonstra, a Police officer in Groningen, Amsterdam who refused to arrest Yooden died in Sept. 1944, in Herzbruck concentration camp after being tortured. Ref. *Anne Frank in the World Exhibit 1929-45*, Sandy Springs, Georgia).

Such luminaries are out-numbered by the Y'hudi-haters, such as:

H. L. Mencken ("The Jews could be put down very plausibly as the most unpleasant race ever heard of." Dershowitz, p. 112)

George Bernard Shaw ("Stop being Jews and start being human beings." Dershowitz, p. 112)

Henry Adams ("The whole carcass is rotten with Jew

worms." Dershowitz, p. 112)

Francois Voltaire (Viewed by many today as one of the intellectual godfathers of modem anti-Semitism and racism. Writing in the eighteenth century he called the Y'hudim "an ignorant and barbarous people, who might someday become deadly to the human race." Dershowitz, p. 112)

H. G. Wells ("A careful study of anti-Semitism, prejudice and accusations might be of great value to many Jews, who do not adequately realize the irritation they inflict." Dershowitz, p. 112, 113)

Denis Diderot ("Brutish people, vile and vulgar men." Dershowitz, p. 113)

Theodore Dreiser ("New York is a kyke's dream of a ghetto," and "Jews are not pure Americans and lack "integrity." Dershowitz, p. 113)

T. S. Eliot (A social as well as literary anti-Semite, even after the Holocaust. Dershowitz, p. 113)

Immanuel Kant ("The Jews still cannot claim any true genius, any truly great man. All their talents and skills revolve around stratagems and low cunning.... They are a nation of swindlers." Dershowitz, p. 113)

Henry Ford (America's best-known anti-Semite declared in 1921: "Jews are not sportsmen. Whether this is due to their physical lethargy, their dislike of unnecessary physical action, or their serious cast of mind, others may decide.... It may be a defect in their character, or it may not; it is nevertheless a fact which discriminating Jews unhesitatingly acknowledge." Ford also published an anti-

Semetic periodical called the *Dearborn Independent* and circulated countless copies of a pack of lies called **The Protocols of the Elders of Zion** in a reworked American version.

I will cite just one example to disprove Henry Ford's opinionated 'fact' of the Jewish lack of athletic abilities: Sandy Koufax. Mr. Koufax, a Y'hudi who was born in Brooklyn, New York, was a star pitcher for the Brooklyn and later Los Angeles Dodgers baseball team between 1955 and 1966. His performance and records for the last six years of his short career, pitching with a sore arm I might add, has never, and I predict, will never be surpassed—111 wins, 1.95 ERA, .766 winning percentage, 1,444 strikeouts, 33 shutouts, 4 no-hitters, 1 perfect game, 3 time Cy Young award winner, and 2 MVP awards. Ref. **Sandy Koufax, A Lefty's Legacy** by Jane Leavy, p.121,179 and Dershowitz, p. 115, 116.)

Also I might add that the main reason most Y'hudim do not play silly American games is because these games invariably violate the weekly Shabbat which is written about later in this book.

Franklin D. Roosevelt (Although Roosevelt was president of America during most of WW II, he was not a friend of the Y'hudim. Our war against Germany had nothing to do with Nazi atrocities against the Y'hudim. After *Kristallnacht* in November 1938, President Roosevelt said in a press conference: "The news of the past few days from Germany has deeply shocked public opinion in the United States. Such news from any part of the world would inevitably produce a similar profound reaction among Americans in every part of the nation. I myself could scarcely believe such things could occur in a twentieth-century civilization."

But it was just political lip-service to placate Y'hudi American voters because nothing was done about it. There were still about a half million Y'hudim remaining in Germany in November, 1938, who were frantically trying to leave but had no place to go; just as the Y'hudim in Spain in 1492 had no place to go. Nobody wanted them, including the United States.

At the same press conference at which President Roosevelt decried *Kristallnacht,* he was asked if any place had been found for the Jews who wished to leave Germany. He replied, "No, the time is not ripe for that." When he was asked if he would propose a loosening of immigration laws to allow more Y'hudi refugees to come to the United States, he said he would not.)

Y'hudim in the United States held rallies, signed petitions, and sent letters to President Rooselvelt, but polls conducted at the time found that most Americans were against letting Y'hudi refugees into the United States, even refugee children. And the U.S. government refused to open its gates to the Y'hudim.

In 1939, a plan was proposed by a U.S. senator and a congresswoman to save twenty thousand Y'hudi children under the age of fourteen by bringing them to the United States. It was supported by former President Hoover and by Eleanor Roosevelt, the president's wife, but not by the President. It never passed Congress.

On May 13, 1939, the German luxury cruise ship *SS St. Louis* sailed from Hamburg, Germany with 936 passengers, 930 of whom were Y'hudim with tickets and visas for Cuba. Right before the ship left harbor, Cuba's president (a good Catholic Christian) bowed to German propaganda and invalidated the Y'hudi landing permits.

Captain Gustav Schroeder appealed to the U.S. government for a haven while U.S. Coast Guard ships patrolled the waters to prevent anyone swimming ashore as the ship passed very close to Florida. On their return to Europe most of the Y'hudi refugees were let into Holland, Belgium, France, and England.

These countries were still free at the time so the refugees felt safe, but within a year Holland, Belgium, and France were conquered by the German Army and subjected to Nazi rule. Only the 288 who were let into England survived (Ref. *We Remember the Holocaust* by David A. Adler, p. 40-45 and *The Breman Museum* in Atlanta, Georgia)

Ronald Reagan (Yes, even the venerated Republican Party icon was anti-Y'hudi). As president, Reagan visited an SS cemetery in Bitburg, Germany in 1985 where he said that the SS dead buried there were victims, just as surely as the victims in the concentration camps, i.e. he pardoned the Nazi murderers for their genocide of the Y'hudim by saying they were just 'following orders.'

What kind of warped mind equates mass murderers to their victims? Reagan refused to go to the Dachau concentration camp in Germany because he was not interested in "reawakening the memories and so forth." Dershowitz, p. 134, 135)

Patrick Buchanan, an orthodox Catholic Christian who is a nationally syndicated columnist and former White House director of communications under Ronald Reagan. "In one of his columns, regarding the Jewish outrage arising subsequent to the Catholic Church establishing the Carmelite convent at Auschwitz in 1984 in the very building that housed the poison gas used to murder more than a million Jews between 1942 and 1944 at the Auschwitz-Birkenau complex, Buchanan invoked 'Catholic rage' against the Jews. Instead of urging his readers to understand the pain that some Jewish survivors of Auschwitz must feel at Polish efforts to de-Judaize Hitler's final solution, Buchanan declared that, to orthodox Catholics, the demand that we be more sensitive to Jewish concerns is becoming a joke. Then, in a tone reminiscent of an incitement to a nineteenth century religious pogrom, he prophesied that, 'the slumbering giant of Catholicism may be about to awake.' Lest there be any doubt about the target of this giant's wrath, Buchanan pointed to 'those who so evidently despise our Church—'namely 'the Jews.'

Mr. Buchanan had, in the past, come to the defense of such genocidal killers as Klaus Barbie, Karl Linnas, and the SS killers buried at Bitburg. Buchanan had even expressed doubts about whether Jews were gassed at Treblinka." Dershowitz, p. 150, 162, 163)

Mel Gibson (This Catholic actor rants against the Y'hudim when he is stopped by a policeman for drunk driving. He also produces anti-Y'hudi movies such as *The Passion*). I will boycott and oppose everything written, said, or produced by anti-Y'hudi people such as these aforementioned vermin. They are anathema to me and more importantly, as will be shown in the next section, they are anathema to Elohim.

The Ill-Treatment of Blacks in America

The United States of America, a self-professed Christian nation, had legal forced slavery of Negro, or Black African, people exclusively for its first hundred years and then legalized segregation of only Black African people for another hundred years after slavery was abolished.

Both slavery and segregation were wholeheartedly supported by the mostly Protestant Christian churches in the USA during this 200 year period. The demise of both slavery and segregation had to be brought about by military force of the government, with no help or encouragement from Christianity.

On the contrary, the Christian churches were dragged into integration kicking and screaming the whole time. Christianity condoned and sanctioned both slavery and segregation and both were evil because they demeaned, abused and persecuted another group of people simply because of their origins and skin color and viewed them as less human and inferior to the white Caucasian Christians. That's the height of arrogance and also a lie, and both are sins against Elohim.

I witnessed, and unfortunately to my regret, was part of the ugliness of legal segregation and separation of Black people from the rest of the population in the Heart of Dixie city called Birmingham, Alabama, during the 1940s, 1950s, and 1960s.

It was like they were quarantined with a deadly communicable disease. It is hard for me to believe today that it actually happened, but unfortunately it did. I will list a few examples, that I personally recall, of the demeaning inhumanities directed against Black African people during the early years of my life that were just accepted and rarely questioned by me and everyone else, even most Blacks. It was as the Hank Williams, Jr. song says "just family tradition":

1.) Public drinking fountains always came in pairs, one

labeled 'White Only' and the other labeled 'Colored Only'.

2.) Public restrooms were always in groups of four, White Men, White Women, Colored Men and Colored Women.

3.) Movie theaters, mostly downtown, were white-only unless it was one of the fancy larger theaters such as the Ritz or the Alabama which would admit Black people but restrict their seating to the balcony or "peanut gallery" as it was jokingly referred to. The drive-in theaters were segregated as well.

Blacks detained for attending a white-only movie theater. [New York Public Library Digital Collection]

4.) Public transportation such as buses, streetcars, trains, and planes were partially segregated. For instance: Black folks were allowed on the same City of Birmingham buses as White folks but had to sit in the rear behind the movable wooden, two-pronged, "Colored" sign that fit into two holes on the top of the seat back tubing. The sign could be moved forward or aft as required to accommodate the ratio of Whites and Blacks riding the bus or streetcar at any one time. This is what I call "onboard segregation"

Cab stand for blacks. [New York Public Library Digital Collection]

similar to the nicer theaters. I don't recall exactly how the train and plane segregation policy was implemented, but I can assure you there was never a black person seated next to a white person on either one.

5.) I attended a lot of AA Southern League professional baseball games of the Birmingham Barons, usually with my grandfather, at Rickwood Field. Black people were allowed to attend but, there again, were segregated from within by having to sit in the right field bleachers, which was also mockingly referred to as "the peanut gallery."

I recall there actually being a pro baseball team named the Birmingham Black Barons that was allowed to play at Rickwood Field, but I never attended any of their games so I don't know what the seating arrangements were. I don't think White people were restricted to the right field bleachers though, but they sure as hell couldn't sit next to Black people, so I presume they just weren't allowed to attend.

6.) Restaurants were strictly segregated with most being White-Only, of course, with a few of usually lesser quality for Colored-Only. A Black person was not allowed into a white restaurant, cafeteria, cafe, bar, pub, nightclub, etc.—there weren't any fast-food joints at the time except for Krystal and Dairy Queen—and a White person was not allowed into a Black establishment. I'm sure it was a law or local

Black-only bar. [New York Public Library Digital Collection]

ordinance and presumably you could be arrested if you violated it.

7.) Public and private schools at all levels, kindergarten, elementary, high, college, university, trade, technical, business, etc.—I never attended one class in my 17 years of public schooling in Alabama, including Auburn University from 1957 to 1962, where there was a single Black student in my classroom or even enrolled in the school itself—there were foreigners, some with very dark skins from India, Pakistan, Middle Eastern Arabs, Mejico, Central and South America and even some Japanese and Germans, whom we had just defeated in a very bloody world war, but not one American citizen of African Negro descent was ever in any of my classes, dormitories, or boarding houses.

8.) The public swimming pools were all strictly segregated and like the eating-places there were a few inferior Colored-Only pools. The very idea of sharing pool water with a Black person was abhorrent to most whites at the time. I don't ever remember any Black people on the Gulf of Mejico beaches when we vacationed in Panama City, Florida every summer. I guess they were White-Only beaches, besides, they would have no place to stay in these coastal resort cities anyway since....

9.) Hotels and motels—motels, or motorcourts, were just coming into their era—were, of course, strictly segregated. There again, the Blacks were consigned to a few inferior flop-house hotel accommodations for Colored-Only.

10.) Public libraries were also segregated. I don't know where Black people got their books to read, perhaps they weren't expected to read books.

11.) Hospitals, doctor's and dentist's offices were also segregated. I never remember seeing a Black person in any hospital, as a patient, visitor, nurse or doctor that I ever entered, which in my case was mostly West End Baptist (Christian) Hospital.

12.) The Young Men's Christian Association or YMCA was segregated big time, as was the Young Women's Christian Association (YWCA). Notice these are both Christian organizations. My only experience with the Birmingham YMCA was a trip one time as a guest of some of my high school classmates to swim in their pool. To my surprise they required that the young men swim without bathing trunks. It was my first and last visit to the YMCA. Not only were they perverted racially with their segregation policies but they were also probably perverted sexually with their nude swimming policy—maybe some Christian Catholic priests were in charge.

13.) Even our private family automobile had "onboard" segregation; my mother's twice-a-week Colored maid had to sit in the back seat when being transported to and from our house by my mother—my favorite maid was Callie, who was like another mother to me. Callie, who was an excellent cook, would usually prepare our meals, in addition to cleaning our house, washing and ironing our clothes, and washing our dirty dishes, but she wasn't permitted to eat with us at the table; rather she would eat the left-over food later by herself. I asked my father onetime why Callie couldn't eat with us, and he replied, "We just don't eat with Colored people," or something like that.

My dad had to transfer to Oklahoma City for a year circa 1950, and my mother wanted Callie to come with us, which she did. The trip was a bit awkward of course because she had to sit in the back seat during the entire trip, next to me and my brother and sister, but I didn't mind.

Of course, she wasn't allowed into any White-Only restaurants, so my mother would get her food to go, and she would usually eat in the car. I don't recall the motel accommodations along the way, but she wasn't in our room or motel so she either slept in the car or stayed in a Colored-Only motel in the Colored district. All the main motels along the highway between Alabama and Oklahoma were segregated.

We lived in a rental house in a northern suburb of Oklahoma City, and Callie was there every day doing her usual duties, but she lived in the downtown Colored quarters at night in a rooming house, I think. She wasn't allowed to sleep in our house even though there was room for her. One day our family, including Callie, went on a visit to the Oklahoma City Zoo. I have a vivid recollection burned into my brain of what happened next: Callie was refused admission into the zoo! Even as an eleven-year-old boy, that struck me as really bad. I still remember it like it happened yesterday. Sad to say, we went ahead with the zoo visit while Callie waited outside.

14.) I don't remember subdivisions in the 1950's in Birmingham but White people and Black people could not live in the same neighborhood or share the same apartment complex. My recollection of a black neighborhood was the large Negro (actually, this word was usually misspelled and mispronounced with an Ni, two g's and an er) "quarters" in West End near where my father worked. It was nothing but a disgraceful overcrowded ghetto of shacks and shanties with unpaved streets.

I heard many stories about young men going into the quarters and throwing water filled balloons or firecrackers at the poor frightened Black residents. This was considered good sport and evoked much laughter when recounted later to their White friends.

15.) The worst example of how bad segregation was in the Southern states of the United States of America was the lily-white Christian churches. The churches were all strictly segregated, both small and large, plain and ornate, conservative, and liberal. No intermingling of Blacks and Whites was allowed—just like I never had a Black student in a public school class with me, I never saw a Black person in any Church of Christ I ever attended until about the year 2000, and even then it was frowned upon by a lot of die-hard segregationist White Christian members. The Christian churches were the last institutions to desegregate and some are still just dejure integrated even today.

Black church. [New York Public Library Digital Collection]

The mostly Protestant Christian churches in the South should have been leading the fight to abolish both slavery and segregation, but instead they held on to both evils until the bitter end. Can you imagine people who claim to be followers of Elohim refusing to let another human being into their church to worship and praise Elohim with them just because of their skin color resulting from their Black-African roots? It's crazy; it's disgusting; it's disrespectful; it's bad fruit, and it's just plain wickedness. It's more proof that Christianity is not of Y'HoVaH but is of the Adversary, haSatan.

The Ill-Treatment of Native Americans

Still more hapless victims of Christianity are the Native American Indians. It was mainly Catholic Christianity at work in South and Central America and Catholic and Protestant Christianity at work in North America, but the purpose, methods and results were pretty much the same: plunder, raping, looting, stealing, lying, death and destruction of the vulnerable, honorable, truthful, but naive Indians in their dealings with the dishonorable, greedy, avaricious, lying, scheming, theiving, forked-tongue European Christians.

The basic message of the Christian conquistadors was the same as always: "convert to our religion or die." Of course, conversion to Christianity included surrendering yourself and your property to them. The Indians who surrendered were renamed with Christian names, dressed in Christian clothes, introduced to White man's booze called "firewater," and the children were sent to re-education schools or camps where they were force-fed Christian lies.

Those who refused to surrender were murdered or massacred by the Christian invaders—including women and children—in "the name of Jesus Christ." It was total annihilation, just as they had previously dealt with others that they hated such as Y'hudim and Heretics.

Of the 340 so-called treaties the White man made with the North American Indians, 340 were violated by the lying forked-tongue White man devils. The victors always write the history, so the Indians are always portrayed as ruthless, blood-thirsty savages, when in fact these characteristics describe the Christian soldiers and politicians. Christianity on the American continent was the largest land-theft in history, and the few surviving Native North American Indians are mostly living in abject poverty on small uninhabitable lands called "reservations." Their culture has almost been completely wiped out but is miraculously still extant.

Thomas Jefferson, one of the American 'founding fathers,' summed up this religion rather well, "Christianity was the greatest fraud ever perpetrated on mankind." I agree with him.

The history and ill-treatment of Native Americans, something about which my father had strong feelings
By Laura Dobbs Pemberton

Introduction

This section examines the incidents known as Wounded Knee I and II, which will provide some historical context for what else follows. A review of the extraordinary case of Leonard Peltier and AIM is presented next. It includes his illegal extradition from Canada; the details are from a Freedom Of Information Act (FOIA) document from the minister of Justice of Canada.

Further detailing the shabby treatment of native Americans is the more recent case of the Dakota Access Pipeline. A review of the 2014 Wisconsin tribunals concerning Indian Boarding schools follows. The section concludes with a discussion of the genocide committed against native American children via abduction by the Department of Family and Children Services (DFCS).

Wounded Knee I (1890) and Wounded Knee II on Pine Ridge Reservation (1970)

The first battle of Wounded Knee took place in 1890 when U.S. Military troops and Lakota Sioux Indians fought at Wounded Knee Creek in South Dakota. It resulted in the deaths of 300 Sioux men, women, and children, many of whom were defenseless.

Fourteen years earlier, Sitting Bull had led thousands of Sioux away from the reservations, resisting forced relocation, but they remained under constant pursuit by the U.S military. The confrontation which followed began with the discovery of gold in the Black Hills, an event which lured unprecedented numbers of miners and settlers into the area.

In response, the U.S Army ignored previous treaty agreements and allowed this new movement into the region. As a result, many Sioux and Cheyenne tribesmen were forced to leave their reservations. A great number joined Sitting Bull and Crazy Horse in Montana.

More than 10,000 Native Americans from a variety of tribes camped along the Little Big Horn River in defiance of a U.S. War Department order to return to their reservations or risk attack. Rather than give up, they chose to battle the soldiers sent to force them back to the reservation. On June 25, 1876, some 3,000 warriors overtook General Custer and killed his entire command.

Thirteen years later, in 1889, many Sioux Indians gathered at Wounded Knee Creek on the Pine ridge Reservation to participate in the Ghost Dance. The ceremonial dance was intended to bring back the Buffalo and send the white men away. The dancers wore special charms they believed would protect them from bullets.

The U.S. military, fearing large numbers of Indians gathered in one place, brought in troops but were unsuccessful in stopping the Ghost Dance ceremony. The soldiers viewed the Indian ritual as preparation for armed conflict and described the participants as wild and crazy. In addition to the Ghost Dance, the U.S. Government feared Sitting Bull as a leader due to his great influence over the native people.

Believing that Sitting Bull was organizing a new effort to lead the people from the reservation, the U.S. government had him arrested on Dec. 15, 1890. The aim was to take him into custody and remove him from the reservation, but a cadre of Sioux men rallied to his side to prevent it. The conflict ended in an exchange of gunfire that resulted in the death of the great Sioux leader, and triggered the conflict of Wounded Knee I.

Wounded Knee II began on Feb.27, 1973. According to internet sources and the book *In the Spirit of Crazy Horse* by Peter Mathieson, it involved about 200 Oglala Lakota people and members of the American Indian Movement (AIM) on Pine Ridge Indian reservation. The incident amounted to a 71-day standoff between the U.S government and native American Indians. Both sides were armed, though the government troops were backed by tanks.

Tribal leader Dick Wilson, considered by many Lakota people to be a puppet of the U.S. government, intended to sell off roughly an eighth of the reservation land for the mining of gold and uranium. The traditional Lakota people on the reservation strongly opposed the land sale. Wilson, with the aid of the government, established the "Guardians of the Oglala Nation" the acronym for which--GOONs-- proved accurate. Over a three-year period, this private army was suspected of being responsible for many of the 60 deaths which occurred among Wilson's vocal opponents. GOON tactics included arson as well as drive-by shootings. In one such incident, a young boy was shot in the eye in front of his house.

In addition to their opposition to the land sale, the

Native Americans and AIM also addressed the government's failure to fulfill treaties and demanded the reopening of treaty negotiations. It was a brutal and scary time for anyone on the reservation willing to stand up for their rights and land. In all, about 240 mysterious deaths occurred.

The Saga of Leonard Peltier

During the infamous standoff at Wounded Knee II, the Pine Ridge Reservation asked AIM to come to their aid. Leonard Peltier was one of many who answered the call, living in tents at various campsites in the area. Not long after his arrival, two FBI agents were shot to death, presumably by protestors. A native American bystander, Joe Stuntz, was shot and killed by a police sniper. Leonard Peltier was charged with murdering the FBI agents, but the identity of the person who murdered Joe Stuntz remains a mystery.

The details leading up to the shootings are unclear, but according to most reporting sources the two FBI agents were looking for a man named Jimmy Eagle who had been in a fight with two ranch hands. Eagle reportedly stole a pair of boots from one of them. While in pursuit of the subject, the agents came under fire and were killed.

Afterward, events cascaded in an avalanche of turmoil. SWAT teams and a variety of agents swarmed the reservation. Years later, it was discovered through a Freedom of Information (FOIA) release that the agents and SWAT units had been assembled *prior* to the shootout in a pre-planned operation.

Peter Mathieson, author of ***In the Spirit of Crazy Horse***, claims it was planned in coordination with Richard Wilson's surrender of a large tract of tribal land in the northwestern section of Pine Ridge reservation to the U.S. government. The FBI involvement was intended to divert attention away from Wilson's giveaway of mining rights. The deal was in violation of the 1868 treaty which required the approval of three-fourths of all the adult males in the tribe for the transfer of any Lakota land.

Another theory held that the raid was intended to incite gunfire from the Indians and thereby provide an excuse to move a paramilitary force onto the reservation which could then attack AIM and its supporters.

The timing of the shootout and the raid was no mere coincidence. Few fair-minded people would believe the government's claim that its well-armed agents just happened to turn up near the AIM camp two days in a row to investigate the theft of a pair of boots or an argument between drinking buddies. If petty theft had become a priority for the FBI, the word never reached the public. In addition to the FBI's interest, the Bureau of Indian Affairs (BIA) "just happened" to be conducting maneuvers near the Jumping Bull property, scene of the altercation, on the day of the shootout.

According to Edgar Bear Runner, paramilitary forces had surrounded the Oglala Sioux region all that morning. Included were approximately 150 white men—state troopers, U.S. marshals, and SWAT teams. According to a report in *The New York Times*, and later confirmed in a FOIA release, there were 250 government agents in all, a fact which the government still denies.

Leonard Peltier while in a Federal prison in Florida.

Leonard Peltier, a native American activist and member of AIM was imprisoned in 1977 for the 1975 murders of the two FBI agents. Four years after his incarceration, a FOIA suit resulted in the release of previously undisclosed documents which prove his innocence and the FBI's use of its infamous Counter Intelligence Program (COINTELPRO) to "neutralize" members of the movement.

An FBI teletype revealed that the FBI's own ballistics experts knew the gun attributed to Peltier could not have fired the bullets that killed the agents, and that this critical evidence was withheld from the defense at Peltier's trial. The government conceded that they "do not know who killed the agents," and that there were no eyewitnesses or direct evidence against Mr. Peltier.

In 1985, the government changed its original charge, that Peltier killed the agents, and claimed instead that he aided and abetted the killer.

The appellate court stated there was a "clear abuse of the investigative process" which "cast strong doubts on the government's case." Yet, each of his four appeals ended with Peltier being denied justice or a new trial based on the merits and validity of his arguments rather than one based on legal loopholes.

Peltier, who had fled to Canada in 1975, was not included in a Cedar Rapids, Iowa, trial of two other native Americans charged with the same crime. The defendants pleaded self-defense and presented compelling evidence about FBI and prosecutorial malfeasance. The jury found them not guilty.

This outcome didn't sit well with the FBI which then used false affidavits to extradite Peltier from Canada. In the process, they stripped away his right to claim self-defense and then moved him to a different state for trial before a judge known to have issues with native Americans.

In extraditing Peltier, the government produced an affidavit from Myrtle Poor Bear, a woman they claimed was an eyewitness to the shooting. In an earlier affidavit, however, she claimed not to even know Leonard Peltier and was nowhere near Pine Ridge on the day of the shootout. She later admitted she had been coerced and her children threatened if she told the truth.

The following is taken from a flier published by the International Leonard Peltier Defense Committee (www.whoisleonardpeltier.info): "Leonard was a close associate of Dennis Banks (one of the founders of AIM) and showed signs of potential leadership. All AIM leadership was targeted. The FBI wanted desperately to destroy the movement and force native people into assimilating into the white culture and allow the Government control of their mineral (oil, uranium, gold) rich land. Peltier so concerned them that a memo was sent out in which Peltier's occupation was described as "Manager of AIM." Not only was Peltier *not* the manager of AIM (he was a mechanic), no such position even existed."

Leonard Peltier is imprisoned in the Federal Correctional Complex, Coleman (FCC Coleman) in Florida, stripped of his freedom and rights as a human being. He has suffered greatly due to a problem with his jaw stemming from a case of lockjaw in his youth. Unable to eat at times, or close his mouth, while in prison and early on, he was denied medical treatment that was offered free of charge by the Mayo clinic, even though it was his legal right to have it. It has been noted by an independent physician that "the type of radiation treatments given to Leonard while at Springfield, under the auspices of the penal system, are not normally associated with treating his problem."

In his book, **Prison Writings**, Peltier says, "You see, this is how it's done. Target us, set us up, arrest us, beat us, hang a phony rap on us, drag us off to court and jail, impoverish us with legal expenses, even if we never did a darn thing. We later learned it was called FBI neutralization." It seems clear the FBI also used COINTELPRO tactics which the U.S. Senate declared illegal in 1976.

Peltier goes on to say, "...and let me tell you, so long as you have nothing but contempt for the law and the U.S. Constitution itself, it can be a very effective strategy indeed." And, he remarked further, "I felt no more guilty running from my oppressors than a Jew in Nazi Germany would have felt running from the Gestapo. Like them, I was being targeted for WHO I was."

He believes the FBI "...hid behind their usual cloak of National Security to do their dirty work. ... it works like this: their first tactic, forget the law, the law's for suckers. Subvert the law at will to get your man, however innocent he may be; suborn the whole legal and judicial systems; LIE whenever and wherever you have to, to keep the focus of inquiry on your victims, not on your own crimes."

In a larger context, he says, "The FBI itself is a victim of the energy wars, having strayed far beyond the bounds of legality and human decency in its misguided eagerness to serve the interests of the multinational invaders in their continuing assault upon Mother Earth. All these things are acts of war against the Lakota people, against all the Indian people, against all indigenous people everywhere, against all of humanity. We must continue to oppose these forces of destruction with every fiber of our being, with every breath we take."

Laura Dobbs Pemberton and companion at a 2009 rally in Washington, DC, sponsored by the International Leonard Peltier Defense Committee. [Dobbs family photo]

The Illegal Extradition

The following is based in part on information received from the Canadian Minister of Justice in response to a FOIA request regarding Peltier's extradition.

Still stinging from the not guilty plea awarded at the Cedar Rapids trial, the FBI concentrated their efforts on Peltier. This was a result of Leonard running off to Canada while the others stayed in the US and were charged. The FBI got busy trying to get Peltier back so they could pin the entire shoot out ordeal on him. This conveniently took the attention off the FBI and their involvement in all of it. In order to justify the extradition order, they came up with five criminal charges against him, all of which have proven to be false.

1) The attempted murder of state trooper Ron Hlavinka in Milwaukee, Wisconsin, on 11/22/72.

2) The murder of the two FBI agents on the Pine Ridge Reservation on 6/26/75.

3) The attempted murder of a state trooper in Ontario, Oregon, on 11/14/75.

4) A burglary in Nyssa, Oregon, on 11/15/75.

Canada threw out item #3, the attempted murder charge that occurred in Oregon because if the incident had occurred in Canada, it would not have justified committal for trial, and a jury would most likely have rendered a not guilty plea. However, the court agreed to extradite Peltier based on the other charges, the most damning of which involved two affidavits from Myrtle Poor Bear.

It is critically important to point out that all of these charges are demonstrably false. They involved coerced witnesses, hidden affidavits, and COINTELPRO tactics. Many of these same prevarications were sent to the police in an effort to make Peltier look guilty. Canadian judicial authorities later learned of this, and they have tried on numerous occasions to have Peltier returned to Canada. All such efforts have failed.

The charge of murder in the case of the two FBI agents on the Pine Ridge Reservation was based on three sworn affidavits from Myrtle Poor Bear, a native American woman suspected of having mental health issues. A fourth affidavit, which actually predated the others, was withheld. In the original document which was suppressed, Myrtle Poor Bear testified that she had not been present the day of the shootout and had left Pine Ridge the day before.

In the first of the three bogus affidavits, Poor Bear claims to have overheard Peltier and others planning the ambush of the two agents.

In the second affidavit, Poor Bear claims to have been Peltier's girlfriend, and that she actually saw the agents being murdered.

In the final affidavit, which was presented to the Canadian court, Poor Bear's testimony was limited to what she supposedly witnessed. There was no mention of her overhearing any ambush plans or being in any way related to Peltier.

Myrtle Poor Bear later said she had been coerced in her affidavits and that the lives of her children had been threatened.

When these facts were later brought up during Peltier's trial, the prosecutors denied that Poor Bear had been coerced. They claimed she was too incompetent to be a witness at the trial and further, that they did not believe her story about being a witness.

When Attorney General Janet Reno was asked if the government should have spotted Poor Bear's incompetence *before* the extradition proceedings, she responded with,

"...that question cannot be finally answered on the record before the court and is a question which need not be answered to resolve the issues of appeal." Did she think if she used enough words to answer a simple question people would get confused and forget the question?

One cannot help but wonder why the question couldn't be answered in court, and the Canadian court certainly had the right to an answer. The second part of her answer is equally spurious. The whole point of an answer to the question regarding Poor Bear's competency was that it would likely have caused Peltier's appeal to be granted. I submit that is precisely why Reno refused to provide a real answer.

Why couldn't Reno answer the question? Let us take a closer look at the possible reasons: A) Because she didn't know the answer, or B) Because she didn't *care* to know the answer, or C) Because she did not want the rest of us to know the answer since it would not make her look good.

Reno said she couldn't answer the question on the record, but from a legal standpoint, wouldn't it then be useless? To break it down further, I would conclude that she lied, because it's blatantly obvious from the evidence that she knew the answer, and that answer in fact had *everything* to do with Peltier's appeal as opposed to having nothing to do with it, as she claimed.

It was quite clear she knew a fourth affidavit had been suppressed by people who worked for her and that Poor Bear's mental state did not go from competent to incompetent in that short time span. My conclusion? She lied; she knew the answer and withheld it as well as covering up the FBI's lies. Instead of letting the wheels of justice turn to ensnare the real criminals, she chose to whitewash it all. I submit that is the answer Janet Reno did not want to reveal.

Here are *their* "facts:"

1) Myrtle Poor Bear was fully competent on Feb. 19, 1976.

2) Myrtle Poor Bear was fully *incompetent* by the first trial in June of 1976.

By subtraction, that comes to just 4 months, and people simply do not go from being in a state of full competence to full blown incompetence in that short a time span, and it's nothing I would sign off on if I were the so-called professional.

How is it that the prosecutors believed Poor Bear was competent during the extradition process but incompetent during Peltier's trial? Could it be Reno felt entitled to ignore questions that might be incriminating?

A copy of Reno's non-answer wasn't forwarded to Canadian authorities until 1993, despite requests from the Canadian Department of Justice for information concerning fabrication of Poor Bear's affidavits.

CONCLUSIONS: The U.S. Justice Department admitted they did not know why or how the first two of the three affidavits cited above would not be used and further, the US prosecutors did not think the affidavits were even contradictory. And yet they felt justified in suppressing the original affidavit because it would have prevented Peltier's extradition.

One is left to ponder whether or not these people can read or write. Their statements are too contradictory to be merely accidental. They said they didn't think the differing affidavits they themselves prepared were contradictory. Anyone in law enforcement who cannot distinguish between a direct eyewitness from one who was nowhere near a crime scene, should probably look into some other line of work. It would save not only taxpayers and innocent people, but would also save them from embarrassment. Former Justice Department prosecutor Bill Halprin remarked during oral arguments that the FBI had engaged in misconduct. The FBI claimed Halprin was aware of all the affidavits, and it was his idea to only use two of them.

When asked for his response to the FBI on 6/7/79, Halprin said he was unaware of the original affidavit until the hearing before the Federal Court of Appeals when council for Mr. Peltier introduced it as fresh evidence. He went on to say the FBI's statement was incorrect though he admitted to having the original affidavit withheld because his director, Steven Harding, needed more information.

He concluded that he thought the bureau was covering up the suppression of the affidavit by Myrtle Poor Bear in which she claimed to have been off the reservation at the time of the shooting.

It seems the FBI simply found it convenient to leave this piece of evidence out. On June 28, 1979, Canadian investigator Rutherford asked the Justice department to address the Poor Bear issue in light of Halprin's comments about the FBI cover up and the factually incorrect statement they provided.

The justice department told Rutherford his query had been "passed on"—sometimes know as "thrown in the trash"—to none other than the FBI and the U.S District Attorney of South Dakota for their response. Rutherford responded that neither were forthcoming with additional information.

To me, that would be the equivalent of a judge asking a convicted criminal, in jail, for a review of his own crime, and expecting him to be forthcoming with additional evidence that could be used against him.

On January 29 of the following year, the FBI finally did respond, but said they had no additional comments and that their letter of May 10, 1979, was as accurate as possible and was based on the recollection of their agents and a review of their files.

Frankly, their files—for lack of a better word—are creepy. And who turns an investigation over to the criminal's side to see if they want to fess up to their own crime? Yes, the question was about the FBI's misconduct which is a crime. Just like Homeland Security, where laws are set up for them to conduct their own oversight. Of course they wouldn't find anything wrong!

Such a set of denials, non-answers, and circular logic is all too common in bureaucratic circles, but one would hope the FBI is above it. Clearly, they're not.

The question was about the FBI's misconduct, which in itself is a crime. What legitimate investigator seeks the opinion of the very people who broke the law in the first place?

In 1986, Rutherford exhausted his sources trying to pull an answer out of the FBI (much as I was exhausted just reading about the confusion). In the face of mounting demands by Peltier supporters to the Minister of Justice, he wrote a letter to the Office of International Affairs (OIA) stating he had made repeated requests to the Justice Department, that assistance was not withstanding, and that no satisfactory explanation had been received in response to Canada's inquiries about the Poor Bear affidavits. In 1989, after the Supreme Court of Canada dismissed Peltier's appeal, they noted that the Poor Bear issue raised serious questions about the bona fides of the U.S Extradition Process.

Rutherford wrote the OIA a second time and requested a further review. He was told the matter had been referred to the FBI for review. In 1990 the National Law Library published an article claiming that the prosecuting side and the FBI had admitted the Poor Bear affidavits had been fabricated during oral arguments. Rutherford immediately wrote the OIA with concern and requested an explanation.

Lynn Crooks, one of the original prosecutors, responded with an excerpt from the National Law Journal in which he stated, "We have never admitted the affidavits used in the extradition were fabricated." He went on to say, "We never fabricated evidence and neither did the FBI."

So, even after it goes on the record that they admitted to fabricating evidence, they still go on to deny it at a later date. That strikes me as a level of ultimate deceit with a twist of arrogance. That's a stiff drink to swallow in the "house of justice."

One is left to assume that Crooks is saying the FBI may be guilty of using false affidavits, but since they never admitted using them, it doesn't matter. Presumably, this "Get Out of Jail Free" card extends to any other laws they might break. Nor is the irony of Lynn Crooks' name lost on this writer.

Crook also claimed that Poor Bear was as incompetent at the initial interview as she obviously was at trial. In other words, he's admitting that the first affidavit was more accurate, which is the one the FBI withheld during the extradition. Therefore, Peltier was extradited illegally.

Judge Heaney wrote that there was merit in consideration for clemency for Mr. Peltier when the FBI used improper tactics during extradition and during the investigation, as well as during his trial. Lynn Crooks' response was that he confirmed his position that the Poor Bear affidavit was taken in good faith, and there was no misconduct.

I believe the summary presented above speaks volumes about the injustice done here and the lack of credibility which stains everyone involved in the prosecution of Leonard Peltier. In my view, while Peltier remains locked up, no one is free, and there is only injustice for all. That should anger every American--to the bone.

Next we'll examine the other two trumped up extradition charges, one of which was an attempted murder charge in Oregon. Canada recognized it was a phony rap and threw it out. Evidently, there is still some justice in this world. The other charge, however, was much more involved.

The attempted murder charge in Milwaukee, WI, was the only one not mentioned in detail in the Canadian FOIA. Peter Matheison reported on it in detail in his book, *In the Spirit of Crazy Horse*. The story begins with Peltier and a companion having dinner in a Milwaukee restaurant. Two men sat at a nearby table and harassed Peltier, laughing, pointing, and calling him a "dirty, filthy Indian."

When Peltier got up to leave after eating, the two men blocked the exit. Before Peltier could ask them why he'd been stopped or what they thought was so funny, one of them drew a .357 magnum handgun and held it to Peltier's head. Peltier raised both hands and walked back into the restaurant saying, "I give up" hoping other patrons would hear him.

Only then did they identify themselves as off-duty police officers. They marched him outside and into custody where he was frisked. They found a damaged Beretta which Peltier had purchased for twenty dollars. One of the officers claimed Peltier had pointed the gun at him and pulled the trigger, but the weapon jammed. This charge was proven false as the weapon was unusable.

Later, it was also revealed that one of the arresting officers had injured his hand while beating Peltier after the arrest. He required several days off for the injuries to heal enough for him to return to work. And during the subsequent Milwaukee trial, a conversation between one of the lawmen and his girlfriend was brought up. In that exchange, the cop waved a photo of Peltier and bragged about how he was going to capture "a big one" for the FBI.

Recruiting local law enforcement to assist in the FBI's plans for "neutralization" of AIM and its leaders was a standard tactic. The Milwaukee incident is merely one compelling example. Having spent five months in jail, Peltier was convinced his trial would be rigged, as demonstrated by the phony charges, and he jumped pretrial bail in hopes of avoiding further imprisonment.

If Peltier was such a menace to society, one can only wonder why the FBI had to manufacture evidence in order to convict him. Yet, they claimed his conviction was fair and just, though he wasn't allowed to plead self-defense, as the others in the Pine Ridge Reservation shootings had, a plea which was ultimately upheld. It's highly unlikely the founding fathers had these kinds of bullying tactics in mind when they penned the Constitution unless they were thinking about the oppressive policies and procedures of our former British overlords.

In a fair and impartial world, the Canadian Minister of Justice would not have extradited Peltier as his offences were characterized as being of a political character. The following are definitions for such offenses:

1) An offense against a sovereign power or an attack against a custom or institution held sacred.

2) Political violence used by political radicals in terms of the individual conscience versus the power of the state.

3) The judiciary would still determine whether there was a possible cause that the offense was committed, which protects against extradition based on fabricated charges. With the political offender, penal sanctions do not deter his actions. He is committed to the principle of political change through his actions and does not consider his actions blameworthy. He attacks the status quo and denies legitimacy of the particular laws, claiming instead the

allegiance to a "superior legitimating principle."

However, political offenses are not recognized as extraditable offenses. The political offense exception to extradition generally prevents a person from being extradited to face prosecution for crimes committed in furtherance of a political uprising, movement, or rebellion in the country in which such occurrences took place[xii].

[i] Commonwealth v. Hare, 36 Pa. Super. 125 (Pa. Super. Ct. 1908).

[ii] State ex rel. Brown v. Stewart, 60 Wis. 587 (Wis. 1884).

[iii] White v. Marshall, 11 Ohio Dec. 779 (Ohio C.P. 1901).

[iv] State v. Hudson, 2 Ohio Dec. 15 (Ohio C.P. 1893).

[v] Haxhiaj v. Hackman, 528 F.3d 282 (4th Cir. Va. 2008).

[vi] Id.

[vii] Factor v. Laubenheimer, 290 U.S. 276 (U.S. 1933).

[viii] Gallina v. Fraser, 278 F.2d 77 (2d Cir. Conn. 1960).

[ix] In re Extradition of Lin, 915 F. Supp. 206 (D. Guam 1995).

[x] Id.

[xi] 18 USCS § 3184.

[xii] Koskotas v. Roche, 931 F.2d 169 (1st Cir. Mass. 1991).

One could argue that Peltier was acting against a sovereign power since the various agents all represented a different sovereign power than the tribe.

The U.S government funded Dick Wilson's GOON squad which was used against traditional native members of the tribe. This was evidenced by the fact that US agents surrounded the area prior to the shootout. The agents entered the Jumping Bull property illegally since they had no warrant, and used the bogus claim of tracking down a stolen pair of used cowboy boots. Petty theft has never been the responsibility of the FBI.

If the FBI upholds the U.S. Constitution, then they must accept Indian Sovereignty under Article 1 Section 8 which grants the power to make decisions regarding relations with other nations and control internal government. The Federal Crimes Act of 1885 (18 U.S.C. § 1153) specifies that if certain major crimes are committed by Indians on Indian land the accused will be placed under Federal jurisdiction. These offenses include murder, arson, maiming, assaults, burglary, and robbery, all of which occurred before the shootout at Wounded Knee II. However, since the equipment and supplies used in the above offenses were provided by the U.S. Government, and its agents ignored Federal statutes involving crimes against traditional natives, the law allowing for their intervention should have been nullified.

Leonard Peltier sits today in a maximum security prison as an old man and as a political prisoner. He should have been released by now, especially in light of the FOIA releases in which judges have admitted the government engaged in serious misconduct in trying to convict Peltier. At the very least he should be released from maximum security due to his age; the law is clear on this. Even the FBI agents involved admitted they have no idea who shot those agents and that Peltier's charge is only for aiding and abetting. This being the case, Peltier should not be serving a life sentence, much less be forced to serve it in a maximum security prison.

It would seem the government agents who oversee such things have a vindictive nature. Though they "have no idea who shot those agents," they are unwilling to give him any relief. They claim he aided and abetted in the crime, but are certainly not treating him as if that was the sole extent of his involvement. If so, we would need many more maximum security prisons to house all the people given similar life sentences.

Protesters at a 2009 rally in Washington, DC, sponsored by the International Leonard Peltier Defense Committee. [Dobbs family photo]

A number of reasonable people believe the FBI is actually responsible for the murders of their own agents. Meanwhile, we have political figures in our government who shake their fingers at other countries for having political prisoners, all the while ignoring their own. In my mind, this is the worst kind of hypocrisy.

The Keystone Pipeline

At the time of this writing, 2018, the same type scenario is going on with the roll-out of the keystone Oil Pipeline, which runs from Canada to the United States. It carries oil to refineries in Illinois and Texas and to oil tank farms and distribution centers in Cushing, Oklahoma. The route of the pipeline cuts right through the Standing Rock Indian reservation, a sovereign nation. The people there have protested strongly against the project since its inception.

Many protesters have camped out in frigid cold temperatures and stood up against the tyrannical people behind the construction of the pipeline. In addition to outright trespassing, the project has the potential to contaminate the tribe's drinking water since the Mississippi river runs right alongside the designated pipeline route. Many natives call themselves "water protectors." Around 850 water protectors have been arrested during the protests. 650 cases were dismissed or offered plea deals.

I believe people have a legal right to protest when someone trespasses on their property, no matter who it is.

Attorney Daniel Sheehan has also been involved with the Dakota access pipeline issue and helped represent the native people on this issue. In his youtube.com video, "Daniel Sheehan on Standing Rock, DAPL, and its Unlawful Criminal Conspiracy," he explained what the people living in the Standing Rock area had to face. His team filed some 3,000 pages of situation reports, internal emails, interviews, and documents with the court proving that Tiger Swan, a privately owned paramilitary concern hired by the Energy Transfer Partners, changed the route of the Dakota Access Pipeline moved the pipeline from Bismarck, ND, an almost all-white town to the reservation because of whites protesting possible harm to their water supply.

Tiger Swan chose the alternative route based solely on the racial makeup of Standing Rock. In the video, Sheehan explained that he had been working on the unlawful abductions of native children by the Department of Family and Children Services (DFCS) from 2004 to 2016. He was renting office space in the Dakotas while working on that when the Keystone pipeline issue arose, and he was asked to help out with it as well.

Sheehan is a noteworthy civil rights lawyer who has worked on cases like the Iran Contra Affair, the Three Mile Island incident and the Karen Silkwood case where his team won a $10.5 million dollar lawsuit against the Kerr-McGee Chemical Co., thus ending all new nuclear power plant construction in the U.S for 30 years.

In the video, he explains that the pipeline was originally routed through the town of Bismarck, ND, which has a population that is 92% white. There were so many complaints by residents of Bismarck that the U.S. Army Core of Engineers deemed the route unsafe as a possible leak would fowl the community's water supply. As a result, the oil conglomerate revised the route to go 10 miles farther south, through the Great Sioux nation and directly *underneath* the lake which supplied the native population with water.

An order signed by President Clinton in 1997 declared that no longer could toxic waste dumps, recycling, rubber plants, or the like could be built in minority communities. Prior to that, over 90% of these plants would be purposely placed in minority locations. Due to the new ordinance, the Energy Transfer Partners fabricated a report to give to the EPA stating they had studied the area, and that no minority groups would be affected because the pipeline was a half mile north of the Standing Rock reservation.

The judges chose to ignore the fact that water runs downhill, and the Missouri river, along which the pipeline would be built, runs directly into the reservation. Furthermore, the Sioux Nation had a right to be concerned since the pipeline was only designed to detect leaks over 1%. With an anticipated flow of over 900,000 gals per hour, the pipeline could leak over 9,000 gallons of oil--per hour--and no one would be alerted.

There is no question the land belongs to the Sioux tribe and yet 843 people, mostly natives, have been arrested for trespassing while protesting peacefully. Of the 843 arrests, 700 were dismissed or acquitted. One judge noted that no one owns one of the sites were people were arrested because no one had the right to even claim trespass.

When the townspeople of Bismarck complained, the pipeline was promptly rerouted, and yet when the natives legitimately complained about the same thing, they were attacked and arrested. That is clearly an example of racial profiling. And it was used as part of a criminal conspiracy to deprive them of equal protection under the law. (Just to be clear, a conspiracy occurs when two or more people work together on an illegal project. In this case, it was a violation of Title 18, Sections 241 and 242 of Civil Title 42 of 1985.) In response to a legally filed charge, Energy Transfer Partners should have had to stop the construction of the pipeline.

Many of the police sided with the protesters and were seen dancing with them and engaging in other ways. Ath the very least, those lawmen had no major complaints about the protesting. The serious problems arose when Energy Transfer Partners hired Tiger Swan, a private paramilitary concern similar to the infamous Blackwater security company.

The founder of Tiger Swan headed the anti-terrorism unit of Blackwater during the war in Iraq. Not surprisingly, Tiger Swan characterized the native protesters as terrorists and viewed everything they did as acts of terrorism. They even labeled them as "potential terrorists" who opposed development of valuable infrastructure and who stood against private industry. Swan's propaganda about the natives to police, the news media, and the national guard, among others framed the Lakota people and their supporters as evil.

Tiger Swan even claimed that the Lakota are anti-Christian, much like the middle East Jihadists. As such, they were religiously motivated, and therefore the Lakota were terrorists, or potential terrorists. It didn't matter that the natives had permits to be there.

Tiger Swan also lied about the Lakota dumping sewage in the river. These tactics were developed by the CIA to turn neighboring people against those who protested, just as they did at Wounded Knee II in the late 1970s. They lied about the shootout to hide the illegal land deal and to get people to forget about all the laws they broke on Pine Ridge Reservation up until that point.

The native protesters have been sprayed with water cannons in sub-zero weather; they have been tear gassed; they have been assaulted with concussion grenades and hit with rubber bullets stored under snow to make them rock-hard. When the natives held up shields to protect themselves, Tiger Swan declared they were being used to "impede law enforcement." This gave them an excuse to charge the protesters and make arrests.

Chase Iron Eyes, a Lakota attorney, was arrested for asking people to come out and help in the protest. Tiger Swan fabricated the charges by claiming he was inciting people to riot and inviting them to engage to stop the pipeline. He is one they especially seem to hate. They even charged him with inciting an insurrection against the military.

Chase Iron Eyes was found not guilty in August of 2018.

More racial profiling became evident due to Tiger Swan's comparisons of the protesters to Jihadists. This tactic was used in a criminal conspiracy to deprive them of equal protection under the law. Taken together, Tiger Swan's statements amounted to criminal conspiracies. First, to reroute the pipeline for the whites who complained in Bismarck but not for natives who complained, and second, by claiming native protesters were anti-Christian and as such amounted to Jihadists.

In the end, Chase Iron Eyes and other protesters relied on a lesser known law called the "necessity affect."

As an example, the Necessity law says that even though jaywalking is illegal, if one can show they had to jaywalk in order to save a child walking in a busy intersection, the jaywalking charge can be dismissed by virtue of necessity. In the case of the pipeline protesters, if it could be shown that even though it may be illegal to protest (which we do not believe), the charge can be ignored since the act attempts to prevent a much worse scenario, like a massive oil spill contaminating the water supply. So, even if a jury believed the natives were trespassing (which they weren't since the U.S holds no title to that land) such minor trespassing or ceremonies held in open fields in the dead of winter, don't compare with the negative effects of a major oil spill.

The Indian Boarding Schools and Tribunals of 2014

There is another example of genocide in which the US government has blood on its hands, the Indian boarding schools and tribunals held on Oct. 22, 2014, in Oneida, Wisconsin.

Three Sioux boys on arrival at the Carlisle Boarding School. [New York Public Library Digital Collection]

Indian boarding schools were established with the goal of assimilating the native American children into the Euro-American culture, and to a smaller degree, provide them with a basic education in English subjects. However, it is the opinion of the author that obtaining an education was the least of their motives, based on all the unnecessary horrors and abuses which took place, none of which had anything to do with receiving a "proper" education.

These schools were established during the 19th and 20th centuries. The Government paid religious orders (primarily the Catholic church) to run them. Later, the Bureau of Indian Affairs operated some of the schools.

The first thing they did to children entering these schools was cut their hair and forbid them to speak their native language. No symbols of their cultural heritage were allowed, this included their given names. Instead, non-native names were assigned.

The same three Sioux boys after three years at the Carlisle Boarding School. [New York Public Library Digital Collection]

In testimony given at the Tribunals (see following section), many native children were ridiculed in these schools by the priests and nuns, much like the Jews were in Germany during WWII. Indian names were replaced by European names for the sake of "civilizing and converting them to Christianity." This harkens back to the time when Jewish or Yahoudi names and places in the bible were changed.

These schools were not intended to civilize and convert children to Christianity, but rather to destroy their culture out of fear and hatred. Both races, native American and Yahoudi, were well established, healthy, intelligent and successful in their own right before the white men came along.

Many of the abuses suffered in Indian boarding schools ended in death, a chilling reminder of what happened to so many innocent Jews in Nazi Germany. Later investigations revealed and documented sexual, manual, physical, and mental abuses which occurred primarily in the church-run schools.

On Oct. 22, 2014, Indian Boarding School Tribunals were held for three days in Green Bay, Wisconsin. They focused on the ill treatment of native American children who were taken away from their parents. The following excerpts are from the testimony of native Americans who either attended such schools or whose parents did. Most were derived from direct experiences which detail the devastating impact of the schools.

Dennis Banks, who is an Anishinaabe, urged native young people to take the lead in AIM (American Indian Movement. See also the last testimony of Leonard Peltier for more information about AIM). It was an organization intended to reclaim broken treaties with the US government and to overhaul the Bureau of Indian Affairs which was known to be taking land, among other things, and to help correct injustices and the racism shown toward native people.

Dennis Banks was in an Indian boarding school from age 5 to 16. As an adult, he described hearing screams in the night from the beatings and rapes of Indian children in his school. Banks also had a grandchild taken by social services later in life. According to Banks, Social Services will make decisions based on the non-Indian structure of families and does not take into account the extended family. Banks recalls never receiving any letters while he was at boarding school, and it wasn't until much later that he finally got them after papers from boarding schools were discovered. One of those letters contained a $5 bill and a note from his mother saying, "I want you to send my son home."

At the Tribunals, Banks went on to say that the memory of whippings have never left him, and yet he was called a terrorist later in life by the FBI. It makes one wonder the real terrorists are. I believe the true history answers that question quite well.

Jean Whitehorse Dine' (a Navajo) spoke on native rights and the sterilization of Indian woman. She said she went to the hospital in intense pain and was asked to sign papers which resulted in not only the removal of her appendix, but also her sterilization without her knowledge. This took place at the Gallop Indian hospital. During this time the US government published a pamphlet promising horses to native woman who did not have many children. Jean Whitehorse Dine' also spoke of heroes like the native woman who resisted relocation to Big Mountain.

Kim Oseira, 73, is an Alaskan native and survivor of the Holy Cross Mission Orphanage in Holy Cross, Alaska. Said she and others were punished often, so she learned how to lie since telling the truth would result in punishment. Around the age of 9 or 10 she recalled being punished and having to scrub brown floors until they were white. One day she wanted to finish one small area when a nun grabbed her by the wrist and threw her down. She claims the nuns starved her. According to church records, the Holy Cross Mission was called an orphanage. It was founded in 1880 near the villages of Athabascan and Yupik Eskimos. Oseira's earliest memories are of being alone at age 5 when she was also the primary caregiver to her sister, Della Mae, who was two year younger. She was responsible for feeding her, changing her diapers, and potty training.

Madonna Thunderhawk, a Lakota from Cheyenne River, South Dakota, recalled hearing about her mother's experiences. She describes how the abuse caused the freezing of emotions. If one child ran away, for instance, all the others were put in a room, their hair was cut, and they would be tied up and flogged. If they were caught speaking their own language they would have to kneel on beans on the floor for long periods of time. She thanked AIM for breaking the cycle of guilt and left-over emotions because of the abuse.

Thunderhawk went on to recall her own experiences with boarding school. She said her head had been dumped in Kerosene and then wrapped in towels. No one said a word. She remembered being told, "You don't cry. You don't show emotion." In her generation, abuse came from other children, bullies who grew up without parenting skills due to the boarding school abuse which resulted in inter-generational trauma and dysfunctional families.

Similar stories abound about the treatment of native people in Australia, some of which still goes on today! For example, review an article by John Pilger in the April 9, 2016 edition of *The Observer*. The title of the article is "Australia's Treatment of Aboriginal People is Its Dirty Secret."

Thunderhawk now devotes herself to halting abuses carried out by US Social Services, or should it be US Dysfunctional Services?

Yvonne Swan is from the Binixt people of the Arrow Lakes of Colville Confederation of Tribes from Washington State. Parents there were told that sending their children to boarding school would give them an education. Swan's grandfather told her he named the kids after their ancestors and said it was necessary so that when one died, the spirits would recognize them. Swan also recalls getting sick from the boarding school food. She would sneak off and climb into the hills and eat roots and sunflowers for healing. The boarding school rarely took them to a doctor. The school also censored letters from their families. Swan later learned she never got all the letters sent from her family. Once, while cleaning the kitchen, she saw the steaks and fresh fruit the staff got to eat. The children were fed a mush called "dynamite." When Swan's cousins wet their beds they would be shamed and forced to sit in a tub of ice water. The pattern was to ridicule them, beat them down, and make them lie to avoid being punished.

The priests had two straps. "Little Susie" was used on the girls for punishment, and "Black Might" was used on the boys.

The nuns hit the children's hands so hard they would bleed. Swan said many of the children later turned to alcohol and died of suicide or in car accidents.

Swan's niece hung herself in jail, and her three nephews shot themselves. She described how a priest would grab and hold her sister, and that the unwanted embrace ended only when someone walked in on them. Swan's hunger led her to ask another child for their orange peelings to eat, and a staff person who overheard her said, "Go get them, you pig."

Swan testified that her brother was kicked in the back causing him to run away. It took him ten days, during which time he walk in the snow and over a mountain. Another child was knocked down a flight of stairs for speaking her own language.

Roxanna Banguis Ed.D. (Tlingit, Haida, and Sechelt), said her mother was very sick for a long time and was never cared for by a doctor, so the other children would bring her food. Her mother was sexually molested by some other boys. Those boys learned they could get away with such sexual acts from the people who worked at the boarding schools including priests. She said the boys were repeating the sexual abuse they themselves suffered.

When the school was partially burned down, skeletons of babies were found in the walls. Here was government sanctioned employment for sexual predators and child abusers. It was never determined if the babies were natives or from the nuns. According to Banguis, the nuns were not celibate.

Next, Grand Chief Terrance Nelson of the Southern Chiefs Organization and chairman of AIM. He writes, "The reason my heart is in AIM is because they won't put up with the crap that has been done to our people." He also spoke of his trips to Iraq and Iran and the Indian kids killed there by the US. Chief Nelson spoke of the children killed by the United States in Iraq during his trips there and to Iran. He went on to say he understands the psychology of abuse used to control people which was what was used on Indian children in the boarding schools. Nelson said, "In order to control people, you must first dehumanize them, then you have to take their children."

He told the story of James, a 10 year old boy, who had been in a boarding school with Chief Nelson's mother. The first time James ran away, they shaved his head. The second time he ran, they made him stand weighted down with a ball and chain in the hall, where he would feel shame as the other kids passed by. Then, James ran away a third time.

The principal hit him with a strap up and down his arm, but James didn't cry. So the man strapped his other arm, too. It took a long time, but they finally got James to cry. Years later, when James had become an alcoholic, he was stabbed to death on the road.

Nelson said the reason offending kids were strapped was to control the other kids. He recalled his mother's words, "She learned to cry, and cry fast," so they would leave her alone. When you want control, you make sure there are consequences.

Milton Grasshopper spoke next. He came from Mackinac Island in northern Michigan. Milton remembered being sexually abused by a priest at the age of 5. He recalled his shame and the heartache he felt standing there with blood running down his leg. He carries a lot of pain to this day. The Catholic priest threatened to kill him and his family if he told anyone.

Milton said he found his way back to himself through

Indian culture and the Sundance. He claimed if he hadn't been a Sun Dancer he would not be alive today.

In testimony, Bill Means, the brother of Russel Means, recalled that their parents were at Flandreau Boarding School. He said they would tie sacks of marbles on their knees and make them scrub the basement floor with a scrub brush just for speaking their language. Means' father worked with the horses at the school and on one occasion, a horse was spooked by him and a friend. The prized animal hit a barbed wire fence and suffered cuts. The staff person who owned the animal beat Means' friend to death. The killer was never charged with a crime and simply moved to a different boarding school.

With the help of the boarding schools, many run by the Catholic church, the military could keep track of who was still speaking their native language or singing their native songs. According to an article entitled "Assimilation Through the Indian Boarding Schools" by Amanda McAllister and Taylor Krawczewski, native American children were strictly monitored and often punished for speaking their language or practicing their culture. Punishments included confinement, deprivation of privileges, and threat of corporal discipline. The article goes on to say that the widespread abuse dealt blows to the traditional social structure of native communities.

Before colonization, native woman enjoyed a high status, perhaps more than in any other culture. The McCallister/Krawczewski article also pointed out that violence against woman, children, and elders was virtually non-existent. Today, sexual abuses and violence have reached epidemic proportions among native communities along with alcoholism and suicides.

Researchers are just beginning to establish the quantitative links between these epidemics and the legacy of the Indian Boarding Schools. Victor Herald from the

Cheyenne River Tribe in South Dakota, was four years old when he was taken. He recalls dump trucks coming in the late 1940s. All the children in his family were taken, and their hair was cut.

According to Mary Wahpeton, a native American from North Dakota, the schools checked incoming children for "nits and bugs" and then used or kerosene to get rid of them. Though DDT had been phased out as a remedy elsewhere, it remained in use for several more years at the schools.

The horror stories continued. Victor, at age 4, wet his bed. The dorm attendant kept throwing him against a wall until some of his bones were broken. He broke several ribs and his nose but never received medical treatment. As a result, Victor would stay awake at night so he would not wet the bed. At age 70, he still has scars on his back.

Finally, Dorothy Ninham, a former Leonard Peltier Defense committee member whom I know and assist in non-profit work on Leonard Peltier's behalf, read Leonard Peltier's notes on his experience at Indian Boarding school. As mentioned earlier, Leonard is still being held as a political prisoner by our Government simply because he was connected with AIM and went to Pine Ridge to protect the Lakota people.

Leonard recalled being nine years old when he, his sister, and a cousin were taken from his family. He had been living with his grandmother at the time. Peltier had been taught to run when authorities came, but he was curious. When he heard the words "boarding school," he wanted to run into the woods, but he didn't want to leave his grandmother, sister, and cousin for fear his grandmother would be taken to jail.

Peltier froze even though his grandmother had told him, in Chippewa, to run and hide. He says he will never forget the day the black car drove up to take them to the BIA boarding school in Wahpeton, North Dakota. When they arrived, staff people cut off their long hair, stripped them, and doused them with DDT powder. Leonard says he thought he would die there, and it was more like a reformatory than a school. He considers his days at Wahpeton as his first imprisonment. And it was for the same crime as all the others: for being an Indian.

While at Wahpeton, Peltier was tasked with taking care of a younger boy. He remembers being punished for not scrubbing the boy hard enough with a stiff brush because the child began to cry. Later, his cousin Pauline was placed in an insane asylum. The school claimed she fell and hit her head.

Dorothy Ninham summed up the era quite well. The Indian boarding schools were set up to prepare Indian children either for the military or prison. It seems everything was geared to make the native people go from one institution to another. The boarding schools instituted identity theft, taking away culture, language, and a way of life. Ninham believes, as I do, that there should be a class action lawsuit against the US government and the churches involved because of the shameful things which happened in the Indian boarding schools.

In his book, **My Life is My Sundance**, Leonard Peltier states: "I know what I am; I am an Indian; an Indian who dared to stand up to defend his people. I am an innocent man who never killed anyone, nor wanted to. And yes, I am a SunDancer. That too, is my identity. If I am to suffer as a symbol of my people, then I will suffer proudly, I will never yield."

I urge readers of this book to read Peltier's work as well. May we all show Peltier's integrity and bravery in the face of tyranny and abuse. May we reside "In the Spirit of Crazy Horse."

Genocide Against Native Americans By Abducting Their Children

In a recent article by *Health Impact News*, a common scenario is spelled out in an article bearing the headline, "South Dakota Commits Shocking Genocide Against Native Americans by Abducting Their Children." (See also, the youtube.com video entitled "Daniel Sheehan: South Dakota Exposed.")

This is how it works for natives nowadays and sometimes for whites as well: The Department of Family and Children Services (DFCS) receives a report of child neglect on a reservation and without any legal authority removes the child without any notification to the child's relatives. In one such case, a boy was taken from a restroom while family members were attending a high school graduation ceremony. It was weeks before his family found out where he had been taken.

There is a financial motive driving this insanity. For each native child taken, the state of South Dakota receives $79,000 compared to $9,000 for a white child placed in a foster home. Indian children make up for 13.8% of South Dakota's population, but they represent 56.3% of the foster care population.

Department of Social Services (DSS) workers warn native children that if they become emotional during a visit with their parents, the visits will be discontinued. One Indian mother had 62 hearings and was never allowed to present any witness testimony, nor was she allowed to see the petition filed against her.

This is a huge violation of the long established U.S. Law of Due Process. Also, the Indian Child Welfare Act mandates that native children shall first be placed with tribal relatives, non-related tribal members, or members of other tribes before non-Indian families can be considered.

There's more, according to Daniel Sheehan, attorney at law, from his video, "South Dakota Exposed" taken from the front page of the same *Health Impact News*. Sheehan toured the countryside interviewing native mothers and grandmothers about the abductions. They had no access to any upper echelon government groups or agencies to find out why it was happening, they just knew that it was. Sheehan met with then-chairman Ted Klaudt of the state legislative committee which oversaw the Department of Social Services. He served from 1999 to 2006.

When Sheehan asked about the high numbers of native children being taken into foster care, Klaudt responded, "Oh, it's a lot more than that" and claimed it was "an epidemic" though he didn't know why. When Sheehan asked if he would get an ombudsman to investigate the matter, Klaudt responded, "Oh no. That's a lot of money coming into the state each year and might have legal consequences." He went on to tell Sheehan he would have to get an investigations cleared with the state Attorney General.

Klaudt then called the Attorney General and told him a lawyer in his office was asking about "all those Indian kids." The Attorney General appeared within fifteen minutes and said they could not look into the matter because there was too much money coming into the state for each of the foster kids, and Sheehan would have to sue them to find out any details.

With the help of Native Americans Joe Cross and Madonna Thunderhawk, Sheehan managed to have an investigation started. Madonna Thunderhawk was also involved in the Indian Boarding School Tribunals.

The investigation revealed that the process began after George W. Bush became Governor of Texas in 2000. His administration instituted a requirement that any child entering the Texas foster care system had to first pass a mental health screening test. Since 98% of native children failed this test, they could be labeled as "special needs." The state received $79,000 per child per year provided the child remained in foster care, something strictly against DFCS and DSS rules and standards. Not only was the practice illegal, but more importantly, it was hugely immoral.

The children were "treated" with various drugs ranging from Ritalin to Prozac to much stronger ones like Reserpine and Adderall. Some children were given up to five drugs at the same time, and often to kids less than a year old. One boy recalls taking his medications in foster care, and that it was like "lights out after 15 minutes." He complained about this years later saying it was a terrible thing to give medications to foster kids, and that he was not "mentally off" but upset because he was in foster care. I contend most people would find this reaction quite reasonable.

In an article by Fox 40 entitled "Foster Children Given Powerful Psychiatric Drugs Without Proper Safeguards" and another by National Public Radio entitled "Foster Kids Given Psychiatric Drugs at High rates," the people doing the testing complained that after given the cocktail of drugs, the children "still acted like Indians."

When Bush went to Washington, DC, after being elected president, he formed a handpicked committee and asked them to see if he needed to establish as a condition, that before any federal funds went to any state under the Adoptions and Safe Families Act, those states first had to implement the Texas Mental Health Algorithm test. Not surprisingly, the committee recommended just that.

Bush's good friend, Bill Janklow, who was Assistant Attorney General for South Dakota and was the one who called in the Nixon administration for assistance in the Wounded Knee operation, got invited to the Bush inauguration in 2001. While there, Bush asked Janklow if he realized what he was sitting on. According to Sheehan, Bush went on to inform Janklow he was sitting on a bonanza, and that for every Lakota child he could receive $79,000. He then went on to say he could give part of that money to the pharmaceutical industry who in turn would contribute to the Republican party.

According to Sheehan 742 native children were taken annually from their families and their culture, and were placed in white foster care homes. A disturbing law was proposed which would authorize the state to perform protocols on native children to determine what affects various drugs had on them. This bit of sponsored legislation seems to have come directly from Nazi Germany where the same sort of experiments were performed on innocent Jews. The bill ignored an FDA warning and an existing law which made it illegal to administer these types of drugs to any child under the age of 18.

At the time, the head of the Child Protection Division of South Dakota, Regina Weasler, allowed such drugs to be given to underage children. As a result, many drooled on their clothing, cut themselves and/or became suicidal, classic symptoms as defined by the FDA for why these dangerous drugs should not be given to children.

It is interesting to note that Ted Klaudt, who was questioned by attorney Daniel Sheehan, was convicted in May, 2007, for raping two foster children aged 17 and 19. Bill Janklow was also accused of raping one of his own native American foster girls but was never charged. Makes one wonder who puts such people in charge.

According to Sheehan, "This group of criminals are fundamentally racist and derive their whole sense of being and value by opposing some other [race]. ... They take great pride in their intellect, and they've alienated themselves from any type of organic relationship with the universe, with the Earth, and with the natural processes of the planet.

They view the aboriginal people as being an absolute, fundamental threat to them, and that is why they want to extinguish those people." These quotes are from Daniel Sheehan's youtube.com video, "South Dakota Exposed."

In Georgia, the foster care system known as Department of Family and Children Services (DFCS) is an entity which former Georgia State Senator Nancy Schaefer, described as "needing to be shut down." It is my belief her words and ideas resulted ended in her death. Both Schaefer and her husband were gunned down in their home. Officials called it a double suicide carried out by Nancy's husband.

I find the GBI's investigation to lack competence and credibility. They contend that Schaefer's husband shot her and himself with a foreign, unregistered gun, even though he had access to his own firearm right in the house. Those who knew from church said he would never have done such a thing.

Investigators concluded that no one could have gotten past the locked, front entrance security gate even though a concerned citizen posted a youtube.com video of him easily reaching the Schaefer home from the back entrance to the property. He provided video of himself simply walking around the small gate which led to the Schaefer's backyard. (youtube.com video by William Wagener, "Murder of State Senator Nancy Schaefer, #1."

Is it possible that Nancy Schaefer's documentary about widespread corruption within the Department of Family and Children Services which was to be released in a week might have spurred someone to kill her? She had also written a book revealing many of the cases she had looked into where she found no justification for taking children from their families. Could that have triggered an attack? Or was it because she believed the corruption was all about money? Her book would identify all the people involved and explain how they placed children in the hands and homes of known pedophiles. To this day, her book has not been released.

What we have instead are a number of videos in which she offered to give up her senate seat in order to have more time to work on the issues of malfeasance and nonfeasance within the DFCS.

In his book, *Medical Kidnapping, A Threat to Every Family in America*, writer Brian Shilhavy discusses what is going on under the table or which just skirts the law. According to him, in recent years countless children have been kidnapped by DFCS. They have used a wide array of "reasons" but more recently have utilized doctors.

Medical kidnapping is defined as the state taking children from their parents and putting them in state custody or the foster care system, simply because the parents did not agree with a doctor regarding their prescribed medical treatment. In some cases it as simple as telling a doctor you are going to seek a second opinion on a suggested medical procedure.

My own theory is that it is used intentionally to take a child away and is sometimes done with the cooperation of some doctors.

Shilhavy says medical kidnapping is part of a larger problem of state-sponsored child kidnappings. The state decides they know what is best for a child or a group of children in a family, and then removes them without any formal charges being brought against the parents. The parents lose their children immediately, often without a warrant being issued by a judge. They are not afforded the rights of a trial by a jury of peers. They are then subjected to so-called Family Courts where different rules are in place. The worst of these is that the accused is assumed guilty until proven innocent.

They take the children based on a presumption of

guilt leaving the parents with no options to regain custody without incurring huge legal bills. The agency is cloaked in secrecy and secret laws demand no accountability from them. Even if parent do get their children back, the kids are traumatized.

Hundreds of these cases are covered in Shilhavy's book. I know of personal accounts myself, like my husband's friend from work who had his kids taken away and put into the foster home of a known child sex offender. After he got a lawyer, DFCS worked out a deal, and he was able to get his kids back, but that was because he had an aggressive lawyer. A lawyer I know claims that all too often, the attorneys involved in these cases are tied into the system and only take money from less well-off parents who are too scared to speak out against the system.

I have intimate knowledge of just such injustice. An acquaintance of mine whose kids were taken was asked to take a psychological evaluation. I urged her to bring a recorder to capture the entire ordeal, which she did. In court, the social workers lied under oath and said she never showed up for the evaluation. When she tried to give her lawyer the recording, he said, "I cannot play that tape. I will get into trouble." This lawyer withheld evidence which could have helped this mother and her kids because he was afraid of the system. She should have turned him over to the state bar.

The rules are so slanted in favor of the state that at trial they often use no court reporter. The judge simply takes the word of the social worker over the parent without having to show any proof. I have seen this first-hand myself.

In another case from Shilhavy's book, a couple with a premature baby fed the child formula suggested by an Alabama doctor. The baby was doing well but when the family moved to Massachusetts, a Women Infant Children (WIC) pediatrician insisted they use a different formula. The baby didn't do well, and her weight declined. The parents went back to Alabama immediately, to be with the pediatrician who had specified the right formula.

Massachusetts DCF followed their case to Alabama, contacting Alabama DHR. Alabama DHR investigated the family and cleared them after seeing how well the baby was doing. But this was not good enough for Massachusetts DCF which allegedly threatened the family with criminal charges if they did not return to Massachusetts. Even though Massachusetts had no jurisdiction due to the case originating in Alabama, the parents were cowed into moving back to the northeast where the child was put in Boston Hospital and the parents lost custody. This, to me, smells of collusion between the state and some doctors and hospitals.

Shilhavy goes on to say that recently people have come forward with adult medical kidnapping issues. These include the kidnapping of seniors and the seizure of their assets to cover medical expenses. This goes along with the recent Federal "kickback" laws involving hospice care and nursing home room and board fees. It's a "scratch my back" relationship to gain financially by claiming Medicare and Medicaid payments.

I also am familiar with a case where a young adult cancer patient at a major hospital was kidnapped by a Hospice, namely Hearth Hospice located in Fort Oglethorpe, GA and Parkside Nursing home located in Rossville, GA. She was taken even though the parents and the patient told a physician, Doctor DePasquale, as well as the Hearth Hospice liaison, Lorinda Thompson, that they were not interested in going to their "death camp" facility. When the patient was heavily drugged and the parents were away, they slipped her out anyway. Once they had the patient at Parkside in Rossville, where Hearth Hospice rents rooms through a cozy relationship the staff, especially administrator Susie Kellett and Head of Nursing Angela, they refused to let her go even when the mother got Power of Attorney. They also refused to transfer her closer to the family, since Hearth and Parkside were located a hundred miles away. The administrator told the mother her daughter had to stay 30 days or die, or else somebody would get stuck with the bill, and Parkside wouldn't get paid. A nurse, Bobbie Gilreath, lied to the mother about the existence of an earlier Power of Attorney naming the patient's parents, which was drafted by a social worker and supposedly left at the front desk for the parents to sign.

This hospice and nursing home also drafted another Power of Attorney and gave it to the pro-hospice grandmother behind the parents' backs and against the patient's wishes. This was revealed in a Freedom of Information Act document. The nurse had asked the patient who she wanted to grant her Power of Attorney, and she named her parents. The nurse drafted it that way and left it at the front desk to be signed by them on their next visit. However, the nursing home and hospice hid or destroyed it. When the patient's parents asked about signing the document, the nursing home claimed to know nothing about it. Further, they told the parents they would need a lawyer to draw up the document, which is not a requirement in the state of Georgia. In fact, the hospice didn't hire an attorney for their fraudulent document which granted those rights to the grandmother.

This patent received little care other than drugs for pain. Her requests for water were largely ignored leaving her mother to help her when she could. But the insensitivity didn't end there. The parents needed four months to claim her body for burial since the grandmother had filled out forms specifying cremation. It was also discovered by the family that certain narcotic drug dosages were left blank on the medical records. I theorize that some of these hospice facilities and nursing homes may be involved with Medicaid and Medicare fraud along with possible fraudulent organ donation.

The family had a state investigator look into this particular hospice who was able to substantiate the allegations, so at least that will go on their record. Hopefully people will think twice before putting their loved ones in Hearth Hospice or Parkside Nursing home and be leery of doctors at major hospitals who push hospice and deny natural treatments like a $30 vitamin C drip like the one this family requested, instead of the death camp.

We will never know who, or what group of people, will be the next target for organized oppression. It has been the case throughout history from the Jews to the native Americans, and now, according to Nancy Schaeffer and others, to our children, the elderly, and the sick. It reminds me of a quote from *The Complete Jewish Bible* (Mattityahu 18:5-6) "So the greatest in the Kingdom is whoever makes himself as humble as this child. Whoever welcomes one such child in my name welcomes me; and whoever ensnares one of these little ones who trust me, it would be better for him to have a millstone tied around his neck and be drowned in the open sea!"

What Most People Don't Know About Homeland Security

By Laura Dobbs Pemberton

In a recent article published by *The World Traveler* entitled "Nazification of Germany versus Nazification of America" author Norman D. Livergood compares the U.S. government's response to the 9/11/2001 attacks and the process of German Nazification.

Phase 1: Nazification of Germany

A) Seizure of power

B) Hitler appointed Chancellor even though the Nazi party represented only a small minority in German government.

C) On his first day as chancellor, Hitler dissolved the Reichstag and instituted the complete takeover of all governance and functions of the State thus making Germany a totalitarian dictatorship.

Phase 1: American Nazification
A) George Bush appointed president by the U.S. Supreme Court after massive election fraud perpetrated in Florida in which thousands of voters were disqualified when Jeb Bush and his Secretary of State compiled a false list of felons who were then unable to vote.

B) Bush appoints convicted criminals, racists, and corporate-controlled underlings to his cabinet.

C) Bush pushes tax cuts to the wealthy and begins his assault on the environment and commands the FBI to stop investigations concerning the bin Laden family along with other terrorists cells.

Phase 2: German Nazification -- Subdue the German People
A) Hitler was dining at Herman Goebbels' apartment when the Reichstag caught fire and burned down. Hitler claimed "...the fire was a beacon from heaven and the beginning of a great epoch in German history." Author Klaus P. Fischer believes the Nazis set the fire.

B) Exactly one day after the fire in 1933, Chancellor Hitler invoked Article 48 of the Weimar Constitution, which permitted the suspension of civil liberties in time of national emergency. If this sounds familiar check current U.S. Law.

C) A decree by Hitler for the "Protection of the People and State" abrogated the following protections or simply eliminated them:
1- Free expression and opinion
2- Freedom of the press
3- Right of assembly and association
4- Right of privacy of postal and electronic communications
5- Protection against unlawful search & seizures
6- Individual property rights
7- State's right of self-governance.

D) Hitler's supplemental Decree created
1- SA (Storm Troops)
2- SS (Specialty Security) Federal Police agencies

The Reichstag fire destroyed a democracy by creating a law and order crisis and offering a solution, the abdication of civil liberties and state's rights to an unaccountable central dictator. The men of wealth who put this tyrant in power were then able to reap the obscene profits of war.

Phase 2: American Nazification -- Subdue the American People

A) It is postulated that the September 11, 2001 World Trade Center attacks were an inside job, planned and executed from within the federal government. Evidence of this has been found in numerous areas, one being large amounts of a substance called thermite found within the debris. To further prove this, numerous spheres of molten iron were identified using an electron microscope. Also, samples tested in a calorimeter produced graphs of huge, high, narrow peaks indicative of being highly ignitable. Whereas, normal fires just burn over time and do not ignite. This is not to mention the other obvious signs from the photos and video of the buildings going down demolition-style. Many engineers have come forward with evidence supporting this theory.

Many Americans are unaware that a third structure, Building 7 of the World Trade Center, also came down demolition-style. The building was not hit by a plane.

One day prior to the attacks, it was announced that 2.3 trillion dollars had gone missing from the pentagon. The next day the offices responsible for tracking that money down were also destroyed. Moreover, the only off-site backup for the missing money for black budgets was located in building 7 of the World Trade Center. Building 7 also housed information about Federal investigations involved in large scale stock market and accounting fraud. Building 7 was the first to be cleaned up and evidence destroyed.

Debunkers point to a recent article in *Popular Mechanics* which claims it is ridiculous to think that nanothermite could be used to demolish a steel structure. It's interesting to note that an article from the November, 1935 edition of the same magazine talked about nanothermite doing just that, with the Sky Ride Tower being demolished in exactly the same way. For detials, see the YouTube video "Never Forget Thermite-The Real Proof."

B) No military aircraft were scrambled to intercept the four commercial airliners, even though there was plenty of time to do so. (V.P. Cheney gave a stand down order.)

C) No genuine investigation into the Sept. 11 attacks suggests a gigantic cover-up.

D) Hundreds of suspects were immediately jailed without Habeas Corpus or other rights.

E) Exactly one day after the Sept. 11 attacks, Bush forced Congress to pass the Patriot Act without giving them time to even read the bill. (This same Patriot Act had been proposed on several occasions but it was never approved.)

The patriot Act suspended civil liberties and abrogated the following constitutional protections:
       1- Free expression of opinion
       2- Freedom of the press
       3- Right to assembly and association
       4- Right to postal and electronic communications
       5- Protections against unlawful search and seizure
       6- Individual property rights
       7- State's right of self-governance

F) Presidential decrees made it possible for military forces to be used to monitor and control civilian populations in abrogation of the Posse Comitatus Act.

Phase 3: German Elections Ended, Dictatorship Begins

A) The Enabling Act of 1933 granted Hitler dictatorial power. Elections were no longer needed because the Fuhrer made all the decisions. Prior to March 5, 1933, the Nazis held only a 44% plurality in the Reichstag elections. Herman Goring became head of the German armed forces and declared no further need for state governments. He replaced the leadership of all German states with Nazi Reich commissioners. The Enabling Act gave Hitler power for four years. To ensure the law would pass, the Nazis imprisoned communists and created propaganda campaigns to influence public opinion. Just days before the vote, they staged a ceremony where Hitler was depicted as a conservative national leader and not the head of a radical party. The moment the bill passed, the German democratic constitution was abrogated, and Nazi rule became absolute power.

B) The Hitler regime established the first concentration camps. Organized by Himmler, they held 5,000 prisoners, mostly communists, social democrats, and homosexuals. The Bavarian police guarded them until the SS took over. The slave labor camps were so hideous, the

German people didn't want to hear about them, and became an efficient tool in silencing opponents of the Hitler regime. Dachau was a political camp and held the first Jewish detainees. Not surprisingly, the Jews were among the most vocal political opponents of the Nazis. Over 10,000 Jews from all over Germany were interned there the Kristallnacht pogrom. When the genocide of the Jews began, Jewish prisoners were deported from Dachau and other prisons to the extermination camps.

Phase 3: America's Homeland Security Act Becomes Law

A) Beginning in 2000, the electronic voting process has taken away our right to have our votes counted. In Florida during this time, 94,000 people, over half of them black Americans, had their names added to a scrub list which blocked from voting in the 2000 election. Florida never rectified the situation, even for the 2002 election. Electronic touch screen voting is the basis for election fraud. Votes can easily be lost through software glitches. Democrat votes can become republican votes. Touch screens are made by ES&S vendor chosen by people who are pro Bush. ES&S machines failed to work in black precincts in 2002. With electronic voting, there is no paper ballot back up.

B) The Homeland Security bill was pushed through one day after the Sept. 11 attacks which gave Bush dictatorial powers. Presidents may now make decisions without judicial or legislative restraints. The executive branch can now carry on its meetings in secret without scrutiny from the press. Homeland security agents can now intrude in any part of the citizens' lives, an element slipped into the bill at the last moment. The Homeland Security law allows police to conduct internet and phone eavesdropping without asking for a court's permission. It also requires internet service providers to share subscriber records with law enforcement, thus overturning previous legislation which outlawed the practice. The Homeland Security Awareness office will be run by a former convicted felon. 850,000 jobs were privatized knocking out union or civil service oversight. In 2002, Senator Byrd spoke out vehemently against the bill calling it "...Bush's grab for dictatorial power and the worst tyranny he had seen during his 50-year tenure in congress."

C) In a revealing admission in 1997, the Director of Resource Management for the U.S. Army confirmed the validity of a memorandum relating to establishment of civilian labor camps. Congressman Henry Gonzales said we have stand-by provisions in the name of terrorism prevention under which the military can arrest Americans and put them in detention camps.

D) In his quest for war in Iraq, Bush sent 250,000 troops to the Middle East; 265,000 National Guard personal would be called to active duty. Most of the national guard would be deployed in the United States. One wonders if Bush was at war with Iraq or America?

The Homeland Security Debacle

Brenden Gallagher penned an article entitled "The Case for Abolishing The Department Of Homeland Security" in the internet newspaper, *The Daily Dot*. In it, he describes a dreadful example of waste, the so-called Fusion Centers. These are regional hubs used to support info sharing and facilitate cooperation. But in a 2012 Senate Homeland Security Committee report, it was revealed that the Fusion Centers often produce irrelevant, useless, or inappropriate intelligence to the DHS. Moreover, many produced no intelligence reporting whatsoever. In short, Fusion Centers expand the vast surveillance network in America but provide no tangible benefits.

Perhaps the reason the government keeps details of its budget classified is because the waste is so huge. It spends $50 billion a year, and while most of the budget technically belongs to agencies like the CIA, FBI, and NSA, the intelligence wouldn't shrink even if DHS were abolished.

Making matters worse, DHS budget failures account for some of the worst treatment of minority communities. Simply consider the failures connected to hurricane Katrina when FEMA merged with the DHS and both overlooked the disaster's impact on communities of color.

Recent evils of ICE are too numerous to provide, but with its abuse of data, separation of families, and massive arrests there's enough evil done at ICE to justify the end of the DHS.

Surveillance is a huge element of the DHS, and without that agency we could still rely on the CIA, FBI, NSA, etc. Ending the DHS would at least eliminate one of the numerous agencies which spy on American citizens. Almost every mandate of the DHS has a surveillance component, and the American Civil Liberties Union has accused various components of DHS with civil rights violations, from laptop searches to behavior profiling.

The DHS does not have a history of success. In its first five years of existence, the organization had $15 billion in canceled contracts. It's reward? Our tax dollars are now being spent on a brand new building for DHS in Washington, DC. Apparently they were having too hard a time conducting meetings, and the answer, apparently, is a 4.5 million square foot building, the largest construction project in GSA history. Maybe now they'll be able to coordinate get-togethers with a few of their 14,000 employees.

Other than building massive structures to accommodate an ever-increasing army of bureaucrats, one might ask, just what is Homeland Security up to now? They seem to be becoming the jack of all trades with monopolies on immigration, FEMA, and when they aren't too busy spying on all of us, they now control our weather along with other pastimes like buying up bullets by the millions. Simply outstanding work! They ought to be on the cover of *Time* magazine's corporate conglomerate business of the year!

According to Harold Saive in a *Veterans Today* article entitled "NEMO Blizzard a Product of Homeland Security Aerosol Geoengineering Program HAMP," while there are many questionable weather control strategies, the most disturbing is the deployment of black carbon aerosols to intensify hurricanes. So the word is out that they are using geoengineering to produce a weapon and not as a mitigation.

In 2008, DHS received $64 million to test the effect of aerosol Geoengineering on hurricanes. In October, 2012, *Infowars* writer Mellissa Melton pointed to hurricane Katrina as the basis for Project HAAMP (Hurricane Aerosol And Micro-physics Program). In it, Project Storm Fury veteran Joe Golden and a panel of other experts tested the effects of aerosols on instruments and intensity of hurricanes. Harold Saive concluded that the evidence is too strong that "Frankenstorm Sandy" and "NEMO the Blizzard" were created by DHS as deliberate weapons of mass destruction and climate terrorism. He said, "It all comes down to one motive: to persuade voters as the globalist carbon tax and climate change agenda come up for a vote."

In addition, Jason Box, a glaciologist, has identified black carbon soot emitted from natural wildfires as a major cause of polar ice melts. In his paper, "Bounding the Role of Black carbon in Climate System," Box concludes that soot can melt Greenland's ice caps faster than methane. Pair that with all the carbon soot dumps into fabricated hurricanes and storms, along with the contention of "Truth by Grace" (a YouTube.com video) that wildfires in California were started by laser technology possibly combined with smart meters and the like. One can only conclude from this that if there were such a global warming trend, the government would likely be the #1 suspect.

Even NOAA (National Oceanic and Atmospheric Administration) has concerns about DHS meddling with the weather. In "Engineering Frankenstorms: Obama Ordered Homeland Security to Control Hurricanes," an article published by aircrap.org, they point out that in 2009, Richard Spinrad, NOAA's Assistant Administrator for OAR (Oceanic and Atmospheric Research), sent a memo to the last DHS program manager for advanced research, William Laska, regarding OAR's review of a "Statement for Work" for HAAMP. Spinrad wrote, "While OAR recognizes that weather modification in general is occurring through the funding of private enterprises, NOAA does NOT support research that entails efforts to modify hurricanes." Spinrad went on to say, "Any collaboration with DHS must occur within NOAA's mission, which NOAA felt HAAMP did not do."

NOAA houses the national hurricane center, the primary organization responsible for tracking and predicting hurricanes. Budget cuts are expected to slash NOAA's satellite program and weather forecasting systems by $182 million. It certainly looks like there's a price to be paid by anyone who says "No" to DHS. Subsequently, though the DHS plan was disapproved by NOAA, DHS simply moved ahead with their research without NOAA's participation.

At a recent DHS symposium they discussed the topic: "DHS HAAMP Overview of Proposed Hypothesis

Testing" which entailed the following:
* Seeding with small aerosols suppressing rain.
* Seeding with radiation absorbing aerosols at storm periphery.
* Seeding with radiation absorbing aerosols at storm top.
* Pumping cool water to ocean surface in front of hurricane.

They concluded that carbon black could increase hurricane intensity. The idea goes back to Gunn and Phillips' 1957 *Journal of Atmospheric Sciences 14,* (pages 272-280) where they looked at air pollution on initiation of rain clouds. Aerosols can increase floods or decrease rain. In the video from article above from aircrap.org titled DHS Hurricane Aerosol Micro-physics (HAAMP - Weather Modification Association Conference 2010) he starts to say aerosols can affect the way both weakening uh uh of hurricanes. but stopped himself from saying the word strengthening. This comes from the same agency who holds symposiums on hurricane steering.

Aaron and Mellissa Melton, in a video called "The Real Reason Weather is Manipulated," describe how Kurt Vonnegut's book, **Cat's Cradle**, was taken from real life accounts by his brother who worked at General Electric with Irving Langmuir. They both worked on project CIRRIS where they sprayed silver iodide into a hurricane. Kurt had worked at GE, too, but quit after writing a critical article about the company. He describes Langmuir, portrayed as Hoenikker in the book, as being "an eccentric man."

Project CIRRIS involved personnel from GE, the Office of Naval Research, the U.S. Air Force, the U.S. Weather Bureau, the U.S. Army, and the Signal Corps. They were all involved in dumping silver iodide into a hurricane in 1947. At the time it was a couple of days away from shore in the Atlantic, but the experiment caused it to change both its direction and speed. It smashed into Savannah, Georgia causing extensive damage.

The public was furious, and as a result the Department of Defense (DOD) put a 13-year-long moratorium on weather modification efforts. In 1955, while the moratorium was still in effect, Langmuir continued doing research. His goal was to make it possible to use weather as a weapon. Under Operation Popeye, in Vietnam, he was responsible for technology that involved 2,600 cloud seeding sorties and expended 47,000 silver iodide flares over a 5-year period at an annual cost of $3.6 million. When congress finally found out about the secret program in 1973, the U.S. Senate formed a resolution prohibiting the use of environmental or physical anomalies as weapons of war.

In the last YouTube video from the aircrap.org article entitled "Hurricane Florence Engineered," a weather map is displayed and the speaker points out gray clouds with soot aerosol dumps sprayed ahead of the storm, ripple aligning in different directions due to magnetic waves hitting metals inserted into clouds seeded with metals. It looked like a magnet next to a pile of iron shavings. Outflow of chemtrails and dark gray clouds with aerosol dumps of coal ash. NASA's daily budget is $52 million. What a waste of tax dollars!

The secret world of Government was created after 9/11 and has become so large, so unwieldy, and so secretive that no one knows how much it costs. Nor does anyone know how many people it employs, how many programs exist, or how many agencies overlap and do the same jobs.

These findings are from a two year investigation by the *Washington Post*. This amounts to a top secret America hidden from public view and lacking any oversight. After five years of unprecedented spending and growth, the result is that the system is so massive, its effectiveness is impossible to determine.

Other Findings

* Some 1,271 government and 1,931 private companies work on programs related to counter-terrorism, homeland security, and intelligence in about 10,000 locations across the U.S.

* 854,000 people hold secret clearances

* Navy security and intelligence agencies do the same overlapping work creating redundancy and waste. 51 Federal and municipal agencies track the flow of money to and from terrorist networks.

* Analysts who make sense of documents and conversations obtained by foreign and domestic spying share their judgement by publishing 50,000 intelligence reports each year. With a volume so large, many go ignored. In the DOD, where more than two thirds of the intelligence programs reside, only a handful are "Superusers." Superusers have the ability to know about all the departments and their activities. But as two Superusers put it, there's no way they can possibly keep up with all of it. One said he would not live long enough to be briefed on everything; another recounted that for his initial briefing, he was escorted into a tiny dark room seated at a small table and told he could not take notes.

Next, program after program began flashing on the screen until he yelled out to stop in frustration! He couldn't remember any of it.

Then Director of the CIA, Leon Panetta said he had begun to map out a five year plan for his agency because the levels of spending since the 9/11 attacks were not sustainable. In all, at least 263 agencies have been created or reorganized after 9/11, each needing their own secretaries, administrators, logistic reporters, phone operators, librarians, architects, carpenters, air conditioning mechanics, construction workers, and even janitors who hold top secret clearances. Each day, a collection of NSA systems intercept and store 1.7 billion emails, phone calls, and other communications. The NSA sorts a fraction of those into separate databases. Other agencies have similar, if smaller, systems. It seems there is no end to the number of people reading our email and eavesdropping on our conversations.

Many of these top secret operations are housed in office parks or are intermingled with neighborhoods, schools, and shopping centers and thereby go unnoticed.

A SCIF has become the Crème of the crop in status when it comes to secrecy. SCIF stands for "Sensitive Compartmented Information Facility." In Washington, DC, everyone talks SCIF, and you can't be a big boy unless you have a three-letter agency and a big SCIF. The new bling of the national security world, SCIFs are equipped with command centers, internal TV networks, video walls, armored SUV's, and personal security guards.

Some of the most important but less well paid users of SCIFs are analysts in their 20s and 30s making $41,000-$65,000 a year. They are the core of what top secret

America tries to do. They command computers which sort and categorize data. However, human judgement is often needed in these data searches. The agents are trained straight out of Corporation headquarters. They know little about priority countries like Iran, Iraq, Afghanistan, and Pakistan and are not fluent in their languages. Yet they still generate an overwhelming number of intelligence reports on these countries.

For instance, 60 classified analytic websites are still in operation that were supposed to have been closed down for lack of usefulness. The problem with their intelligence reports is they "re-slice" the same facts already in circulation. Even the analysts at the National Counter-Terrorism Department, whose positions are the most difficult to obtain, get low marks from intelligence officials for not producing original reports. At the very least they should be better than the reports already written by CIA, FBI, NSA, or DIA, but they are not.

To conclude, there is no question that America is reading the Nazi playbook--same book, different day. The only difference is that Hitler was open about his plans unlike Homeland Security which operates in secrecy, often denying their own existence. It is disturbing that not only is Homeland Security acquiring monopolies on agencies like Immigration, whose power lies within the court system and were much more competent and knowledgeable than the eavesdropping secret agency which has taken over, there are overlaps, too. FEMA, FBI, and the NSA overlap, and when they are not too busy spying on all of us, they are now trying to control our weather and hide behind words like "terrorist" and "never forget" and "necessary to be safe" as if the constitution was drafted to be open for negotiation and business pay-offs and trade-offs. In their world of money and greed

I guess it is.

The problem lies with this: when you start consolidating a bunch of agencies into one like Homeland Security, just as Hitler did, and he even called it "the Homeland," you've got a clear example of the abuse of power. It is made only more egregious because there is no oversight. They're not going to call themselves out for wrongdoing.

The worst spy grid is on the way in the near future which also doubles as a kill grid. It's the 5G rollout. People will be tracked in real time through the "Internet of Things" where everything is connected to everything, down to cell phones communicating with floor tiles, and even milk jugs. The current 4G is already responsible for bad health effects on the public. Brain cancer is now the #1 disease now among people aged 15-19. And for ages 19-29, it's brain, thyroid, and testicular cancers, all from electromagnetic wave energy dispersed from WiFi and cell towers.

5G will radiate every 3rd house or so due to interference with antennas being mounted if companies are allowed to go through with this plan. It should be called 5G's Spy and Death plan. Who's protecting us from this dangerous microwave energy? No one, since it is all being covered up by the FCC which is currently in charge and which has a conflict of interest since they are tied in with the telecommunications industry which is making massive profits from cell phones and WiFi. The laws seem set up to protect them and not us.

The FCC has not one scientist on their payroll, and Congress took oversight away from the EPA which was looking into the non-thermal dangers. This is the reality even though thousands of published scientific studies show the dangers of electromagnetic frequencies.

The most alarming and less talked about danger is that at 5Gs, 60GHz is the same frequency as the Oxygen molecule's absorption, thus affecting Oxygen's bonding to the hemoglobin molecule and pineal gland in the body. This will affect the oxygen we breath and our health. 5G will also alter the iron and magnetic function of hemoglobin and the pineal gland. This magnetic field disruption is already happening with the current 3 and 4G which was an earlier theory of mine. However, 5G will greatly amplify this negative affect.

I urge everyone to spend a little time and visit the website www.5GRemedies.com; watch the video "Real Dangers of 5G Wireless Radiation." Find out not only what the dangers are, but more importantly, what we can do about it. Note: Senate Bill S19 mentioned in video is now called S1968 ("The Spectrum Now Act"). The House version is HR3475. These and other bills concerning 5G will soon be up for votes.

To conclude, I would say that Homeland Security has been effective at normalizing racial profiling and demoralizing human beings. An agency created on the back of one of America's greatest tragedies--the attacks of 9/11--has been used to justify the oppression of the country's most vulnerable communities. I say shame on them.

Part – 3 Shabbat

Question: Which day of the week is a kodesh day of Elohim?
Answer: The seventh day which Elohim named Shabbat.

Proof #1:

[B'resheet 2:1-3] "Thus the heavens and the earth were finished along with everything in them. On the seventh day Elohim was finished with his work which he had made, so he rested on the seventh day from all his work which he had made. Elohim blessed the seventh day and separated it as kodesh; because on that day Elohim rested from all his work which he had created, so that it itself could produce."

Proof #2:

[Sh'mot 20:8-11] "Remember the day, Shabbat, to set it apart for Elohim. You have six days to labor and do all your work, but the seventh day is a Shabbat for Y'HoVaH Elohekha. On it, you are not to do any kind of work—not you, your son or your daughter, not your male or female slave, not your livestock, and not the foreigner staying with you inside the gates to your property. For in six days, Y'HoVaH made heaven and earth, the sea and everything in them; but on the seventh day he rested. This is why Y'HoVaH blessed the day, Shabbat, and separated it for himself."

Proof #3:

[Sh'mot 31:12-17] "Y'HoVaH said to Moshe, 'Tell the people of Yisra'el, You are to observe my Shabbats; for this is a sign between me and you through all your generations; so that you will know that I am Y'HoVaH, who sets you apart for me. Therefore you are to keep my Shabbat, because it is set apart for you. Everyone who treats it as ordinary must be put to death; for whoever does any work on it is to be cut off from his people. On six days work will get done; but the seventh day is Shabbat, for complete rest, set apart for Y'HoVaH. Whoever does any work on the day of Shabbat must be put to death. The people of Yisra'el are to keep the Shabbat, to observe Shabbat through all their generations as a perpetual covenant. It is a sign between me and the people of Yisra'el forever; for in six days Y'HoVaH made heaven and earth, but on the seventh day he stopped working and rested.'"

Proof #4:

[Sh'mot 34:21] "Six days you will work, but on the seventh day you are to rest—even in plowing time and harvest season you are to rest."

Proof #5:

[Vayikra (Vah-yeek-rah, i.k.a. Leviticus) 23:1-3, 32] "Y'HoVaH said to Moshe, 'Tell the people of Yisra'el; the designated times of Y'HoVaH which you are to proclaim as kodesh convocations are my designated times. Work is to be done on six days; but the seventh day is a Shabbat of complete rest, a kodesh convocation; you are not to do any kind of work; it is a Shabbat for Y'HoVaH, even in your homes.... It will be for you a Shabbat of complete rest, and you are to deny yourselves; you are to rest on your Shabbat from evening the ninth day of the month until the following evening.'"

Proof #6:

[B'midbar (Buh-meed-bar, i.k.a. Numbers) 15:15-17, 30-35] "For this community there will be the same law for you as for the foreigner living with you; this is a permanent regulation through all your generations; the foreigner is to be treated the same way before Y'HoVaH as yourselves. The same Torah and standard of judgment will apply to both you and the foreigner living with you.... But an individual who does something wrong intentionally, whether a citizen or a foreigner, is blaspheming Y'HoVaH. That person will be cut off from his people. Because he has had contempt for the word of Y'HoVaH and has disobeyed His command, that person will be cut off completely; his offense will remain with him. While the people of Yisra'el were in the desert, they found a man gathering wood on Shabbat. Those who found him gathering wood brought him to Moshe, Aharon and the whole congregation. They kept him in custody, because it had not yet been decided what to do to him. Then Y'HoVaH said to Moshe, 'This man must be put to death; the entire community is to stone him to death outside the camp.' So the whole community brought him outside the camp and threw stones at him until he died, as Y'HoVaH had ordered Moshe."

Proof #7:

[Yesha'yahu 56:2-7] "Happy is the person who does this, anyone who grasps it firmly, who keeps Shabbat and does not profane it, and keeps himself from doing evil. A foreigner joining Y'HoVaH should not say, 'Y'HoVaH will separate me from his people; likewise the eunuch should not say, 'I am only a dried-up tree.' For here is what Y'HoVaH says: 'As for the eunuchs who keep my Shabbats, who choose what pleases me and hold fast to my covenant: in my house, within my walls, I will give them power and a name greater than sons and daughters; I will give him an everlasting name that will not be cut off. And the foreigners who join themselves to Y'HoVaH to serve him, to honor the name of Y'HoVaH, and to be his workers, all who keep Shabbat and do not profane it, and hold fast to my covenant, I will bring them to my kodesh mountain and make them joyful in my house of prayer.'"

Proof #8:

[Yesha'yahu 58:13,14] "If you hold back your foot on Shabbat from pursuing your own interests on my kodesh day; if you call Shabbat a delight, Y'HoYaH's holy day, worth honoring; then honor it by not doing your usual things or pursuing your interests or speaking about them. If you do, you will find delight in Y'HoVaH."

Proof #9:

[Yesha'yahu 66:22-24] "'For just as the new heavens and the new earth that I am making will continue in my presence,' says Y'HoVaH, 'so will your descendants and your name continue. Every month on Rosh Hodesh and every week on Shabbat, everyone living will come to worship in my presence,' says Y'HoVaH. 'As they leave, they will look on the corpses of the people who rebelled against me. For their worm will never die, and their fire will never be quenched; but they will be abhorrent to all humanity.'"

Proof #10:

[Lukem 13:10; 23:56:] "Y'shua was teaching in one of the synagogues on Shabbat.... On Shabbat the women rested, in obedience to the commandment;"

Proof #11:

[Acts 13:13-16, 42-44:] "Having set sail from Paphos, Sha'ul and his companions arrived at Perga in Pamphylia. There Yochanan left them and returned to Yerushalayim, but the others went on from Perga to Pisidian Antioch, and on Shabbat they went into the synagogue and sat down. After the reading from the Torah and from the Prophets, the synagogue leaders sent them a message, 'Brothers, if any of you has a word of exhortation for the people, speak!' So Sha'ul stood, motioned with his hand, and said: 'Men of Yisra'el and Elohim-fearers, listen! The Elohim of this people Yisra'el chose our fathers'.... As they left, the people invited Sha'ul and Bar-Nabba to tell them more about these matters the following Shabbat. When the synagogue meeting broke up, many of the born Y'hudim and devout proselytes followed Sha'ul and Bar-Nabba, who spoke with them and urged them to keep holding fast to the care and kindness of Elohim. The next Shabbat, nearly the whole city gathered together to hear the message about HaAdonay;"

Proof #12:

[Ma'asheh 17:1-4:] "After passing through Amphipolis and Apollonia, Sha'ul and Sila came to Thessalonica, where there was a synagogue. According to his usual practice, Sha'ul went in; and on three Shabbats he gave them drashes (homilies) from the Tanakh, explaining and proving that the Mashiach had to suffer and rise again from the dead and that 'this Y'shua whom I am proclaiming to you is HaMashiach.' Some of the Y'hudim were persuaded and threw in their lot with Sha'ul and Sila, as did a great many of the Greek men who were 'Elohim-fearers,' and not a few of the leading women."

Proof #13:

[Ma'asheh 16:13:] "Then on Shabbat, we (Sha'ul and Timothy) went outside the gate to the riverside, where we understood a minyan met. We sat down and began speaking to the women who had gathered there."

Proof #14:

[Ma'asheh 18:4] Sha'ul also began carrying on discussions every Shabbat in the synagogue, where he tried to convince both Y'hudim and Greeks.

Another major part of haSatan's theological deception is the change of Elohim's kodesh day Shabbat (Shah-baht), the seventh day of the week, to Sunday, the first day of the week, by over 99% of Christian churches.

Elohim named the seventh day Shabbat—the only day Elohim named—and made it kodesh. HaSatan named the first day Sunday—in honor of the pagan Sun God; in fact all the days of the week are named after Pagan Gods—and made it the special day of Christianity. No mention is made, none, nada, in the entire Bible from B'resheet through Hitgelut about the first day of the week being a kodesh day or a day of rest. Christendom is all about Sunday. Sunday identifies them just as much as the mark of the beast on their foreheads. Have you ever thought about why Sunday, mostly the first day of the week, is considered part of the weekend?

Let's use some common sense. The 'weekend' is the end of the week. Therefore since the weekly cycle of seven days beginning with day number one and ending with day number seven that Elohim inaugurated at creation has never changed, then the last day of the week is day number seven. If you want two days in your 'weekend' it would be day six and day seven. Right?

So how did Sunday, which is mostly the first day of the week—actually only about three-fourths of Sunday from its beginning at midnight Saturday to sundown on Sunday is part of the first day—worm its way into the so-called 'weekend'? I'll tell you how, the same way that Sunday became a substitute for the seventh day Shabbat, by decree of the Roman Emperor Constantinus and his Roman Catholic Christian Church that followed.

The Catholic officials even brag that they are the ones who instituted Sunday in place of Shabbat and that it is proof of their power. It is simply, once again, people and churches putting tradition of man over command of Y'HoVaH. Y'shua asked the question of the religious leaders of the day in Mattiyahu 15:3: "Indeed, why do you break the command of Elohim by your tradition?" The same question can be asked of the religious leaders and their followers today: why are you breaking the fourth commandment of Elohim, as quoted above in Proof #2, by substituting Sunday for Shabbat?

Elohim set aside the seventh day as a kodesh day at creation as shown in proof #1.
As shown in Proof #2, Y'HoVaH commanded, first by speaking in Ivrit and then by writing in Ivrit with his finger on two stone tablets, that man should rest on the seventh day of the week which he then named Shabbat.

Y'shua and his talmidim kept Shabbat as shown in Proofs #10, #11, #12, #13, and #14.

In the Scripture quoted in Proof #9, Y'HoVaH said that

everyone living in the new heavens and earth—the saved—will come to worship him each week on the seventh day called Shabbat. Shabbat is eternal: from creation to Noach, from Noach to Avraham, from Avraham to Ya'akov, from Ya'akov to Moshe, from Moshe to David, from David to Y'shua, from Y'shua to today, from today to the new heavens and new earth, from the new heavens and new earth to eternity. It will never be changed or replaced; it will never end!

The seventh day, just like the other six days of the week, begins and ends at sundown. This is Elohim's timekeeping started at creation as shown in B'resheet 1:5, 8, 13, 19, 23, 31: "So there was evening, and there was morning, one day.... So there was evening, and there was morning, a second day.... So there was evening, and there was morning, a third day.... So there was evening, and there was morning, a fourth day.... So there was evening, and there was morning a fifth day.... So there was evening, and there was morning, a sixth day."

Elohim's day begins at the beginning of evening, just as the sun sets; then you have a short period called twilight between sunset and complete darkness or night; then you have the night hours between evening and morning. Morning begins at sunrise, then you have the daylight hours until sunset again.

Shabbat is not equivalent to Saturday—named after pagan god Saturn—which runs from 12 o'clock midnight to 12 o'clock midnight. There is, of course, some overlapping, but they are not the same day. You must start your rest period and devotion to Y'HoVaH at sundown of the sixth day, or Friday—named after pagan god Frigg—evening, and continue till sundown of the seventh day, or Saturday evening, at which time day one begins.

Adonay also tells Moshe in the latter part of Proof #5 that Yom-Kippur, which occurs every year on the tenth day of the seventh Y'Hudi month, runs from evening of the ninth day to the following evening. This special day of atonement is also a day of rest and is therefore called a Shabbat just like the weekly Shabbat.

The Scripture quoted in proof #9 talks about the corpses—the lost—of those who rebelled against Y'HoVaH. If you willfully and knowingly continue to disobey Y'HoVaH, you are in rebellion against Y'HoVaH! This is something you do not want to be guilty of because the blood of Y'shua is of no use for you anymore, as plainly stated in Ivrim 10:26,27: "For if we deliberately continue to sin after receiving the knowledge of the truth, there no longer remains a sacrifice for sin, but only the terrif'ying prospect of Judgment, of raging fire that will consume the enemies."

If you have read up to this point, then you are no longer ignorant of Y'HoVaH's instruction regarding His weekly Shabbat. So a continuation of Sunday in lieu of Shabbat is rebellion against Y'HoVaH. Please don't do it. Put obedience to Y'HoVaH first and foremost in your life—above wife, children, parents, grandparents, friends, job, etc.—Mattityahu 10:34-39.

Build your house on the bedrock of obedience to Y'HoVaH not the sandy foundation of disobedience to Y'HoVaH: "So everyone who hears these words of mine and acts on them will be like a sensible man who built his house on bedrock. The rain fell, the rivers flooded, the winds blew and beat against the house, but it didn't collapse, because its foundation was on rock. But everyone who hears these words of mine and does not act on them will be like a stupid man who built his house on sand. The rain fell, the rivers flooded, the wind blew and beat against the house, and it collapsed—and its collapse was horrendous!" Mattityahu

7:24-27

Please don't be misled by haSatan's soothing message emanating from his Catholic and Protestant Christian churches that, "You don't have to be obedient to God to be saved"—this was haSatan's message to Havah in the garden of 'Eden. This is an evil lie but it increases membership in Christian churches. You cannot be saved if you don't obey Y'HoVaH. There is nothing else you can do for Y'HoVaH but obey his mitzvot.

Y'shua answers a question put to him by a P'rushim Torah expert in Mattityahu 22:37, 38 regarding which of the mitzvot of Y'HoVaH is most important by quoting from D'varim 6:5: "You are to obey Y'HoVaH Elohekha with all your heart and with all your soul and with all your strength. This is the greatest and most important mitzvah."

Y'shua's disciple Yochanan explicitly defines what it means to obey Elohim in 1Yochanan 5:3: "For obeying Elohim means obeying his commands." Elohim has always demanded obedience in his covenants with man. It will never change because Y'HoVaH doesn't change as stated in Mal'akhi 3:6, "But because I, Y'HoVaH, do not change."

I started keeping Shabbat about ten years ago and it has been a delight and a real blessing in my life, just like obedience to any of Y'HoVaH's mitzvot will enrich your life and put you at peace with Adonay. I am a Goyim, or foreigner by birth, and as such am still learning how to properly observe Y'HoVaH's kodesh day, but I pretty much shut down my normal day-to-day activities—which aren't much in my case since I am an old man—but no chores or honey-dos on Shabbat. No going to the grocery or eating at a restaurant, which would require others to work for me. In general, you should refrain from pursuing your own interests and doing your usual things on Shabbat, as directed in the Scripture of Proof #8.

I would recommend looking to the observant Y'hudim, both Mashiachic and non-Mashiachic, for guidance regarding what to do and what not to do on the seventh day, as well as many other things, such as the correct pronunciation of names and places. The remnant Y'hudim have been "set as a light for the Goyim, to be for deliverance to the ends of the earth." (Ma'sheh 13:47). They are the leaders in Y'HoVaH's spiritual army and as such have been hated since Y'HoVaH selected them and will continue to be hated by haSatan and his followers.

This is the only explanation I can come up with to explain the irrational hatred of the Y'hudim by evil people and their evil institutions such as Christianity and Islam. HaSatan knows that salvation comes from the Y'hudim and he is determined to try to thwart Y'HoVaH's purpose.

In Proof #9 Y'HoVaH directed Moshe to tell the people of Yisra'el which days are the designated times of Y'HoVaH when the people of Yisra'el were to have kodesh convocations (assemblies). The first one mentioned in verse 3 of Vayikra 23 was the weekly Shabbat. The others that followed in this chapter were: Pesach (i.k.a. Passover), Shavuot (i.k.a. Pentecost), Rosh HaShanah (Feast of Trumpets), Yom Kippur (Day of Atonement), and Sukkot (Feast of Tabernacles or Booths).

Mr. Neil Lash, a Mashiachic Yehudi, asks and answers the following rhetorical question in his August 2009 issue of *Jewish Jewels*: "Are these Feasts only for the Y'hudi people? No, absolutely not! They are Elohim's holy moedim, His appointed times to meet with his children in a special way. If you are His child, they are for you. But make no mistake: Celebrating the Feasts of the Lord will set you apart, make you different and 'separate.' You may have to wrestle with the 'fear of man' vs. the 'fear of HaAdonay.' Follow the leading of the Ruach HaKodesh. He will not lead you astray!... It is interesting to note that the FIRST of Elohim's feasts is a WEEKLY FEAST, called HaShabbat. 'Six days shall work be done, but on the seventh day is a Shabbat of solemn rest, a holy convocation....' (Vayikra 23:3).

On a Hebrew calendar, the first six days have numbers, not names. Only one day has a name, the seventh day. It is called Shabbat. Sunday never was nor is—or ever will be—the biblical Shabbat. The Elohim of Yiisra'el was referring to what we know as sundown Friday to sundown Saturday when He said.... ' Surely My Shabbats you shall keep, for it is a sign between Me and you throughout your generations, that you may know that I am the Adonay who sanctifies you. You shall keep the Shabbat, therefore for it is kodesh to you....' (Sh'mot 31:12-14). The weekly Shabbat was proclaimed by Elohim to be a 'special day' to be observed by his people throughout their generations as a perpetual covenant. Keeping the weekly Shabbat has kept Yisra'el as a separate people throughout the ages. In Yisra'el, the week revolves around Shabbat. Preparations begin on Wednesday or Thursday and by Friday afternoon, the fresh flowers, linens, special foods, etc., are almost ready in anticipation of the weekly 'guest' who is about to arrive.

Shabbat is seen as a gift from Elohim to his people. Elohim himself rested and was refreshed on the seventh day. When His people do likewise, they are demonstrating that they are no longer slaves to work, but free people, whose Elohim has given them a day to give thanks, reflect, re-create, and delight in their Creator. Observing Shabbat is a way to honor Y'HoVaH and acknowledge Him as Creator of all things. Our Mashiach Y'shua Immanuel El observed Shabbat, and never commanded the observance of Sunday as a special day. The Apostle Sha'ul's custom was to meet on Shabbat (Ma'sheh 17:2; 13:14, 42, 44; 16:13; 18:4).

Neither Y'shua nor Sha'ul ever spoke about the creation of a new 'Christian Sabbath.' Sunday became the Christian day of worship centuries after the resurrection, as part of the general Church rejection and replacement of everything Y'hudi. Bibically, however, there is no such thing as a 'Christian Sabbath.' There is only one weekly Shabbat, Y'HoYaH's seventh-day Shabbat."

My goals, as a foreigner are as follows: to be happy by trusting in HaMashiach, Y'shua Immanu El; to obey all of Y'HoVaH's mitzvot, including the fourth commandment, thereby not profaning Shabbat; keep from doing evil; to become a fellow citizen in Y'HoVaH's kingdom by joining his people, the Yisra'elim, as directed by Yesha'yahu in Proof #7; to serve Him; to treasure His name and not profane it as directed in the third commandment; to be His worker; to hold fast to His covenant; to thereby be brought to His kodesh mountain where I will be eternally joyful in His house of prayer as outlined by Yesha'yahu in Proof #7.

As plainly shown in Proofs #3 and #6, violation of the weekly shabbat is a serious offense and is punishable by death.

Part 4 – Diet

Question: Is it a sin to eat pig meat (ham, pork chops, pork roast, pork sausage, pork hot dogs, pork bacon, pork bologna, pork ribs, etc.), pig fat (lard), pig intestines (chitterlings), pig brains, pickled pig feet, pepperoni, pig skins, rare-cooked meat, raw meat, blood pudding, horse meat, camel meat, dog meat, cat meat, bear meat, rats, squirrels, chipmunks, rabbits, carrion, hawks, crow, blackbird pie, vultures, road-kill, catfish, sharks, oysters, shrimp, lobsters, crabs, clams, scallops, alligators, snakes, lizards, chocolate covered ants, roaches, etc.?
Answer: Yes!

Proof #1:

[B'resheet 7:1,2; 8:20] "Y'HoVaH said to Noach, 'Come into the ark, you and all your household; for I have seen that you alone in this generation are righteous before me. Of every clean animal you are to take seven couples, and of the animals that are not clean, one couple; also of the birds in the air take seven couples—in order to preserve their species throughout the earth.... Noach built an altar to Y'HoVaH. Then he took from every clean animal and every clean bird, and he offered burnt offerings on the altar."

Proof #2:

[Vayikra 3:17] "It is to be a permanent regulation for you through all your generations wherever you live that you will eat neither fat nor blood."

Proof #3:

[Vayikra 11:1-47] "Y'HoVaH said to Moshe and Aharon, 'Tell the people of Yisra'el, These are the living creatures which you may eat among all the land animals: any that has a separate hoof which is completely divided and chews the cud—these animals you may eat. But you are not to eat those that only chew the cud or only have a separate hoof For example, the camel, the coney and the hare are unclean for you, because they chew the cud but don't have a separate hoof; while the pig is unclean for you, because although it has a separate and completely divided hoof, it does not chew the cud.

You are not to eat meat from these or touch their carcasses; they are unclean for you. Of all the things that live in the water, you may eat these: anything in the water that has fins or scales, whether in seas or in rivers—these you may eat. But everything in the seas and rivers without both fins and scales, of all the small water-creatures and of all the living creatures in the water, is a detestable thing for you. Yes, these will be detestable for you—you are not to eat their meat, and you are to detest their carcasses. Whatever lacks fins and scales in the water is a detestable thing for you. The following creatures of the air are to be detestable for you—they are not to be eaten, they are a detestable thing: the eagle, the vulture, the osprey, the kite, the various kinds of buzzards, the various kinds of ravens, the cormorant, the great owl, the horned owl, the pelican, the barn owl, the stork, the various kinds of herons, the hoopoe, and the bat. All winged swarming creatures that go on all fours are a detestable thing for you, except that of all winged swarming creatures that go on all fours, you may eat those that have jointed legs above their feet, enabling them to jump off the ground. Specifically, of these you may eat the various kinds of locusts, grasshoppers, katydids and crickets. But other than that, all winged swarming creatures having four feet are a detestable thing for you.

The following will make you unclean; whoever touches the carcass of them will be unclean until evening, and whoever picks up any part of their carcass is to wash his clothes and be unclean until evening: every animal that doesn't have a separate and completely divided hoof or that doesn't chew the cud is unclean for you; anyone who touches them will become unclean. Whatever goes on its paws, among all animals that go on all fours is unclean for you; whoever touches its carcass will be unclean until evening; and whoever picks up its carcass is to wash his clothes and be unclean until evening—these are unclean for you.

The following are unclean for you among the small creatures that swarm on the ground: the weasel, the mouse, the various kinds of lizards, the gecko, the land crocodile, the skink, the sand-lizard and the chameleon. They are unclean crawling creatures; whoever touches them when they are dead will be unclean until evening. Anything on which one of them falls when dead will become unclean— wooden utensil, article of clothing, leather, sacking—any utensil used for work; it must be put in water, and it will be unclean until evening; then it will be clean. If one of them falls into a clay pot, whatever is in it will become unclean, and you are to break the pot. Any food permitted to be eaten that water from such a vessel gets on will become unclean, and any permitted liquid in such a vessel will become unclean.

Everything on which any carcass-part of theirs falls will become unclean, whether oven or stove; it is to be broken in pieces—they are unclean and will be unclean for you; although a spring or cistern for collecting water remains clean. But anyone who touches one of their carcasses will become unclean. If any carcass-part of theirs falls on any kind of seed to be sown, it is clean; but if water is put on the seed and a carcass-part of theirs falls on it, it is unclean for you. If an animal of a kind that you are permitted to eat dies, whoever touches its carcass will be unclean until evening. A person who eats meat from its carcass or carries its carcass is to wash his clothes; he will be unclean until evening.

Any creature that swarms on the ground is a detestable thing; it is not to be eaten-whatever moves on its stomach, goes on all fours, or has many legs-all creatures that swarm on the ground; you are not to eat them because they are a detestable thing. You are not to make yourselves detestable with any of these swarming, crawling creatures; do not make yourselves unclean with them, do not defile yourselves with them.

For I am Y'HoVaH Elohekha, therefore consecrate yourselves and be kodesh, for I am kodesh; and do not defile yourselves with any kind of swarming creature that moves along the ground. For I am Y'HoVaH, who brought you up out of the land of Egypt to be Elohekha. Therefore you are to be kodesh, because I am kodesh. Such, then, is the law concerning animals, flying creatures, all living creatures that move about the water, and all creatures that swarm on the ground. Its purpose is to distinguish between the unclean and the clean, and between the creatures that may be eaten and those that may not be eaten."

Proof #4:

[Vayikra 17:10-14] "When someone from the community of Yisra'el or one of the foreigners living with you eats any kind of blood, I will set myself against that person who eats blood and cut him off from his people. For the life of a creature is in the blood, and I have given it to you on the altar to make atonement for yourselves; for it is the blood that makes atonement because of the life. This is why I told you people of Yisra'el, 'None of you is to eat blood, nor is any foreigner living with you to eat blood.'"

Proof #5:

[Vayikra 20:25] "Therefore you are to distinguish between clean and unclean animals and between clean and unclean birds; do not make yourselves detestable with an animal, bird or reptile that I have set apart for you to regard as unclean. Rather, you people are to be kodesh for me; because I, Y'HoVaH, am ruach; and I have set you apart from the other peoples, so that you can belong to me."

Proof #6:

[D'varim 14:2-21] "Because you are a people set apart as kodesh for Y'HoVaH Elohekha. Y'HoVaH Elohekha has chosen you to be his own unique treasure out of all the peoples on the face of the earth. You are not to eat anything disgusting. The animals which you may eat are: ox, sheep, goat, deer, gazelle, roebuck, ibex, antelope, oryx and mountain sheep. Any animal that has a separate hoof that is completely divided and also chews the cud, these animals you may eat. But you are not to eat those that only chew the cud or only have a divided hoof. For example, the camel, the hare and the coney are unclean for you because they chew the cud but don't have a separate hoof; while the pig is unclean for you because, although it has a separate hoof, it doesn't chew the cud. You are not to eat meat from these or touch their carcasses.

Of all that lives in the water, you may eat these: anything in the water that has fins and scales, these you may eat. But whatever lacks fins and scales you are not to eat; it is unclean for you. You may eat any clean bird; but these you are not to eat: eagles, vultures, ospreys, kites, any kind of hawk, little owls, great owls, horned owls, pelicans, barn owls, cormorants, storks, any kind of heron, hoopoes and bats. All winged swarming creatures are unclean for you; they are not to be eaten; but all clean flying creatures you may eat. You are not to eat any animal that dies naturally; although you may let a stranger staying with you eat it, or sell it to a foreigner; because you are a kodesh people for Y'HoVaH Elohekha."

Proof #7:

[Yesha'yahu 65:1-4] "I made myself accessible to those who didn't ask for me, I let myself be found by those who didn't seek me. I said, 'Here I am!' to a nation not called by my name. I spread out my hands all day long to a rebellious people who live in a way that is not good, who follow their own inclinations; a people who provoke me to my face all the time, sacrificing in gardens and burning incense on bricks. They sit among the graves and spend the night in caverns; they eat pig meat and their pots hold soup made from disgusting things."

Proof #8:

[Yesha'yahu 66:16, 17] "For Y'HoVaH will judge all humanity with fire and with the sword, and those slain by

Y'HoVaH will be many. 'Those who consecrate and purify themselves in order to enter the gardens, then follow the one who was already there, eating pig meat, reptiles and rats, will all be destroyed together,' says Y'HoVaH."

Proof #9:

[Acts 10:9-14] "The next day about noon, while they were still on their way and approaching the city, Kifa went up onto the roof of the house to pray. He began to feel hungry and wanted something to eat; but while they were preparing the meat, he fell into trance in which he saw heaven opened, and something that looked like a large sheet being lowered to the ground by its four corners. In it were all kinds of fourfooted animals, crawling creatures and wild birds. Then a voice came to him, 'Get up, Kifa, slaughter and eat!' But Kifa said, 'No sir! Absolutely not! I have never eaten food that was unclean or treif.'"

There's not much I can add to the above Proofs from Y'HoVaH's Word since Y'HoVaH is very detailed and specific regarding His dietary instructions of what man is and isn't to eat. Y'HoVaH even forbids the touching of a carcass of an unclean animal; so don't touch or handle pork bacon or pork sausage or ham.

As shown in proof #5 a person makes themselves detestable to Y'HoVaH when they eat unclean creatures. Y'HoVaH refers to unclean land animals, unclean creatures of the air and unclean water creatures as disgusting.

The clincher for my wife was Proof #8. She had quit preparing unclean meats many years ago out of respect for my beliefs, but she would still eat an occasional pig sausage biscuit at McDonalds restaurant. But once she saw that Y'HoVaH classed eating pig meat with eating reptiles and rats she was convinced it was sin, and she hasn't eaten any pig meat since. Besides, if you must eat sausage or bacon, there are plenty of alternatives now, such as turkey sausage, turkey bacon, beef sausage and beef bacon.

The bottom feeders of the waters such as the shrimp or "sea-roaches" are not only unclean but unhealthy and even deadly in some cases. The shellfish have concentrations of impurities and toxins that are in the water. A co-worker of mine at Lockheed, who was from coastal North Carolina, once told me about the tragic deaths of a number of people and the severe illnesses of dozens more, including himself, who participated in a local raw oyster eating fest. "The scaleless fish and all shellfish including the oyster, clam, lobster, shrimp, etc., modern science discovers to be but lumps of devitalized and disease producing filth, because of inadequate excretion. These are the scavengers, the garbage containers of the waters and seas.... Scientists literally gauge the contaminate levels of our oceans, bays, rivers, and lakes by measuring the mercury and biological toxin levels in the flesh of crabs, clams, oysters and lobsters." (Ref. *God's Key to Health and Happiness* by Elmer Josephson, p. 37, 47).

Another scavenger that is very popular in the Catholic/Protestant Christian diet is the swine—I ask you, why is ham the meat of choice for the Christian Easter meal but lamb is the meat of choice for the Pesach Seder meal that Y'shua partook of with his followers just before his death? Doesn't the swine always represent evil and the lamb represents good in the Bible? Y'shua is referred to as "Elohim's lamb" by Yochanan the Immerser in Yochanan 1:29. The demons fled into a herd of pigs, not a flock of sheep, in Mattityahu chapter 8.

In my opinion, the pig is the perfect representative or mascot of the Christian religion. "Some ask, why did Y'HoVaH make the unclean animals? They were created as scavengers. As a rule they are meat-eating or carrion animals that clean up anything that is left dead in the fields, etc. But scavengers were never intended for human consumption. The flesh of the swine is said by many authorities to be the prime cause of much of our American ill health, causing blood diseases, weakness of the stomach, liver troubles, eczema, consumption, tumors, cancer, etc.

"The pig's single stomach arrangement is very simple in design and function and is combined with a limited excretory organ system. Four hours after the pig has eaten his polluted swill and other putrid, offensive matter, man may eat the same swill second handed off the ribs of the pig.... Did anything biologically happen to the swine since Bible times, or did the digestive tract of man have some kind of miracle transformation? No, the Bible, science, and experience have all proven contrary." (Josephson, p. 46, 49).

The scavenger creatures on land, in water, and in the air, that Y'HoVaH forbids man to eat are essentially flesh and waste product eaters. The flesh can be of animal, fish or fowl and can be freshly killed raw or cooked, rotten and putrified carrion, or even fecal matter. A pig will literally eat anything, including their own feces or vomit, their own young, sick and dead pigs in their pen and even human flesh.

"Much of the wisdom in the Divine Design for meats was confirmed by a 1953 study in which Dr. David Macht of John Hopkins University reported the toxic effects of animal flesh on a controlled growth culture. A substance was classified as toxic if it slowed the culture's growth rate below 75 percent.

The table below is based on Dr. Macht's study. His results show that the lower the growth percentage of the culture, the more toxic the flesh. Note that the flesh of animals and fish given to us by Elohim for food are all nontoxic, but all forbidden animals lie in the toxic range.

Don't get confused! Any number above 75 percent is nontoxic, or clean…. The differences between clean and unclean animals appear to be related to their primary food source and to their digestive systems.

Scavengers that eat anything and everything are unclean, not suitable for food, according to the Bible. Animals described as clean, and therefore good for food, primarily eat grasses and grains…. Note that an animal doesn't have to be a scavenger to be unclean. Horses and rabbits, for example, are unclean because they do not have split hooves. Although they are considered to be good food in some countries, studies show that horse meat often contains viruses and parasites. Rabbits, as innocent as they appear, are the cause of tularemia (an infectious disease in humans).

One reason for Elohim's rule forbidding pork is that the digestive system of a pig is completely different from that of a cow. It is similar to ours, in that the stomach is very acidic. Pigs are gluttonous, never knowing when to stop eating. Their stomach acids become diluted because of the volume of food, allowing all kinds of vermin to pass through this protective barrier. Parasites, bacteria, viruses and toxins can pass into the pig's flesh.

In the United States, three of the six most common food-borne parasitic diseases of humans are associated with pork consumption. These include toxoplasmosis, taeniasis or cysticercosis (caused by the pork tapeworm), Taenia solium and trichinellosis.

In Japan, the source of these infections was traced to the flesh of pigs, bears, horses, raccoons and foxes. All of these animals are listed in Scripture as putrid or unclean. Swine are also good incubators of toxic parasites and viruses—although the animal doesn't usually appear to be ill while carrying these diseases.

A scientist at the University of Giessen's Institute for Virology in Germany showed in a study of worldwide influeza epidemics that pigs are the one animal that can serve as a mixing vessel for new influenza viruses that may seriously threaten world health.

If a pig is exposed to a human's DNA virus and then a bird's virus, the pig mixes the two viruses—developing a new DNA virus that is often extremely lethal for humans. These viruses have already caused worldwide epidemics and destruction.

The 1942 Yearbook of Agriculture reported that 50 diseases were found in pigs, and many of these diseases were passed on to humans by eating the pig's flesh.

Additionally, just handling swine has an element of risk. A large hog raising facility in the area where I live wisely requires its employees to wear gloves, masks and protective clothing while working in the pig barns. The workers are required to shower each day before going home." (Ref. **What the Bible Says About Healthy Living** by Rex Russell, M.D., p. 76-78).

Two interesting observations in the following tables is that the flesh of pigs is more toxic than the flesh of rats, and that the Torah is once more proven to be authentic!

Quadrupeds (Four Footed)

CLEAN (Cloven-hoofed and cud chewing)		UNCLEAN	
calf	82%	black bear	59%
deer	98%	camel	41%
goat	90%	cat	62%
ox	91%	coney (guinea pig)	46%
		dog	62%
		fox (silver)	58%
		grizzly bear	55%
		ground hog	53%
		hamster	46%
		horse	39%
		opossum	53%
		rabbit	49%
		rat	55%
		rhinoceros	60%
		squirrel	43%
		swine	54%

Fish

CLEAN (With scales and fins)		UNCLEAN	
black bass	80%	catfish	48%
black drum	105%	clams	
bluefish	80%	crabs	
carp	90%	eel	40%
channel bass	80%	lobster	

CLEAN (With scales and fins)		UNCLEAN	
flounder	83%	puffer	51%
flying fish	87%	sand skate	58%
goldfish	88%	scallops	
haddock	80%	shark (dogfish)	62%
hake	98%	shrimp	
halibut	82%	squid	
herring	100%	stingray	46%
kingfish	83%	toad fish	49%
mullet	87%		
pike	98%		
pompano	110%		
porgy	80%		
rainbow trout	81%		
rock bass	100%		
salmon	81%		
smelt	90%		
sea bass	103%		
shad	100%		
Spanish mackerel	98%		
spot	80%		
sturgeon	87%		
tuna (bluefin)	88%		
white perch	81%		
Carolina whiting	84%		
yellow perch	87%		

Fowl

CLEAN	UNCLEAN	
	kite	
	nighthawk	
	osprey	
	ostrich	
	owl	62%
	pelican	
	raven	
	red-tail hawk	36%
	sparrow hawk	63%
	sea gull	
	stork	
	vulture	

Insects

CLEAN (Winged, hopping, with four legs)	UNCLEAN (All others)
cricket	
grasshopper	
locust	

Dr. Peter Rothschild, M.D., Ph. D. explains in his book, *The Art of Health,* about the toxic effects of unclean foods: "Do not consume any meat of scavenger animals comprising pork, all shell fish varieties, skin fish which are scale-less fish, scavenger birds, snakes and reptiles. The reason for this Biblical prohibition is dual. The first consists in that the meat of such animals is about ten times more perishable, difficult to preserve, than that of the allowed animals. Frequently people do not realize a piece of meat is already poisonously spoiled until they perceive the toxic symptom and have already ingested it. The second reason consists in the scary fact that the by-products that originate from digesting such scavenger meat are highly poisonous. We're referring specifically to the so-called death enzymes, such as cadaverine and putrescine. These death enzymes are extraordinarily useful in nature. Without their assistance no flesh would revert to dust, they are extremely useful to break down a corpse, but terribly inconvenient in a living human body."

I also highly recommend reading *The Maker's Diet* by Jordan S. Rubin. Mr. Rubin is also a Y'hudi and his diet, as the book title suggests, is based on Y'HoVaH's prescribed diet in the Bible. Not only does he advocate clean red meat, clean fowl and clean fish, but Rubin also recommends eating butter and cheese—called curds in the Bible—eggs, fruits, vegetables, herbs, lentils, properly prepared whole grains, honey, and extra virgin olive oil just to name a few; the natural foods that HaCreator put here for mankind.

No manipulated, refined and processed foods such as oleomargarine—I remember my mother making oleo when it was first introduced about sixty years ago as a substitute for real butter. I say making because she had to mix yellow food coloring with white hydrogenated solid vegetable oil such as Crisco shortening to get oleomargarine.

After promoting oleo, with its high trans-fat content, as a wonder-food replacement for natural cow or goat butter all these many years, the so-called health experts are now finally saying that transfats are unhealthy—but I've never heard any apologies for the damage to people's health by their mistaken advocacy of oleo instead of butter. They have no credibility with me.

It is the same story with eggs and milk. I heard all my life that eggs are bad for you because they are high in cholesterol. Now they are saying that eggs are one of the most nutritious foods there is. Mr. Rubin even says that the cholesterol scare is just that, a scare, and in fact is not responsible for coronary artery disease. Ditto for whole milk and cheese. The problem now is getting milk, butter, cheese and meat from grass fed cows that are free of hormones and steroids.

Likewise for the chickens, no stressed-out chickens in crowded chicken coops unable to move about and shot up with fast growth hormones. Thankfully organic products are gaining in popularity and more and more are available, even at large chain grocery stores.

Mr. Rubin argues it's the unsaturated and transfats that are bad, not the saturated fats. The saturated fats are actually necessary daily for the body for the following reasons: to properly nourish cell membranes, to incorporate calcium into the skeletal system, to protect the liver from toxins such as alcohol, to enhance the immune system, to utilize essential fatty acids such as omega-3, to fuel the heart which is surrounded by saturated fat, to protect against harmful microorganisms in the digestive tract. (Ref ***Nourishing Traditions: The Cookbook that Challenges Politically Correct Nutrition*** and ***the Diet Dictocrats*** by Sally Fallon with Mary Enig, Ph. D., p. 26)

I didn't always know whether some fish, such as tilapia or mahi mahi, had scales and fins; or what fowl or meat were kosher. I was, unfortunately, raised in a Christian, scavenger-eating environment. Therefore, as an aid to the reader, I will list some additional edible fish, fowl, and meat from Jordan Rubin's book, *The Maker's Diet*, and *The Jewish Home Advisor* by Alfred Kolatch that are not listed in the table on pages 115-118 for you.

Fish: scrod, orange roughy, red snapper, white snapper, whitefish, grouper, mahi mahi, wahoo, tilapia, mackerel, sole, red fish, locus, perch, largemouth bass, smallmouth bass, plaice, Pollack, sardines, sable, sunfish, tilefish, turbot, yellowtail, anchovy.

Poultry: cornish hen, guinea fowl, doves, chicken or turkey sausage or hot dogs (no pork casing and nitrite/nitrate free), chicken or turkey bacon (nitrite/nitrate free).

Meat: Veal, buffalo, elk, beef or buffalo sausage or hot dogs (no pork casing and nitrite and/or nitrate free), beef bacon (nitrite and/or nitrate free).

After all, Y'HoVaH made everything, so who is better qualified to determine for humans what they should eat and what they shouldn't? Y'HoVaH or man? If you follow Y'HoVaH's dietary instructions you will not only benefit physically with better health but more importantly you will benefit spiritually by being obedient to Y'HoVa.

The author, James W. Dobbs, with his beloved wife, Joyce.

The author (third from left) standing with co-workers at De Haviland Aircraft Canada where he was employed in 1974. He had the photo on his desk shortly before his death. [Dobbs family photo]

About the Author

James Woods Dobbs, Jr. was born in the Heart of Dixie: Birmingham, Alabama in December, 1938. His blue collar family moved frequently during his childhood as his father built and rented houses as a source of income. Despite the growing pains of constantly trying to make friends, James lived a cozy life.

In 1957, he went to school at Alabama Polytechnic Institute, more commonly known as Auburn University. There he earned a Bachelor of Science degree in mechanical engineering. The five long years of study eventually paid off for him and his family.

He met and married Joyce McIntyer in 1962, a year he considered triumphal. He had just graduated from Auburn, and he landed a job with the Chrysler Corporation as a Systems Engineer, working on the Saturn I rocket destruct systems at NASA's Marshall Space Flight Center in Huntsville, Alabama.

Two years later he landed a new job as an Aircraft Structural Analysis Engineer for the Lockheed Aircraft Corporation, Georgia Division, and moved to Marietta, Georgia. There he worked on multiple projects like the massive Air Force C-5 Galaxy and the C-130 Hercules, both cargo planes of renown. In 1968  he hit another career milestone when he was selected as a member of the engineering team which planned the L-1011, a three-engine, commercial airliner.

James stayed with Lockheed, occasionally traveling to other countries, until his retirement in 1995. He and Joyce were the proud parents of three children. Sadly, his wife of 50 years passed away in 2010.

Though an engineering life might strike some as boring, James was anything but. He had a wild side which took over from time to time. He listed a half dozen such instances which he thought readers might appreciate.

1) While a student at Auburn, he and a friend climbed up a 45-degree, sloping I-beam to the top of a 200-foot long steel truss bridge. They walked the entire length of the foot-wide beam and down the other side, in the middle of the night. The bridge rose 50-60 feet above a shallow, rocky stream. He contends something had to be looking out for him as a fall would have been fatal.

2) Accompanied by same college friend, he swam, floated, and doggy paddled across a mile- wide stretch of the Coosa river without a life preserver. Though thoroughly ill-prepared, they both survived.

3) During a vacation with his wife in the Great Smoky Mountains, James bungee jumped from an 80-foot high tower. He claimed, however, that being aware of his family responsibilities, he had grown safety conscious and chose a location with a fully inflated air bag on the ground below-- just in case the rubber bungee cord snapped.

4) In 1993, at the age of 55, he made a static line parachute jump from a Cessna 172 flying at an altitude of 3,000 feet near Rome, Georgia. His chute opened, fortunately, though he lost radio contact with his instructor during his gentle, 10-minute descent to a soft landing.

5) His next adventure involved a traffic citation and led to a fight with City Hall. Acting as his own defense attorney, James argued that the stop sign he failed to obey was incorrectly placed and should have been a yield sign. The Judge disagreed, and after James voiced his disappointment with the justice system, the Judge had him transported to jail where James spent the next two days. His position on the sign issue was vindicated when the Georgia Department of Transportation eventually changed the signage from stop to yield. However, the record remained: City Hall 1, James Dobbs 0.

6) When all else failed, James would simply take off on his Kawasaki ZX-6R Super Sport racing motorcycle. He claimed it helped him clear his mind after the death of his wife. "A few minutes riding like a

'bat out of hell' relieves a lot of pressure and anxiety." He considered it just "good therapy."

James Woods Dobbs, Jr. died in November, 2017.

Afterward from a Grandchild

Grandparents always have something to teach. That said, if I had known how soon my grandfather's life would end, I would have asked more questions. There was so much more to learn from him. He was smart, quirky, and admirably set. I could write a lot about my Grandad, a man of many complex levels, someone whose stories would make a person laugh.

If there's one thing I know with certainty about my Grandad, it is, without a doubt, his self-assurance. He took his beliefs and stood 12 feet tall with them. He invested himself with facts if he didn't know about a subject, and then soared with it. He was a man who walked with certainty, and on those rare occasions when he wasn't certain, he made it a priority to reach that point. That assurance is a quality I saw in him when I was a child, and now, as an adult, I've learned that most people don't carry that quality. Not the way he carried his--in his eyes, his walk, or in the passion with which he spoke. I will strive, day after day, to grow to be like my grandfather in that respect: to be assured of myself, to *always* be assured of myself. That alone will take me places.

-- Alice Leah Pemberton